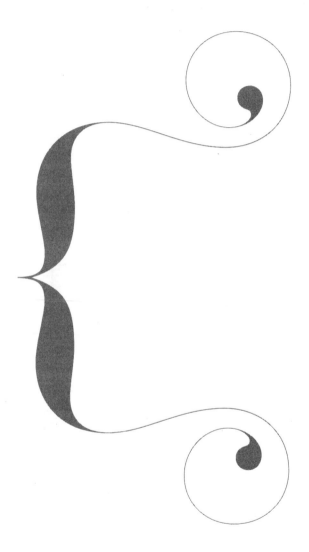

{Avant Desire}

A Nicole Brossard Reader

Edited by
Sina Queyras
Geneviève Robichaud
Erin Wunker

Coach House Books, Toronto

first edition

 Canada Council   Conseil des Arts    ONTARIO ARTS COUNCIL
for the Arts   du Canada   CONSEIL DES ARTS DE L'ONTARIO
an Ontario government agency
un organisme du gouvernement de l'Ontario

Published with the generous assistance of the Canada Council for the Arts and the Ontario Arts Council. Coach House Books also acknowledges the support of the Government of Canada through the Canada Book Fund and the Government of Ontario through the Ontario Book Publishing Tax Credit.

LIBRARY AND ARCHIVES CANADA CATALOGUING IN PUBLICATION

Title: Avant desire : a Nicole Brossard reader / by Nicole Brossard ; edited by Sina Queryas, Geneviève Robichaud, and Erin Wunker.
Other titles: Works. Selections. English
Names: Brossard, Nicole, author. | Queryas, Sina, editor. | Robichaud, Geneviève, editor. | Wunker, Erin, editor.
Description: Collected translations of the original French. | Includes bibliographical references. | Text in English; includes some text in French.
Identifiers: Canadiana (print) 20200198793 | Canadiana (ebook) 20200198947 | ISBN 9781552454039 (softcover) | ISBN 9781770566279 (EPUB) | ISBN 9781770566361 (PDF)
Classification: LCC PS8503.R7 A2 2020 | DDC C841/.54—DC23

Avant Desire is available as an ebook: ISBN 978 1 77056 403 9 (EPUB) ISBN 978 1 77056 636 1 (PDF)

TABLE OF CONTENTS

INTRODUCTION

DESIRINGS

GENERATIONS

TRANSLATIONS, RETRANSLATIONS, TRANSCOLLABORATIONS

FUTURES

AVANT DESIRE,
THE FUTURE SHALL BE SWAYED

An Introduction by
Sina Queyras, Geneviève Robichaud, and Erin Wunker

'I occupy space in Utopia. I can push death away like a mother and a future.'

In the epigraph above, taken from *Picture Theory*, the speaker makes a statement that is both factual and futuristic: *I occupy space in Utopia*. It feels risky even to speak of Utopia when, at the time of this introduction, we see irrefutable evidence of the destructive forces of late capitalism, of heteropatriarchy, of racism and colonialism. None of these structures that fundamentally shape our different lives make space for Utopia, and yet Brossard writes that future into the present. The confidence and power of her speaker is both seductive and generative. Here, in Utopia, the speaker can push death away *like a mother*, without having to be a mother.

Nicole Brossard's work is both thrill and balm – and now, in *Avant Desire: A Nicole Brossard Reader*, readers can encounter the full range and scope of her trajectory. We have worked to curate selections that will be relevant and, we think, exhilarating to new and returning readers of Brossard's work, and we have moved across genres and through time, not in a linear way but in a way that fits the always-aliveness of her work. If Utopia seems impossible to readers in 2020, Brossard's work reminds us that when we gather – either on the page reading, or in rooms together – our co-presence conjures the possibility of Utopia.

Over a fifty-year period, Nicole Brossard has published more than forty works of poetry, prose, essays, and non-fiction. She has broken through the bonds of sexual and linguistic repression, and in doing so has reached across several generations and two solitudes to enchant avant-garde, feminist, and academic readers and writers nationally and internationally, creating a radical, complex, and influential body of literature. It is work that never forgets the importance of pleasure, and that never loses hope in the possibility of Utopia. For the scholar Susan Rudy, Brossard's writing is comparable to Virginia Woolf in being 'uncompromising' in its 'critique of patriarchal reality, unrelenting in her love for women, and unequalled in [its] aesthetic experimentation.'[1] Has any other Canadian writer enjoyed the kind of feverish collaboration and translatory attention paid to Brossard? And has any other Canadian writer had the kind of attention that comes not from the established literary complex down but from the ground up? Poets, writers, and translators have taken up Brossard's work largely as a labour of love. This is quite impressive when you consider that at the core of this fervour is a radical lesbian innovative writer who comes to English only through translation.

Brossard's work was initially made accessible to non-French readers through her collaboration with the late Barbara Godard. In an interview with Smaro Kamboureli, Godard noted that she, a bilingual feminist academic, was working to create 'institutional spaces for intellectual work … and especially feminism in the 1980s when it emerged as an academic discipline.'[2] Godard translated Brossard's poetry for a reading with Adrienne Rich for the Writers in Dialogue conference (1978), as well as her editorial work for *Room of One's Own* (1978). Then, frustrated with the lack of conversation between feminist writers in English and French Canada, Godard held the Dialogue conference (1981), which was designed to bring together 'people across language barriers.'[3] A similar urge for connection between English Canada and Quebecois writers would push Godard and Frank Davey to create the Coach House Press Translation Series, which ran from 1974 to 1986.[4] Brossard's work was among the first to be published in the series. Godard largely introduced Brossard's work to readers in English Canada, translating *L'Amèr* (1977) and in turn introducing her to the writing of continental French theorists such as Gilles Deleuze: 'I recognized in particular the serial system of Brossard's diction and its exploration of

1. Susan Rudy, 'Nicole Brossard in English.' *Fluid Arguments: Essays*. Ed. Susan Rudy. Toronto: The Mercury Press, 2005.
2. 'The Critic, Institutional Culture, and Canadian Literature.' Ed. Smaro Kamboureli. *Canadian Literature at the Crossroads of Language and Culture*. Edmonton: NeWest, 2008. 34.
3. Ibid. 35.
4. Frank Davey. 'A History of Coach House Press's Quebec Translation Series.' ACQL. Montreal, 1995. http://publish.uwo.ca/~fdavey/c/chpque.htm

"surfaces of sense," of making the textual body a virtual surface for the inscription of desire.'[5] The significance of this collaborative moment is striking. Here, Godard underscores not only the labour involved in translating writers from French to English *in Canada*, she also acknowledges Brossard's theoretical influence on her own feminist intellectual development beyond national borders. We see, too, the threads of connection woven between a feminist theorist translating a feminist writer-intellectual in the title of the final publication in the Quebec Translation Series (*Surfaces of Sense*, 1989). Brossard's work has forged transformative connections between English and French feminist writers in Canada, and beyond.

The fabric of Brossard's poetics is one that is also, and importantly so, an invitation to a sensory experience. She has been involved in founding editorial projects like *La Barre du jour* (1965), *Les Têtes de pioches* (1976), and *La Nouvelle barre du jour* (1977). She has helped create numerous anthologies (*Anthologie de la poésie des femmes au Québec*, 1991; *Poèmes à dire la francophonie*, 2002; *Baiser vertige*, 2006; and *Le Long poème*, 2011). She has also been involved in collaborative stage productions and monologues such as *La Nef des sorcières* presented at the Théâtre du Nouveau-Monde in Montreal in 1976 (translated by Linda Gaboriau and published as part of Coach House Press's Quebec Translation Series in 1980 under the title *A Clash of Symbols*), and *Célébrations*, which was also presented at the TNM in 1979, as well as *Je ne suis jamais en retard* at the Théâtre d'aujourd'hui in 2015. There is also her most recent multisensory spectacle and collaboration with Simon Dumas, *Le Désert mauve*, at L'Espace Go in the fall of 2018.

It is hard to oversell the benefits of the kind of space Brossard creates, even as we are in the midst of an exciting feminist publishing renaissance – a space rooted in many particularities of time, politics, aesthetics, and community, but perhaps foremost this space is an example of the potential of what can be created when thinking through language and *in relation* to others. This is crucial and central to both Brossard's work and her position as writer and thinker. In addition to those scores of books, there are countless collaborations, including the documentary *Some American Feminists* (1977), an

5. Barbara Godard. 'Deleuze and Translation.' *parallax*, vol. 6:1 (2000): 57–8.

endeavour between Brossard, Luce Guilbeault, and Margaret Wescott. The collective buoyancy of the feminist moment in the seventies is well captured in the documentary film, which chronicles the uninhibited powers of a feminist utopian imaginary. For Brossard and her contemporaries, establishing a 'system of feminine values, the movement and strategies of feminine and/or writing'[6] became a way of subverting the patriarchal language that occluded them. How can writing, reading, theorizing, and translating be rethought, they asked, and how can language and literature alter or mark one's presence in the world? Collaborative thinking, utopian thinking, desiring thinking: all these theoretical models matter.

As the writer Lisa Robertson puts it in her introduction to the English translation of yet another of Brossard's collaborative engagements, *Theory, A Sunday* (excerpted here), 'theory was not only an institutional discourse but a manual and testing ground for political revolution.' It is our hope that this reader will work as both archive and incentive. As an archive, we aim to show Brossard's artistic and intellectual work both. In turn, we hope that the resonance of her thinking in these texts acts as motivation and material for future revolutions.

Our selection process has been a dynamic one. In addition to working across provincial borders and time zones, we editors have been thinking together across linguistic and lived experiences that differ from each other. We feel this is a strength, and that the dynamism of our process is in conversation with what we see in Brossard's work. *Avant Desire* is organized by thematic sections, which we will go on to describe more fully below. Readers will notice the ways in which these sections cross-pollinate. This is both deliberate and inevitable: Brossard has been orbiting and evolving her writerly attention around some key themes. *Desirings; Generations; The City; Translations, Retranslations, Transcollaborations; Futures*: each of these descriptors hails, for us, some of the central concerns and beautiful obsessions of Brossard's work.

Readers familiar with Brossard will recognize some key texts from her oeuvre. *Mauve Desert*, for example, with its feminist innovations on the form of the novel and its translative play is indispensable to new and

---

6. *The Aerial Letter*, 93.

returning readers. Likewise, the poetic consciousness-raising of *The Aerial Letter* reminds those of us familiar with her work of Brossard's ability to intertwine historical reflection on the effects of heteropatriarchy with a buoyant hope in a feminist future we so desperately need, then and now. We have worked to present some of Brossard's less-known, less-accessible writing, as well as some new translations of her work. Our thinking, throughout this process, has been to highlight the importance of collaboration, of translation, of returning to key themes, images, and concepts over the course of this writer's life. Readers will encounter some of the compromises we have made, as well. For example, in order to make tangible the discursive nature of Brossard's translations, as well as her work *with* translators, we have sacrificed the usual airiness of her layouts in service of more crosstalk. We are confident that our commitment to bringing these particular selections together plots a course full of delicious tributaries for the reader. Our work, which has taken us to archives and libraries, through emails and conversations with each other and with other writers, and, wonderfully, to Brossard's dining-room table, has led to some joyous discoveries.

DESIRINGS

The range and scope of Brossard's work is staggering. We joked that we continually needed to revise this introduction to account for the arrival of new texts and translations! What is staggering is this: Brossard has been insisting on the necessity of pleasure for half a century. Moreover, she has insisted on the humanity of queer pleasure, of lesbian pleasure. Of the pleasure of women. She has insisted on her own pleasure. If it is laudable for us to recognize the importance of pleasure in 2020, imagine the subversiveness and danger of insisting on queer pleasure fifty years ago. This book, and especially this first section, works to pay homage to Brossard's celebration of pleasure which, we believe, hinges around the seductive force of desire in its multiple iterations.

This first section of *Avant Desire: A Nicole Brossard Reader* opens with translations by Jennifer Moxley, Barbara Godard, and Pierre Joris. These poems attend to the multi-faceted nature of the force in Brossard's work. In grammar and syntax, it stretches meaning and makes space for the reality of women loving women. It is rendered as colour; mauve is a homonym that indicates space, possibility, and futurity. Here, we have selected texts that track some of the ways desire has changed in the writer's lifetime. The reader opens with a selection from *Logical Suite* (1970) in which the temporality of desire is already made plural in so far as it is in transit between subjects and bodies.

And what happens when we reject what is considered inevitable? Fixed? Let us allow Brossard to introduce you to Monique Wittig, whose thinking in *Les Guérillères* also courses through these texts: 'Since the day when the lesbian peoples renounced the idea that it was absolutely necessary to die, no one has. The whole process of death has ceased to be a custom' (*Lovhers*). The works in this section renounce heteropatriarchal imperatives in favour of desiring and of pleasure. Desire is ubiquitous. It is fluid. At its best, we want to say, it is *creator of worlds*.

GENERATIONS

We need, and indeed new generations are now creating, new realities. The queer, hybrid, gender-fluid reality is a kinship between bodies and cities in flux. We need dexterousness and fluidity; we need to be able to collide with the contradictions of our lives as we live them. We need to remember where we have been even as we are driving *a fast ca*r (a fuel cell) into the desert, and we must recognize who is with us in the car, on what path, in which sentence. Brossard's thinking reminds us of these variances and urgencies – even as the world is heating and changing and reminding us, too, of its urgencies.

Generations is perhaps the shortest of these thematic sections, but the texts we have placed here are vital. They demonstrate Brossard's attentiveness to the power of the written work to make space in the structures that oppress us. Take, for example, an excerpt of this poem: 'Ardour draws its knots of presence/ here and there in the city we live/ on convictions' (from *Ardour*). The speaker moves across time and space and hails a collective 'we' that survives on conviction. Epistolary, fragmentary, intimate: the texts here perform care for past and future generations.

Always ahead of her time, Brossard's work remains, even when politically adroit, committed to pleasure, something we are seeing in younger writers' such as adrienne maree brown, who writes about pleasure activism.[7] From letters to other generations to meditations on the millennia of oppressive patriarchal systems, Brossard's work manages to ask hard questions about the necessity for pleasure in the midst of struggle. Her work poses these questions without losing hold of the body.

Here, the poetic process of making, of poiesis, invites and performs desire. This invitation and performance are both for and before the desired. Across languages and restrictions, standing before oppressive structures and before beloveds, reaching across oceans and other geographies to find community and connection. As Jennifer Moxley puts it in her introduction to *Nicole Brossard: Selections*, to reinvent language is no glib or novel act. To reinvent language, constantly, is an act of desire for a state freer from oppressions than where we are living now. And, as Brossard herself suggested in our discussions of this reader, writing allows us to create what doesn't exist. It's not the same as speech. Writing allows us to open and expand certain zones in the brain, certain zones of pleasure.

The city, too, is a zone of pleasure: it is both subject and character in Brossard's work, and for this reason it, too, is a thematic anchor of *Avant Desire*. Often, the city is specific; Montreal, for example, is offered here as a complex space of cultural, political, and social richness that has come to seem a lesbian oasis for generations, as we see in the publication of *Theory, a Sunday* by Belladonna*, the innovative feminist New York press. Sometimes, the city is figural, standing in for freedoms of movement of language, and of desire (*Intimate Journal*). Still other times, the city marks a cosmopolitan engagement with conditions and possibilities of elsewhere, as in *Green Night of Labyrinth Park*.

---

7. adrienne maree brown, in her book of the same name, explains that pleasure activism is 'Making justice and liberation the most pleasurable experiences we can have. Learning that pleasure gets lost under the weight of oppression, and it is liberatory work to reclaim it.' https://www.manrepeller.com/2019/03/what-is-pleasure-activism.html

Writing is to 'see one's desire come as far as possible, that is, closer: to the very edge, right to the limits – where it might very well falter.'[8] And yes, there are limits. In her poetic essay '6 December 1989 Among the Centuries,' for example, the reader encounters limits in the real time of the text. For younger readers, this essay performs the collective shock women experienced when a gunman went into a Montreal post-secondary space for learning, separated the women from the men, called the women 'feminists' and then shot fourteen of them dead. Gender-based violence is not new, nor is it being met with the collective and systemic work needed to eradicate it for every person. Brossard's essay makes space for the frustration and rage one may experience when encountering, again, the violence of heteropatriarchy and misogyny. Moving from prose reflections on hope and freedom of movement, the speaker – not in her home city – learns of the violence against women at École Polytechnique, and the line falters. What the speaker desires – freedom of movement, freedom of thinking, freedom of desiring – meets the old structures of patriarchy and misogyny.[9] In an interview about Le Désert mauve, Brossard stated, 'the ending seems very surprising, even gratuitous, but that's exactly what happened at the École Polytechnique, it's exactly the same kind of hatred. So I haven't imagined anything, I have only decoded a pattern that does not explode all the time, but is there all the time.'[10] Met with the limits and refusals of misogyny, Brossard breaks the hegemony of the prose line to reach toward women. In so doing, she subverts patriarchal violence and refuses the proper names of the perpetrators. The text itself becomes a site of struggle to extend the limits and, finally, remove them altogether, if only on the horizon for now. But it is a horizon to reach for, daily.

---

8. The Aerial Letter, 70, and on p. 80 of this book.

9. In her first essay responding to the events of December 6, published in La Presse, Brossard employs a similar tactic: 'All things considered, M. L. was no young man. He was as old as all the sexist, misogynist proverbs, as old as all the Church fathers who ever doubted women has a soul. He was as old as the legislators who ever forbade women the university, the right to vote, access to the public sphere. M. L. was as old as Man and his contempt for women.'

10. 'Order and Imagination,' an interview by Beverley Daurio, Books in Canada, March 1991, 21.

The feminist city has been influential to locations and generations – from Daphne Marlatt and Betsy Warland, Lisa Robertson, Larissa Lai and Rita Wong in Vancouver, to Gail Scott and Erín Moure in Montreal, to Eileen Myles, Rachel Levitsky, Renee Gladman, Akilah Oliver, and the Belladonna* collaborative in New York, among many others, and now to another generation coming into their voices who are searching for a way to be *present* once more in very difficult political times. In yet another difficult time, literature can, we think, provide some roadmaps both for navigating struggle and for pointing to horizons beyond it. Disagreement is a vital aspect of feminist thought. We see Brossard as a model for helping us to confront and encounter these ruptures. As an example we've included a conversation between Nathanaël, Catherine Mavrikakis, and Brossard, which, we think, models productive disagreement. For, as Lisa Robertson points out in her introduction to *Theory, A Sunday*: 'feminist culture, discourse, and resistance has shaped contemporary urban experience and urban space' and while some writers, we three editors included, claim a certain city – Montreal for example – as a feminist city, Robertson reminds us that 'there is no city without our voices' – the city is us, and the city is diversity: diversity of bodies and voices and opinions.

The texts in this section move like the Situationists' *dérive*, always thinking through a feminist lens. Indeed, concepts like *dérive* and *délire* put into play textual and readerly drifts that carry affective resonances, for moving is motion but it is also emotion. The collectivity that marks a 'true' *dérive* comes from the poetic engagement of the reader and the speaker across time, space, and geography. The hologram in *Picture Theory* (1991) or the folded or eroded vocabularies in *Surfaces of Sense* wield deft examples of this motion toward the unthinkable limits of the city as a textual body igniting both pleasure and curiosity, fact and affect. Beyond the conceptual and affective dimensions of mobility, stasis is overcome by narratives that drift just as the characters in her novels are also drifters. From *A Book* to *French Kiss* and *Baroque at Dawn*, her characters are in search of connections, an idea, a lover, a cause. Rather than a linear narrative, these books are composed of perspectives that intersect various vanishing points: a woman's touch, the shape of her body, the curve of her mouth. In *French Kiss*, for instance, we're plunged into an uninterrupted kiss 'in which the text slows down in Camomille's mouth, salivating letters and words of love the better to ... suck on fragments of fiction.' In *Picture Theory*, a book about perspectives, lesbian love, and science-fiction, those connections are holographic; the horizon here no longer operates as the meeting point of vertical and horizontal axes but is transformed into something much more oblique. Lines of desire are material traces of reading and writing, which are superimposed. These lines – drawn between reading and writerly acts – are kept in superposition, able to grasp at disparate realities at once: 'Words begin to turn round on themselves, inciting reflection, inciting thought toward new approaches to reality.'[11]

TRANSLATIONS, RETRANSLATIONS, TRANSCOLLABORATIONS

Brossard's work exists on a spectrum from pure translation to retranslations to what might be called transcollaboration. These are the themes that organize one of the larger sections of *Avant Desire*. *Transcollaboration* is a neologism we offer which gestures to the intimate relationship translation plays in her poetry and prose. We think transcollaboration might also indicate the soft edges we find in her texts that exist between writing and reading, as well as between her texts and the ones she brings into her work as an affirmatory poetics based in collaboration. To trace this generous poetics, we've choreographed a movement in this section – a kind of living pulse between the works – from translations and retranslations to transcollaborations. We see this webwork of translators' engagements woven throughout this book, from Patricia Claxton, Robert Majzels and Erín Moure, Susanne de Lotbinière-Harwood, and Barbara Godard, as well as in a new generation of translators like Jennifer Moxley, Angela Carr, Oana Avasilichioaei, Rhonda Mullins, and Katia Grubisic; we see it, too, in the homage of ideas from Charles Bernstein and in Bronwyn Haslam's anagrammatic translations. These collaborations and translations come from across generations. These translators have made

---

11. *The Aerial Letter*, 68, and on p. 78 of this book.

Brossard's books, in English, possible and we have tried to include as many translators as possible.

Of course, it is crucial to begin with the acknowledgement that so often here translation is a form of collaboration. Some aspects of collaboration are more deeply entangled than others, however. These textual sites are where our use of the term *transcollaboration* comes from. Works of transcollaboration include those moments when the concept of authorship or translatorship is brocaded with various configurations and reconfigurations that complicate the terms *rewriting, rereading,* and *retranslating.*

What we call transcollaboration also has roots in the torrent of feminist interventions in translation and translation theory between Québécoise writers and writers from English Canada in the 1980s. In the feminist bilingual magazine *Tessera's* issue on translation, Barbara Godard describes this subversive and playful approach to translation as 'transformance': 'a mode of performance' that 'emphasize[s] the work of translation, [and] the focus on the process of constructing meaning in the activity of transformation.'[12] This is the same period in which Nicole Brossard and Daphne Marlatt collaborated on two chapbooks, *Mauve* (1985, included in this reader) and *Character/Jeu de lettres* (1986), that were themselves collaborations between the French magazine *La Nouvelle barre du jour* and the English publication entitled *Writing*. Indeed, this was a prolific and empowered period in the history of collaborations between experimental Québécoise and English Canadian feminist writers and literary translators. In their linguistic experiments, these feminist writers/translators used several paratextual strategies (footnotes, introductions, diaries) to underscore the fact that bodies – beautiful, aching, anxious, aging bodies – were ensconced in the translated text rather than the invisible, equivalence-producing translators that the cultural imaginary had relegated to the oubliettes of cross-linguistic literary production. Feminist strategies addressing the invisibility of the translator simultaneously sought to address the invisibility of women as subjects, and the collaboration between Marlatt and Brossard in *Mauve* captures the subversive spirit of that era.

---

12. Barbara Godard. 'Theorizing Feminist Discourse/Translation' *Tessera*. Vol. 6 (Spring/printemps), 1989: 42–53, p. 46.

As we've mentioned, few writers have such an active base of translators as Brossard, an exponentially translated author whose corpus continues to be read and circulated in many more languages than the English translations gathered here: they include German, Spanish, Italian, Japanese, Slovanian, Norwegian, Romanian, and Catalan. Those who have translated her comprise a strong, loyal community of writers and thinkers. *Poiesis*, which derives from the Greek, means to make or to bring into being what did not exist before. *Making*. Brossard's thinking is poiesis if we take the word at face value; it makes and remakes a way of engaging with the world, and we could not conceive of a Brossard reader that did not acknowledge these rich collaborations.

Her collaboration with her translators is an example of what we mean when we say *world-making*. Kate Briggs' beautifully decanted address to the art of translation is illuminating:

> Translation operates, then, as a kind of vital test: an ever-renewable demonstration of the literary value of the novel in [its original language].[13] Which is one way of saying that literature, that quality we call the literary, simply cannot do without translation as a means of repeatedly reaffirming it.[14]

In a world where utopia seems an impossible dream, Briggs' understanding of translation as repeated affirmation is chlorophyllic. Translation works to energize and circulate thinking. Here, translation is acknowledgement, recognition, engagement, and affirmation across differences in languages, temporalities, and contexts. Indeed, there are rich resonances between Briggs' understanding of translation and Brossard's own reflection on the process:

> There are certainly many ways of approaching translation: for me, it involves examining the gears of words, thoughts, images, and meanings and immersing myself in the dreamy meanderings generated by

---

13. The emphasis on the novel specifically rather than any literary form stems from the fact that Briggs' essay stitches together her reflections on being the translator of Roland Barthes' *The Preparation of the Novel* (Columbia University Press, 2011).

14. *This Little Art*. London: Fitzcarraldo, 2018.

any literary reading. It also involves tackling the cultural contours of language, identity, and a certain kind of thinking practice. Simply put, it involves valorizing the constant virtual state in which we live, a state that increases the possibilities of approaching life with intelligence and wonder.[15]

This reflection comes from a new essay (included here) which Oana Avasilichioaei and Rhonda Mullins have translated as 'And Suddenly I Find Myself Remaking the World.' That this long essay is included in the Reader in full, albeit in the 'Futures' section, is itself a result of the literal and figurative dynamism of translation, and the generosity necessary to move a text through language to reach a range of readers. In it, we encounter affirmation, reaffirmation, and wonder. Wonder, 'not because life is necessarily wonderful,' writes Brossard, 'but because life is complex, diverse, and mysterious enough for us to develop an attraction for it that is something other than instinctual.'[16]

Here, dear reader, you will find an excerpt from Barbara Godard's translation of *L'Amèr, ou Le chapitre effrité* (1977), entitled *These Our Mothers, or: The Disintegrating Chapter* (1983), alongside a brand new translation of the same piece by Erín Moure and Robert Majzels entitled *SeaMother, or The Bitteroded Chapter* (2019). In pairing the works together, we want to foreground the way in which translation is an ongoing and active impulse. It is a generous and generative series of conversations that occur over time and through texts. We also see rich and discursive conversation occurring in Norwegian/French poet Caroline Bergvall's English translation of 'Typhon dru' (1997) which we have placed alongside Moure's and Majzels' 'Typhoon Thrum' (2003). This generative energy is discernible in the intervals and repatterned rhythms of Brossard's mutating texts through their retranslations. Mutations, which invite us to look more closely at ways a poem written in the 1980s, for instance, might be read in 2020. As Moure and Majzels remind us in the context of their re-translation of *L'Amèr ou Le chapitre effrité*, '[e]very translation reflects not just an original text, but also a reading. We chose to translate the "figural" series of poems from

15. Ibid.

16. *And Suddenly I Find Myself Remaking the World*, pp. 284–304 in this book.

SeaMother, or The Bitteroded Chapter to see what voice and tenor would arise from a reading of these texts in 2019.'[17]

In the spirit of celebrating and highlighting the dialogue between the works, we have also included moments when we see Brossard in conversation with others as well as with herself, most notably in a rare piece of self-translation ('Polynésie des yeux/Polynesya of the Eyes') as well as a homolinguistic or French to French translation in a work called *L'Aviva*, which we have placed alongside Anne-Marie Wheeler's English translation entitled *Aviva*. This particular work is interesting in that it is not quite a literal nor a normative translation but rather a dialogue between fragments that face each other in a format that recalls the layout of bilingual editions. With Wheeler's English translation we get the complex interaction between the fragments that Brossard orchestrates in her original, and in addition to this textual play we also see the way the translator senses her way through the text as she recreates – indeed rewrites – the links and drifts that are (mis)aligned in the original.

Brossard has also inspired decades of what we're calling transcollaborations – with Fred Wah in the transcreated 'If Yes Seismal/Si Sismal' and *Mauve* with Daphne Marlatt, both included in this book – where original and translation are offered together, face to face on the page. These two works offer examples of translation as a transformative reading practice. In *Mauve*, for example, Brossard has written a short poetic sequence in French that Marlatt converts into English as a creative counterpart. It is less useful here to think in terms of original and translation, or source and target text, than it is to think in terms of two languages, two minds converting the electrical impulses of language, as Marlatt herself observes in her essay on the work: 'Translating *Mauve* became a remarkable illustration of this process, a reading of the depths of the drift, a writing running counter to it, so that i felt as if, in the process, my own cerebral cortext were being marked or written on. *Mauve* stands as a commentary on the act of reading and especially the act of translating.'[18]

---

17. Erín Moure and Robert Majzels, 'Note on Translation,' p. 215 of this book.

18. Daphne Marlatt, 'Translating MAUVE: Reading Writing.' *Tessera* Spec. Issue La Traduction au Féminin/Translating Women. 6 (Spring/Primtemps 1989): 29-30. https://doi.org/10.25071/1923-9408.2358016.

Then there are the texts that walk across the tightrope of translation and straddle the line between translation and something else. We conceive of these as creative responses in an attempt to capture the creative and discursive engagements. Included here is Charles Bernstein's response to Brossard's self-translated piece 'Polynésie des yeux/Polynesya of the Eyes,' entitled 'Polynesian Days,' where familiar words and turns of phrases from the originals appear in drifts and collusions that capitalize on polyphonic and poetic inventiveness. Beyond Bernstein, Bronwyn Haslam's 'Silk Font 1,' an anagrammatic translation of Brossard's French prose poem 'Soft Link 1,' seemed an essential addition to the reader. Here is a text that operates with the (almost) impossible constraint of only using the same letters found in the original. In many ways, Haslam's text captures something of the importance of poiesis to translation and, similarly, to Brossard's work.

Mauve desert, mauve moods, mauve modes of movement. That's the thing about horizons – we move ourselves to their shimmering potential. Desiring, we cross generations, inhabit cities and horizons beyond them, and, if we are fortunate, we translate to encounter one another. We confront the wall of fire. We defend them too. We sprawl ourselves across them. We traverse urban sprawl that compresses the scene of a kiss, in Brossard's novel *French Kiss*, for instance, with simultaneous scenes across Montreal, as though they could all be held together in the space between two ardent mouths opening for each other, or two generations, or ten, all the mouths open for each other.

FUTURES

In a time where the question of who and which bodies matter, we are again struck with the realization that Brossard has insisted on multiple bodies and on creating space for bodies both known and yet to be known. Language has changed in the half-century during which she has been writing, yes, and we have made some editorial decisions to address those changes in language. Pronouns, especially, have been necessarily oxygenated. So too, have terms of identification shifted. Language will and must continue to shift to accommodate our multiple lived realities. Or, as Brossard puts it, 'writing is making oneself visible. To show all forms of experiences.'[19] When we organized the section we named 'Futures,' we were thinking of the ways in which Brossard's work faces horizons, which open outward. We were thinking, too, of the ways in which today's future becomes tomorrow's archive.

There are multiple bodies present here too, in the editorial and curatorial gestures of this reader, and indeed in the crafting of this introduction – not to mention you, dear reader, who have been very much on our mind. So, when we say that Nicole Brossard's work invites the reader to see (and understand that you are creating) the future in the present, it is a cautiously hopeful wager, because perhaps now more than ever that present is so multidimensional – and so easily co-opted and complicit. The present offers a space of anticipation, for the present vibrates in language and vibrates differently for each of us. It is there, in the vibrating present of language, that a space opens in the text. We are reminded of what Nicole Brossard shared with us while we were sitting in her dining room in the fall of 2019: 'Reading turns us on. It's mysterious, but we start to understand how literature works [...] and we also discover what's most interesting about human beings. By meandering in language, as in life, a whole world becomes available.'[20]

Our meeting took place on the day of the massive climate strikes across Canada. Half a million people gathered in Montreal. We had each attended before meeting at Brossard's house to talk about the possibilities and pleasures of thinking together through and across languages – and generations, Geneviève's baby in the arms of Brossard's partner as we wound down from our work. To meander in language, to be turned on by the mysterious power of reading, to be interested in what each person was saying in the moment, and then to try to record it here for you to read – this feels future-oriented for us. This feels vital.

---

19. Nicole Brossard. 'E muet mutant.' *La Nouvelle barre du jour* 50 (1975c): 10-27. Trans. M. L. Taylor. *Ellipse* 23–23 (1979): 45–63.

20. 'Ça nous allume quand on lit. Mystérieusement, on commence à comprendre un peu comment fonctionne la littérature [...] mais aussi tout ce qu'il y a de plus intéressant des êtres humains [...] On peut flâner dans la vie et dans la langue. C'est en flânant qu'on apprend aussi une partie de la vie' (from our interview with Brossard, translated by Geneviève Robichaud).

The question of address too, has seemed vital, and has kept us company throughout the work of curation. Who is this 'we' hailed, sometimes, in Brossard's writing? Who is called – then, now, in the future – by the shifting and often recurrent signifiers of woman, of lesbian, of poet? What if, as readers, we chafe against some of these signifiers, or feel adrift off the coast of them? Sometimes, the poet offers us some signposts.[21] Sometimes these are satisfying maps for a reader. Sometimes, they leave us wanting more. Desiring conversation. Can or should we as readers infer collective subjectivity into the poet's use of the singular pronoun 'I'? Can the individual hail collectives, both imagined and on the edge of what is possible to imagine at a given moment in history?

We are in the midst of climate catastrophe. Abuses of power rage on both global and local levels. Misogyny and fascism feel ever more present. As we finalize this introduction, the rail system in Canada has come to halt by cross-country blockades in support of the Wet'suwet'en. What is the power of poetry, and the possibilities of future-oriented collectivity in the face of these realities? Again, we turn to Brossard, who figures the work of writing as a quest for necessary pleasure in the midst of upheaval and turmoil. Brossard writes, 'For my part, I have always made writing a place of pleasure, of quest, a space of dangerous intensity, a space for turbulence having its own dynamic.'[22] We are living in turbulent times, but there has also always been turbulence at any given moment on our planet. Let's imagine that getting out in front of turbulence, of advancing a teleology of desire – for jouissance, for pleasure, for the 'dreaming parts of us' – is possible, even political.[23] If we imagine that the time we spend together on these pages matters, then we are

21. 'For example, while writing a feminist article, I questioned myself, wondering who is writing my text: the poet, the feminist, or the lesbian. I came up with the answer: the feminist is moral, responsible, fair, humanist, has solidarity. The lesbian is audacious, radical, takes risks, strictly focusses on women. The creative person has imagination and is able to process ambivalent emotion and contradictions as well as transforming anger, ecstasy, desire, pain, and so on, into social meaning' (Brossard, 'Poetic Politics.' *Fluid Arguments*, 35).

22. *Nicole Brossard*. Louise Forsyth, ed. (Toronto: Guernica, 2005). 20.

23. 'Between Plato's body-tomb, the theatrical-body, the body of modernist writing, the feminine body of difference, the lesbian body of utopia, the queer body of performance, the body invents its surviving, its narrative, which is its displacement in the middle of knowledge and beliefs. We need to place the body right at the right place in the dreaming part inhabiting us.' (Brossard, 'Fluid Arguments.' *Fluid Arguments*, 68).

already facing new horizons. Brossard's body of work is one that the reader wants to come back to. That readerly return is a guiding force of our editorial curation here. The sensual dimension of her narratives, in poetry as well as prose, welcome this. It is itself about the measure of desire, the measure of writing. It is easy to become infatuated, to admire the way Brossard's sentences work beyond a single vanishing point, how they multiply desire. It's a question of movement as much as energy, a question of the (d)rift between the writing, the written, and the sensations that gather there. Pleasure is never singular. Never over nor complete. Rattling language to multiply pleasure, there is a refusal to have pleasure denied.

The Brossardian text has the capacity, a clarity, for drilling down into things, for illuminating what's inside the sheath or shell of language, while being, at the same time, never straightforward. Opening vistas and spaces to inhabit, Brossard's poetry and prose offer a radiant gesture, a kind of activism that is working in a different register by refocusing the narrative or by role modelling a new trajectory, a space of clarity, of energy – another way of being. That's part of what's so interesting about Brossard's feminist poetics – that by excavating language in order to seek to uncover or more fully understand the history carried within the frame of a word, her poetry and prose are also always interrupting our expectations, shifting the light in an upward trajectory that is luminous, that illuminates, that penetrates the darkness of/in language.

We have elected to close both 'Futures' and the Reader with another homage to Brossard's innovation. In *Picture Theory* the reader discovers *Hologram*, a book within a book. A similar discovery occurs when we turn the page to find *Mauve Horizon* within the covers of *Mauve Desert*. Books hold worlds of possibility, even other books! *Avant Desire* ends with another book: *And Suddenly I Find Myself Remaking the World*. This full text was translated, as we mentioned, in part by Oana Avasilichioaei and in part by Rhonda Mullins. Each translator leaves something of her imprint on the text she has read and translated. This motion to and fro, from one thinking perspective to another, is part of the invitation we offer in reading Brossard's essay, which crisscrosses translations and translators. Here, too, the electric energy of Brossard's work is made multiple through these engagements in translations, as well as book design.

Deep in the incandescence of language we surface and spiral back and forward to what is the 'avant' of desire: not original, as though existing in some mythic beginning, and yet there is something of the grandeur of myth in the Brossardian oeuvre. What comes before desire? Is there a before or does desire start with desire? This would suggest a kind of impossible trajectory, for how can desire leap toward desire? But perhaps that impossible movement in and out of itself is key to understanding how the concept of avant desire might come to embrace something untranslatable in Brossard's writing (a reminder that tending to the present moment, to the body and word and thinking of the moment, we hold our own power, and in that holding of the present moment we have the possibility of creating our future. Or futures. We, all who are present in the text we have before us, wherever and whenever we are, we have the power. We occupy space in utopia when we are together, thinking, listening, and talking. We are in 'the meeting place of our desires' and 'the future can' and will 'still be swayed.'[24]

---

24. 'Le future, il nous appartient encore [...] il est lié à nos rêves, il est lié à un potentiel, il est lié à des désirs, et donc on peut intervenir dans le future selon la rencontre des désirs' (from our interview with Brossard, translated by Geneviève Robichaud).

{ Desirings }

LOGICAL SUITE

from *Nicole Brossard: Selections*

tr. Pierre Joris

everything gels white
in happy time
deep dark also
all chaos when your hand passes too much
then departure for

belly thus all is there
as sprout as latency
oversteps the mark and never restricts itself
curved line never gels in the past
what the belly espouses up front

in my saying naked
the colour though fictive so true
cuts in the delirious black

⠇

mutual attractions
when intimate renewal
appropriates from
us locks in together
displace the shadow so slowly
around us
that the bonds move very initiatory

⠇

between the lines the liquid slides
and imposes itself novel
thus from the body pleasure gushes
delicious humidity the mauve rests
and inscribes itself radiant fixity

⁝

afterward it's so little
once time's slid out of reach
afterward it's however
to retrace one's steps
when the figures put forward rip

⁝

it's only initial and doesn't stop being so
the movement
displacing distorting
the horizon the horizon broken
always too imponderable

⁝

to act and tend
in the risen night
toward the hidden places
to act swaying between
the world rhythm the authentic
doubly silence pours forth carnal

⁝

again and without cease
entrancing contrast
that reworks the outlines
draws them away from the goal
forces our orientation
again
and time shakes from not being eternal

                                      °
                                      °

there is the palpable night shifts feverish
that is to say disconcerting verbal variant

oh how the invariable 'elsewhere' tames the pronoun
in this imprecise zone of the present
never was the ephemeral so close to the trap

yet it is a matter of the same saying
between charm and trap, it oscillates

                                      °
                                      °

suspension of the act
to understand is a sojourn
excluding any definition
to breathe to show nothing
though everything rushes in

perpetual face
no matter the mask

in these opaque times heaven hauled that many frenzies

with a single signifying stroke when the saying leaks
the word massacre(s)

intensity first of all
            by probing further ahead further
                                            down
                                                farther away

the formula is born
from where does one know it by what by a point
thus vibrant for it nourishes and weighs fully
on the meaning and the counter
in gender agrees with unruly in number
and moves

liaison
the more it precedes the ink
pushes precisely (before) outside and inside

transition
or
droll these signs empty and blue despite
even if (that is to say although)

restriction
nevertheless

explication
vague it is
because too much space between the words
vague and beautiful to consume the liaison

as soon as it enunciates itself
paradoxically future and past engender
at the same time
that moment when it goes without saying that crossing
it happens that black/black badly cross-rules
the white spaces
limit of contrast

thus sparkles the artifice and exposes itself
eventual accomplishment
all on the surface
from riot to fabulous sonorous suites
the said connection erasure
double exasperation
the code struts the code analyses the code dictates
and at the exact opposite the tender code appears

between code and code space is illusory
no place conducive to denunciation
terminology modifies

the code infiltrates
the least attempt at resistance

henceforth meaning will be double
one too many
the artifice is inevitable

here's how.

Suite logique
1970, tr. 2010

THE PART FOR THE WHOLE

from *Nicole Brossard: Selections*

tr. Jennifer Moxley

my lacerating strategist who leads me to fiction
censored in the liar's edits or time
the split: desire's reflection is like this
a lure thrown out in vain
spinning through space until
the 'creature' says: my blood doesn't fit
this version or excerpt anymore

⁝

to save her provocative skin
to lose reason the rush the goods
spread out by the mirror if you attempt
a moon's discretion between your thighs
the liquid outcome
vulva – *lu e(t) vu* – read and seen
in reality you undress her skin
and take it all in

⁝

feigned – the entire bid / fiction –
the injury's intuition (the injured)
her tongue speaks with a hole the one licked
or it's a place to perplex the delicious expert
she trembles in love inversely
her memory perplexes the *slut*story museum
woman / voting booth / stretch marks: what a beautiful baby!
she soaks without quoting, very private

⸭

that tends to flow
the day *drenched in ink*
green or that moment you open your robe
egress illustrated
circadian today and
the moon your condition of rhythm sister
with syrupy insides she depletes
the planet of corridors filled with crossroads
my wife *aroused* a vow circling your passionate neck

⸭

her ass and thank goodness dissolves the
first stone or this erosion of the dismissal
for she cheats all lost time by playing
opposite
silently on the outskirts of town
without context (swallowing but concise)
so she says: *that's senseless*
or irony of the after-effect the abolished
without history and mother tongue in hospital
convulsively white this body speaks
perhaps to amuse herself underground
but at heart charged *without restraint*
she start over from the bottom of the page
filled with the unleashed scents that undress her:
flying

⸭

drying up or fictive the liar opens
her fist this abduction all confined by the masculine
spread out

her withdraw – it depends – at what price
and the beyond amends her history
you get wet and dry up in pleasant parallels
drifting when the net is lifted
or concealed down to your feet you put on the brakes
and yet this pretext intervenes with your hand as process
a gripping sift of the inside or a return to self
this morning shifting history with a silent e

La Partie pour le tout
1975, tr. 2010

CALLIGRAPHER / IN DRAG

from *Daydream Mechanics*

tr. Larry Shouldice

December 1970

text that can be read horizontally as before different in the number of coincidences of the fragments assigned as such to the role will be silenced for revealing herself through the written matter itself fragmentation of meaning fragment this space for what is written glimpsed the spectacle of the written. before the onlooker before the cross-dresser to the birth of ambiguity (aperture from which surges forth life) before the spectacle finally a calligrapher duplicates without erasure before the cross-dresser the mark left vague in the atmosphere left mark curve in movement gesture of writing.   calligrapher in drag intentional double usage of one on / by the other double surface multiple purpose.   before the text travestied with insistence and connotation

⁝

, in the comma sense scar line drawn backwards to its centre (lower belly) and licit mobile link and justification for what follows, in the case in which the visible   the slope of the calligraphy produces quick impatience unanimous   thus I provoke riot   I   in the plural person cause insist riot, opening up of meaning if multiple travesty threat subversive false eyelashes face   new incidence and checkmate

⁝

the allusions understood   the threshold passed to choose an original form of allusive denunciation for with finger with arms to make the facts precise incoherent the *system*   including a meaning   a place in terms of denunciation   a void.   return to the first version   the indecent illegible spectacle repulsing / attracting   in sight and   in knowledge before   inevitable   travestied and anonymous initiators.

the commentary is printed thus in intensifying fervour   the inclination
of the text legible in its beginnings this commentary limited in itself the
present in the flexibility of muscles invested with a hard male resistance in
drag (pleasure and confusion) in the transgression

cancelled everything before this   to haunt your look   rather in form
of abbreviation outlawed

Méchanique jongleuse
1973, tr. 1980

JUNE THE FEVER

from *Lovhers*

tr. Barbara Godard

i read the text of your project. i am writing you now from a sidewalk café on St. Denis where i have been sitting for an hour. it is a fine day and all about there is an air of reality. this café is called La Cour, it has a little yellow fence.

i don't know why, but rather than reading what you have written, i'd like to imagine it. i picture you obsessively in the midst of writing excessively as if nothing could stop you – so, you never worry about anything. when you quote, however, you must stop, it seems to me. for example, when you point out what Y observes: the relationship of thought to language is not a thing but a process, a continuous movement from thought to word and from word to thought, what happens in your eye?

i go at your project in pieces because literally it burns me. each fragment becomes my 'integral' of you, the total work in the sense of an equivalence, of a shared reading facing the certainties i sometimes push away with tears, with forgetting or again with writing so as never to forget even if it is never entirely a question of memory: 'a convenient fiction' to quote Murray whom you quote yourself.

reading the text of your project, i become aware of the extent to which our fictions intersect: looking in our respective circles for the statement of the theory and the theory of play which will put into motion the very emotion of motion.

the waitress just brought me another beer. of course, that doesn't interest you. however, in your text you write *and oriented toward action in everyday life*. i am obstinately looking for traces of everyday life in your work. nothing. everything is in the beyond. entirely real however in each of your gestures/ totally abstract. sometimes i even pronounce 'an abstraction' in your presence. you know however about my fever for everyday life and reality. my desire for words, my appetite for what allows me to imagine the real.

here i am trying to write by exploring all the mechanisms that serve to distract this i (permanent and unexplored) for you have clearly seen in your text of the project that nothing is written about identity without this motivation-mobile as is said about meaning on the look out or about meaning upended, turned back on itself. in reading you i am constantly seeking to displace myself in your words, to see them from all their angles, to find areas of welcome there: *m'y lover, my love.*

if i am writing today it is so i can read you better provocatively so as to speak at last of the systems obsessing us: the brain produces its drugs which are our utopias.

three poets, three women who are poets, have just sat down at the next table. i know them, we greet each other. *Picture theory*: these women and i are products of the same system. our albums of perception are full of complicity. we know the structure. but today, i stay alone at my table because i want to go on reading the text of your project.

i read your text and without second thought i note that you have written your name as a reference among others, with a publication date in parentheses. i put the number (4) before inscribing *Lovhers* and i can only make headway by initials. just imagine a little what *fiction* might mean in these circumstances. an excess of realism compelled to be revealed only behind a screen of skin: mine. it's the tension demanded by any application of emotion. tension that gets a quality of attention. maybe there is a link with what you call the sources of ideological transformation.

my friends have left. there are some men, two i've spotted, who pass back and forth in front of the sidewalk café. they are crazy, i think. madness is on the loose here, scarcely noticed. i think they're all crazy. some are my age, others yours. their bodies are very *affected*. each madness has its own look, as if a crucial incident gives everyone's life its *style.*

since 1972, you say, there has been a tendency to distinguish two types of content in long-term memory: episodic and semantic. on that subject, i refer you back to *Prochain épisode* and *Trou de mémoire* by an author you probably don't know. they are books valuable for exploring what you call the 'forms of consciousness.'

i think all those books you surround yourself with excite you in a vital way. *me too*, mind you. as if each book produced emanations. we play then with the invisible. seduced, carried away or touched to the quick. each time the strategy of the books must be unmasked and we leave foundering there in the course of the reading, our biological skins.

B. N. says in an interview (*exit*, winter 76–77): 'certainly the volcano liberated Lowry, but something unusual happened, a simultaneous relationship between himself and his character, more than an identity, an exchange of personality ... In fact, a passage from one to the other, from the writer into his writing until he actually confines himself, so that he is not liberated in the sense you say, but is put into his own inferno. There is an interview with Lowry where he is asked what he would like to write and he answers: Under, under, under the volcano.'

that's the worst thing that could happen to me. it did happen to me. since then I haven't stopped reading/deliring to climb back up to the surface, to find my surfaces again. which no doubt explains my obsession with surfaces of meaning.

i read the text of your project and i find it provocative. it takes spaces away from me. in what way is it important for you to understand the mechanisms of creativity? gap, uncertainty, excess, ellipsis. everything has to be transposed, doesn't it? especially don't confound the surfaces of meaning and the sense of this text. there is no confidence here though something is being confided to you. i said *text* but it may be a real letter. Y. V. says it plainly in the fire Episode of *La grande ourse*: 'This text was written before it happened to me.'

La Cour is full. a little girl is having fun picking up the plastic arrows they put in our glasses. i think she's very pretty. H. just came out of the Faubourg. in great shape.

when you quote Sullerot: 'Not just the dandies but also the "lionesses"!' what do you mean? has the thought of dying in venice crossed your mind? Your text of the project is full of this type of allusion: that excites me and you know it as on those evenings when you wait for my reaction and you are present, sober, at the metamorphosis. Sober and enraptured, already familiar with the place where you know how to put your hand so as to bring about the effect of reality: lovhers. while i am still trying to read/delirium.

i don't stop reading/deliring: 'After the first time *i love you* doesn't mean anything' – '*Me too* is not a perfect answer, because what is perfect can only be formal, and form is missing here.'

you know if you want to get back to the feminine condition over which you pass so rapidly by the way, it increasingly takes the form of our liaison, that is to say the coherence there is between what you write and what i am writing.

you should say acknowledgement. W. and Z., whom you know, spent three years of their life recognizing the words one by one, not all of course, because some of them are unacceptable, unusable, at least in their present state.

i am telling you about my passion for reading you hidden behind these quotations. the facts are such that your project of the text and the text of the project are completed in the taste of the words, in the taste of the kiss. i know that you are real to me/therefore.

Amantes
1980, tr. 1986

SOUS LA LANGUE/UNDER TONGUE

tr. Susanne de Lotbinère-Harwood

Le corps salive, rien pourtant n'est prévu, ni l'abondance des touchers, ni la lenteur furtive, la fureur exacte des bouches. Rien n'est prévu pourtant c'est à la hauteur des yeux que le corps d'abord touche à tout sans prévoir la peau nue, aussi bien le dire, sans prévoir la douceur de la peau qui sera nue avant même que la bouche signale l'état du monde.

Rien ne suggère ici qu'au moindre toucher le regard déjà défaille à vouloir déjà prévoir un tel rapprochement. Rien n'est prévu sinon que la respiration, la répétition des sons entre les chairs. Fricatelle ruisselle essentielle aime-t-elle dans le touche à tout qui arrondit les seins la rondeur douce des bouches ou l'effet qui la déshabille? Rien n'est prévu pourtant au bout du corps la peau fera image du corps car il n'y a rien sans image au bout du corps ce sont les images qui foudroient l'état du monde.

The body salivates, yet nothing is foreseen, not the wealth of touching, not the furtive slowness, the exact frenzy of mouths. Nothing is foreseen yet at eye level is where the body first touches everything without foreseeing the naked skin, and it needs saying, without foreseeing the softness of skin that will be naked even before the mouth signals the state of the world.

Nothing here to suggest that at the slightest touch the gaze already falters wanting already to foresee such a *rapprochement*. Nothing is foreseen other than the breathing, the sounds resounding flesh to flesh. Does she frictional she fluvial she essential does she, in the all-embracing touch that rounds the breasts, love the mouths' soft roundness or the effect undressing her? Nothing is foreseen yet at body's uttermost the skin will image the body for without image there is nothing at body's uttermost images shatter the state of the world.

On ne peut pas prévoir pencher si soudainement vers un visage et vouloir lécher le corps entier de l'âme jusqu'à ce que le regard étincelle de toutes les fureurs et les abandons. On ne peut pas prévoir l'emportement du corps dans l'infini des courbes, des sursauts, chaque fois que le corps se soulève on ne voit pas l'image, la main qui touche la nuque, la langue qui écarte les poils, les genoux qui tremblent, les bras qui par tant de désir entourent le corps comme un univers. On ne voit que le désir. On ne peut pas prévoir l'image, les fous rires, les cris et les larmes. L'image est tremblante, muette et polyphonique. Fricatelle ruisselle essentielle aime-t-elle le long de son corps la morsure, le bruit des vagues, aime-t-elle l'état du monde dans la flambée des chairs pendant que les secondes s'écoulent cyprine, lutines, marines.

You cannot foresee so suddenly leaning toward a face and wanting to lick the soul's whole body till the gaze sparks with furies and yieldings. You cannot foresee the body's being swept into the infinity of curves, of pulsings, every time the body surges you cannot see the image, the hand touching the nape of the neck, the tongue parting the hairs, the knees trembling, the arms from such desire encircling the body like a universe. Desire is all you see. You cannot foresee the image, the bursts of laughter, the screams and the tears. The image is trembling, mute, polyphonic. Does she frictional she fluvial she essential does she all along her body love the bite, the sound waves, does she love the state of the world in the blaze of flesh to flesh as seconds flow by silken salty cyprin.[1]

---

1. Female sexual secretion. From the French *cyprine* [fr. Gk Cyprus, birthplace of Aphrodite]. We are proposing *cyprin* for English usage.

On ne peut pas prévoir si les mots qui l'excitent sont vulgaires, anciens, étrangers ou si c'est toute la phrase qui l'attire et qui avive en elle le désir comme un flair de l'étreinte, une manière de sentir son corps prêt à tout, sans limite. Rien n'est prévu pourtant la bouche du corps à corps excitée par les mots trouve d'instinct l'image qui excite.

You cannot foresee if the words arousing her are vulgar, ancient, or foreign or if it is the whole sentence that attracts her and quickens in her a desire like a scent of the embrace, a way of feeling her body as truly ready for everything. Nothing is foreseen yet the mouth of bodies commoving aroused by the words by instinct finds the image that arouses.

On ne peut pas prévoir si l'état du monde basculera avec nous dans la saveur et le déferlement des langues. Rien n'est prévu pourtant la blouse est entrouverte, la petite culotte à peine décalée de la fente et pourtant les paupières closes et pourtant les yeux de l'intérieur sont tout agités par la sensation de la douceur des doigts. On ne peut pas prévoir si les doigts resteront là, immobiles, parfaits, longtemps encore, si le majeur bougera ô à peine sur la petite perle, si la main s'ouvrira en forme d'étoile au moment même où la douceur de sa joue, où son souffle au moment où tout le corps de l'autre femme appuiera si fort que le livre qui servait d'appui glissera sous la main, la main, au moment où l'équilibre sera précaire et que les cuisses se multiplieront comme des orchidées, on ne peut pas prévoir si les doigts pénètreront, s'ils s'imbiberont à tout jamais de notre odeur dans le mouvement continu de l'image.

You cannot foresee if the state of the world will topple over with you in the flavour and surging motion of tongues. Nothing is foreseen yet the shirt is half-open, the panties barely away from the cleft and yet the closed lids and yet the inner eyes are all astir from feeling the tender in the fingers. You cannot foresee if the fingers there will stay, motionless, perfect, for a long while yet, if the middle finger will move o ever so slightly on the little pearl, if the hand will open into a star shape at the very moment when the softness of her cheek, when her breath at the very moment when the other woman's whole body will weigh so heavily that the book where it rests gives way under the hand, the hand, at the very moment when balance will become precarious and thighs will multiply like orchids, you cannot foresee if the fingers will penetrate, if they'll forever absorb our fragrance in the image's continuous movement.

Rien n'est prévu car nous ne savons pas ce qui arrive à l'image de l'état du monde lorsque la patience des bouches dénude l'être. On ne peut pas prévoir parmi les vagues, la déferlante, la fraction de seconde qui fera image dans la narration des corps tournoyants à la vitesse de l'image.

On ne peut pas prévoir comment la langue s'enroule autour du clitoris pour soulever le corps et le déplacer cellule par cellule dans l'irréel.

Nothing is foreseen for we do not know what becomes of the image of the state of the world when the patience of mouths lays being bare. You cannot foresee from among the waves the one the unfurling one the split second that will image in the narrative of bodies whirling at the speed of the image.

You cannot foresee how the tongue wraps round the clitoris to lift the body and move it cell by cell into a realm unreal.

Sous la langue / Under Tongue
1987

ULTRASOUND

from *White Piano*
tr. Robert Majzels and Erín Moure

stubborn backbone
that chafes the depth of thoughts

in the plupresent of fear and ecstasy
in the simple present of our intelligent tissues

anon a landscape that rises like an ancient beast
flexible from throat to sex capable of flight and sudden
plunges of inebriate blue

the present wants the present up to the ears
then pain marks who is present; in the distance, cicadas
phrases unfurled 2ice without infinitive

at the time of the best sketches of solitude

to talk no more of coffins and repetition
laments language or quick the eyes above all
to displace the wind, the chic distresses. No one dares
laugh at themselves now because of fragile pronouns
with all our being we head toward elsewhere
to dip the alphabet in new mysteries
simple certainty of shadow
forever in the breast we carry a species overwhelmed
the pain of sincere wishes exchanged in chaos

so we clean the keyboard with our fingers
we disperse slowly solo
each crevice each key certain evenings
to speak in prose to speak dissipates the drownings of origin,

you've seen there are rhinestones
breezes too I was saying who
camouflages what

everyone wanted to enter consciousness
to meddle in the tiniest atoms of frenzy
on the brink of death everyone rolled their anguish
auto marble dice voice the same voice in a loop
to the end of love

⁏

here I started to think again of Venice,
of ordinary scenes from Tiepolo, life of clay

piano and wise songs of water
amid touch screens where
question of instinct

we had to mix tastes,
languages, silks linen
tissue of intrigues
in the evening dig into the universe

cascade of ubiquity
no accumulation
a single longevity

maybe we're true, maybe on the contrary we're tomorrow
how to know if what comes
arises from deep in the throat from a double carnivore tumult
from a supple wrenching into the energy of the cosmos
maybe we're true. The pain is still whole

⁝

nervous depth of sensations
from the anecdote to the others, time flays

we live in the flow of time, don't we
all these sofas sheets and beds where bodies are laid

Piano blanc
2011, tr. 2013

SCENES

from *Mauve Desert*
tr. Susanne de Lotbinère-Harwood

I

Time begins again between Kathy Kerouac and Mélanie. Faces make an effort and lips and the gaze's slant can be seen obliquing their way through words. The heat is high, the pool water blinding.

– It's vague, an effort suffices, or a few words said, or else seeing you in front of this television set.

– It's vague! And yet there are words for saying what you're feeling.

– You look at Lorna and see nothing else around.

– My gaze is wide.

– Vague. You don't see me.

– I see what I love, what is reason to live. You're the centre core of my existence. You have no idea what goes on inside me. Do you think my thoughts are free of your face, of all those memories that settle in our memory over the years?

– Anything to avoid the present, right? But don't worry, I'm leaving. You're both too present and too absent. You exist too strongly inside me because you never talk to me. I'm forced to imagine your tenderness, to invent dialogues in which you tell me of your love, your esteem, your appreciation. But I'm weary of these fantasies. I don't want to spend my life in emotional disorder. I want the horizon very clear before me.

– A girl does not go out into the desert to feed on the sun and the horizon. A girl must not go as far as where the eye is misled.

– My gaze will be vigilant. I'm alert in the questioning state.

– The sun, the heat, the solitude will overcome you.

– The heat originates inside me. I know how to be alone. If only you could imagine in my eyes the splendour of existing!

– You mean that your gut wants to speak.

– I'm saying that my eyes are speaking about existing.

– Your eyes are so full of arrogance and pride that they will necessarily mislead you. Don't you know that …

– No, I don't know anything. I'm leaving because you don't teach me anything. You watch that television. Your attention turns only to Lorna. No, you don't teach me anything.

– You know, eyes, oh! you'll know soon enough.

– What about eyes?

– Eyes that seek to get ahead of the horizon. Impatient eyes will always be disappointed.

– I will be bright and patient.

– There is no outsmarting them. Eyes need to think and when they're thinking, we must yield. Eyes cause the faces they penetrate to crack. You too will yield.

– I'm not afraid of death.

– Mélanie, you mustn't think about death. Death is something somewhere invented by men to forget and to elude reality.

– Don't be ridiculous. Death is an encounter for everyone.

– I'm saying that men invented death because they think about it. They cultivate it raucously.

– Have you never thought about death?

– I became mortal the day I gave birth to you. Death does not come toward us, it's we who in time *quite naturally* go toward death.

– Why are you talking to me like this now?

– I've always wanted you to be able and whole.

– I am.

– Yes, because that's how I wanted you to be.

– You'd like to be everything, wouldn't you? Everything to me, everything to Lorna, everything to your customers. You'd like perfection to begin with you. You'd like to wipe the slate clean, make believe. Reinvent the world and the law.

– I want peace, the end of massacres and forgetting.

– *You are merely a mother.*

– You think a daughter can dictate things to her mother that could make her 'easy'! A mother is never 'easy.' A mother makes all the difference in a life.

– A mother makes a difference if she has taught her daughter well. A mother who doesn't teach her daughter deserves to be forgotten in front of her television set. An ignorant mother is a calamity.

– I taught you through my gestures and my courage.

– It was Lorna who taught me how to swim, how to know the desert. All you wanted to teach me was how to cry. I learned about fear from looking at you. You seem afraid of everything. But what is a life if one is afraid of everything?

– I guess you can go now. We have nothing more to say to each other. Take this silver comb. It will bring you luck and happiness.

– Happiness! It's your looking for happiness that bothers me.

– I'm looking for contentment, well-being, daily wellness.

– Comfort. You're looking for convenience, facility.

– Mélanie, you should leave or keep quiet because you don't know what you're saying. You're violently confusing words, you're appropriating them as though they were sugar cubes you were placing on your tongue and waiting for them to take effect. Forgive me if I've been unable to teach you. I believed that I had. Despite your refusal to talk, your constant running away. I thought my affection was enough, that my voice somewhere inside you could reach the hard knot you have for a soul.

– What becomes knotted in the heart is knotted with the silence of others. You know, *your voice*, your beautiful voice never really spoke to me. Your voice just superimposed itself on the mediocrity which in this Motel precludes all hope. I'm leaving but you know I'll be back. I'll come back because I know you'll be expecting me. You see, our eyes are dry. That's a good thing. Never cry for me. Never do that because then your tears would join with mine and we would be carried away, yes, I believe we'd both be carried away by a single wave.

II

Two hours were all it took for dailiness to become a small dark spot in the consciousness. Kathy Kerouac and Lorna Myher parked the jeep. Vertical section on the horizon, their bodies form a certain presence in the mauve.

– Hurrying up, slowing down. It seems we're either too heavy or light, or does the desert create this impression of confounding the body's real weight?

– By your side I keep my balance. You are this high-density water which keeps the body afloat and keeps it from sinking deep into the whirlpool.

– Do I deserve to be so valorized and celebrated? I'm just an ordinary woman.

– And I'm a great dyke fulfilled with joy by your side. You see, all we need is to get away from that Motel for a while to come alive again.

– We need to leave that damned television set alone.

– You are …

– Don't tell me who I am, even if what I am I can only discover with you.

– Because I'm like you or because we're different?

– Because you're lively and afraid of nothing. Yet [*discomfort in her voice*] you really should learn to read.

– You still can't accept me as I really am. I'm a body. A body happy when in water. Have you never thought that my body would disintegrate if ever it entered the twisted stuff of words? If you only knew how much I prefer my own nimble fingers a thousand times over all those fragile lines a thousand times twisted which men write, which your daughter writes.

– But everyone around us knows how to read and write.

– Everyone around us doesn't do, doesn't think, doesn't bite their shelove's ear like we do. No one around us does what we do. No one feels what we feel.

– I'm an ordinary woman and I feel like others feel.

– Others, who? Poor Kathy, my love. Poor me, your shelove. What will we become if you don't love me as I am, if I want you as you are not? How many caresses, how many times hands over our mouths, how many times the belly's fire before we become exactly what we are? Or is that irrelevant?

– But reading is something necessary. Reading is food.

– Yes! 'What are we eating? What are we eating?' Your daughter often says that. And she runs away, your daughter. As for me, I devour. I take. I don't wait for the twisted lines to make my body breathless and unfit to the point where it can't tolerate good tastes and beautiful images. Your daughter talks about eternity too much.

– My daughter is subtle. She understands things.

– And I'm gross, I suppose! Tell me what you're doing with me then.

– With you I do what's essential. My life. I invent my reality. I outline certainty and weave my faith.

– That's all very abstract. [*Silence*] Do you think it possible to love around the body? To love without smells, without taste, without tongues seeking their salt on the beloved's skin, without the rustling of hands on thighs, without needing to refine our senses? Do you think you could have loved me without considering my body, if I had been just an image at the back of your eyes, if you had had to leave out my body to choose me?

– Yes, I think I would have loved you even never having found your body. Yes, I could have loved you and left out your body.

– But leaving out my body, who would you have loved?

– I would have loved the impossible in myself, even till it bruised me.

– And you would have done it anyway?

– Anyway.

– You disconcert me. I find it unbearable, even for a second, to think of loving without bodies coming in to free or to sustain desire.

– Who said anything about desire? I'm talking about a specific emotion that creates presence way beyond the real body.

– Emotions, we have more than we need to elude reality. Desire is what prompts every encounter, every life impulse.

– I don't desire you. I'm moved by you. I'm keenly touched by everything in you that signifies. That is infinitely more precious than desiring you. I'm vitally touched by you.

– As for me, I say desire and quickly, bodies one on one. Bodies of abundance, caresses, embraces, excitation. I want traces, marks, blood streaming in our veins. Love needs evidence. Carnal evidence otherwise the body languishes, dissolves into the twisted stuff of words, the chaos of emotion.

– Emotion is what pacifies.

– So you don't desire me? In that case what are we doing together? How am I different from what stirs your emotion?

– You are unique.

– No I'm not, and you know it. Nobody is that free. No one woman is that alone in the world.

– Well then I guess there's no explanation and that it's pointless to seek a reason for the love I feel for you. Perhaps it's easier to choose from among the suite of mirrors, costumes, and roles, words that are simpler, softer, less crude, ordinary.

– When it comes to love, one mustn't be ordinary. It offends me to hear you say that you're an ordinary woman.

– You mean it humiliates you to love an ordinary woman.

– I don't think you're ordinary. But yes, it humiliates me to hear you say it. I spent my whole childhood, my adolescence refusing to become an ordinary woman. We were poor but to my eyes that was no excuse for being confined to the ordinary. Look at your daughter, she isn't ordinary either. And you may be sure that that has nothing to do with knowing how to read or not.

– You're giving words quite a turn.

– Can one exist without turning words into sentences!

– You see, you're more twisted than you care to admit.

– I'm in love. I'm doing everything I can not to lose you. For me this goes without saying and without drama.

– Yet terror is everywhere. Ice, the sparkle of cold laughter.

– This isn't something we can prevent. Terror is. We can't escape this cloud. Wired, revolted or resigned, we walk in its wake.

– Can we constrain the story?

– The narrative of our lives, of terror or of the impossible?

– Merely sum up. Quite simply. Without violence, with a few markers along the way.

– We have no markers but ourselves. We are surrounded by signs that invalidate our presence.

– Well then let's say that I would like for us to sum up our presence. Lorna Myher, you great dyke from Ajo, send me into raptures. Adventure me in desire. Do everything that you must, that you mustn't, my trust is absolute.

– I will do only what in you desires. That's the only presence I can offer you.

III

The shoulder is suntanned, the skin smooth, the flesh firm. The neon lighting hugs the chest, slides over the shoulder, exposes the imago a moment, then moves back up toward Mélanie's face.

– It's a beautiful night.

   – Night is what allows sudden changes.

   – Night is concrete.

   – Night is oblique. On one side beings, on the other side beasts. This is why we tremble, when night has come, about not finding our place.

   – Here we are, speaking to each other quite naturally and yet, Angela Parkins, I know nothing about you.

   – I come from the desert.

   – What do you know about the desert, the sun, and men? My mother says that …

   – The desert is a space. Men came there one day and claimed that this space was now conquered at last. They claimed they suffered over their conquest. They suffered because the desert suffers no error. But men confused error with suffering. They concluded that their suffering could correct the error of nature, the very nature of error. This is how they hooked into death.

   – It's a beautiful night.

   – Night is always beautiful for it forces us to feel with our skin and our inner eyes. At night we can count only on ourselves.

   – Night is beautiful in sheer solitude but your presence makes this night even more real for me.

   – Night is strange.

   – That's because the body changes rhythm.

   – At night it is especially necessary to wait for the body to change its trajectory in the universe. To move in such a way that all of our senses can transit freely. Capture the vast emptiness. How old are you?

   – I hope I never become like other people.

   – How do you know you haven't already?

   – I know.

– I'm thirsty. How long have you had the butterfly tattoo on your shoulder?

– A month. It gives me strength for facing reality. It gives me wings. I'm Sagittarius. It makes me feel like somebody put their hand on my shoulder, looked at me, taught me.

– Taught you what? You really want to be taught about life?

– You no doubt desired that once.

– I made my own way. I don't owe anybody anything.

– Do you think that's the way to find joy?

– I'm thirsty. I spend hours and hours resisting thirst. Waiting for sunset. I spend my life watching the horizon in detail. I've never given happiness a thought. I charge ahead. I troat.

– Do you know that animal?

– Which animal?

– The stag. They say it is often compared to the tree of life and that it symbolizes rebirth. For the Pueblos it represents cyclical renewal.

– Mélanie, what are you talking about?

– What I've read.

– Come closer. Let me get a good look at this butterfly. It has the thorax of a great sphinx.

– Well?

– *Nothing.* Why did you say that night changes the body's rhythm?

– Because it's true. Do you think I would have dared to follow you and speak to you in broad daylight?

– During the day I'm far away, way off in the vastness. During the day all my attention is focused on the earth's crust.

– Don't you want to be loved?

– I'm not lovable. My thirst is too great. Mélanie, you're very young. Your mother is probably already worried about your absence.

– My mother knows me. She knows that night and day I feel the need to run. To always go a bit beyond myself to let reality loose.

– I think we look alike.

– Without a mirror it would be hard to tell.

– I think our eyes are better able to tell when there are no reflections.

– There, I'm close to you. Do you recognize me?

– Yes, I recognize you. It's true that you are ageless. You have always existed. Don't go thinking that I'm making things up. I can tell among the signs and the clues what in you is made to last. You needn't fear time. Only speed will damage you.

– Don't say that. I love living fast.

– That's what I recognize in you.

– Rain.

– Stay just a little longer. Rain can only soften our lips and make the night palpable.

– The rain on your lips is fine.

– 'We pray thee send forth rain, blessings, immortality.'[1]

IV

The scene can be imagined by parting the curtain between auther and transla-tor. The distance is abolished by imagining the two women sitting in a café. One is smoking and so is the other. Both like dealing with silence but each one here is looking to understand how death transits between fiction and reality. The language spoken is the auther's.

– I feared for a moment that you wouldn't come.

– Here I am. Don't worry, I took great *pains* to be here.

– I have no rights. You come before me.

– What do you want from me?

– To hear what I can make my own. Everything you tell me will be ...

– Useful?

– Necessary. I've been living with this book for two years. I've only just recently conceived the project of translating it.

– What would you like to talk about?

– One thing only: Angela Parkins' death. I'd like to talk to you exactly the way I imagine Angela Parkins would if she could get out of character, if she were its ultimate presence.

---

1. Veda.

– I'm listening.

– *Why did you kill me?*

– *You're going fast, Angela, you're getting too directly to the heart of the essential. Wouldn't you rather we talk first about you or about me, that somewhere we find the familiar Arizona landscapes again?* [Silence] *So be it, if you like, we can talk about your death right now. But first, swear to me that you didn't see anything coming. Swear it.*

– *Saw what coming? Love, death? Saw what coming? Mélanie or the assassin?*

– *Saw reprobation coming.*

– *What! You would have punished me for what I am.*

– *I'm not talking about you. I'm talking about everything around you. Intolerance. Madness. Violence.*

– *In that case I saw nothing coming. Certainly I saw myself lost, delirious, wary and minotaur, drunk and arrogant, joyous and casual, nostalgic and in love but I never saw that man's madness coming.*

– *And yet you knew him.*

– *I knew him by reputation. He was an inventor, a great scholar, but how could I ever imagine that that man carried such hatred inside him?*

– *You never noticed anything in his ways, in his gaze?*

– *He looked normal. He looked like a normal client. To tell you the truth, I never noticed him. My whole being was involved in the rhythm moving me closer to Mélanie.*

– *Well then I'll tell you. I'll try to tell you why you died so suddenly, absurdly. You died because you forgot to look around you. You freed yourself too quickly and because you thought yourself free, you no longer wanted to look around you. You forgot about reality.*

– *You could have helped me, given me a sign.*

– *It's true that I believed you out of harm's way, safe from barking dogs. I imagined you passionate and as such able to repel bad fate. I believed you were stronger than reality.*

– *But imagining the scene, you could have changed its course. You could have made the bullet ricochet or wound me slightly.*

– *No. It was you or him. For if this man had only wounded you, you would have turned on him with such fury that you're the one who would have put him* to death. One way or another, your life would have been ruined. Self-defence or not. That man, don't forget, had a fine reputation.

– You dare to tell me that in order to protect me from that man, that madman, you chose to get rid of me.

– I didn't kill you. That man killed you.

– But that man doesn't exist. You were under no obligation to make that man exist.

– That man exists. He could be compared to the invisible wire that sections reality from fiction. In getting closer to Mélanie you wanted to cross the threshold.

– I hold you responsible for his actions. For my death.

– I'm not responsible for reality.

– Reality is what we invent.

– Don't be cruel to me. You who are familiar with solitude, ecstasies, and torments. You and I have never thought of protecting ourselves. In this we have come a long way but sooner or later reality catches up.

– I can reproach you for what is in your book.

– By what right?

– Reading you gives me every right.

– But as a translator you have none. You've chosen the difficult task of reading backwards in your language what in mine flows from source.

– But when I read you, I read you in your language.

– How can you understand me if you read me in one language and simultaneously transpose into another what cannot adequately find its place in it? How am I to believe for a single moment that the landscapes in you won't erase those in me?

– Because true landscapes loosen the tongue in us, flow over the edge of our thought-frame. They settle into us.

– I remember one day buying a geology book in which I found a letter. It was a love letter written by a woman and addressed to another woman. I used the letter as a bookmark. I would read it before reading and after reading. For me that letter was a landscape, an enigma entered with each reading. I would have liked to know this woman, I imagined the face of the woman for whom it was meant. It was during that time that I started writing the book you want to translate. Yes, you're right, there are true landscapes that pry us from the edge and force us onto the scene.

– I think there is always a first time, 'a first time when it must be acknowledged that words can reduce reality to its smallest unit: *matter* of fact.' Do you remember those words?

– No, but I think that whoever said that was right. I'm weary. Is there anything else you wish to know?

– I mostly wanted to hear you talk about death. But no matter what happens, we're alone, aren't we?

– Keep to beauty, have no fear. Muffle civilization's noises in you. Learn to bear the unbearable: the raw of all things.

Le Désert mauve
1987, tr. 1990

HOTEL RAFALE

from *Baroque at Dawn*

tr. Patricia Claxton

First the dawn. Then the woman came.

In Room 43 at the Hotel Rafale, in the heart of a North American city armed to the teeth, in the heart of a civilization of gangs, artists, dreams, and computers, in darkness so complete it swallowed all countries, Cybil Noland lay between the legs of a woman she had met just a few hours before. For a time which seemed a coon's age and very nocturnal, the woman had repeated, 'Devastate me, eat me up.' Cybil Noland had plied her tongue with redoubled ardour and finally heard, 'Day, vastate me, heat me up.' The woman's thighs trembled slightly and then her body orbited the planet as if the pleasure in her had transformed to a stupendous aerial life reflex.

Cybil Noland had felt the sea enter her thoughts like a rhyme, a kind of sonnet which briefly brought her close to Louise Labé, then drew away to pound elsewhere, wave sounds in present tense. The sea had penetrated her while whispering livable phrases in her ear, drawn-out laments, a life-long habit with its thousand double exposures of light. Later, thoughts of the sea cast her against a boundless wall of questions.

⁂

In the room, the air conditioner is making an infernal noise. Dawn has given signs of life. Cybil can now make out the furniture shapes and see, reflected in the mirror on the half-open bathroom door, a chair on which are draped a blue T-shirt, a pair of jeans, and a black leather jacket. On the rug, a pair of sandals one beside the other.

The woman puts a hand on Cybil Noland's hair, the other touching a shoulder. The stranger at rest is terribly alive, anonymous with her thousand identities in repose. Cybil Noland turns so as to rest her cheek comfortably in the curve of the other's crotch. Neither thinks to move, much less to talk. Each is from somewhere else, each is elsewhere in her life of elsewhere, as if living some life from the past.

⁑

Cybil Noland had travelled a lot, to cities with light-filled curves shimmering with headlights and neon signs. She loved suspense, the kind of risk that might now take as simple a guise as strolling about among the buildings of big cities. She had always declined to stay in the mountains or the country or beside a lake, even for a few days. Her past life had unfolded at a city pace, in the presence of many accents, traffic sounds, and speed, all of which sharpen the senses. Over the years she had come to love sunsets reddened by carbon dioxide. It had been so long since she had seen the stars that the names of the constellations had long ago vanished into her memory's recesses. Cybil Noland lived at information's pace. Information was her firmament, her inner sea, her Everest, her cosmos. She loved the electric sensation she felt at the speed of passing images. Each image was easy. It was easy for her to forget what it was that had excited her a moment before. Sometimes she thought she ought to resist this frenetic consumption of words, catastrophes, speed, rumours, fears, and screens, but too late, her intoxication seemed irreversible. Between fifteen and thirty years of age she had studied history, literature, and the curious laws that govern life's instinct for continuation. Thus she had learned to navigate among beliefs and dreams dispersed over generations and centuries. But today all that seemed far away, ill-suited to the speed with which reality was spinning out her anxiety with its sequences of happiness and violence, its fiction grafted like a science to the heart of instinct. As a child she had learned several languages, enabling her today to consume twice the information, commentary, tragedy, minor mishaps, and prognostications. Thus she had unwittingly acquired a taste for glib words and fleeting images. All she had learned in her youth finally came to seem merely muddleheaded, anachronistic, and obsolete.

On this July night that was drawing to a close in a small hotel in a city armed to the teeth, Cybil Noland had felt the sea rise up and swallow her.

Something had spilled over, creating a vivid horizontal effect, but simultaneously a barrier of questions. The sky, the stars, and the sea had synthesized an entire civilization of cities in her when the woman came.

There between the stranger's legs, questions arose, insistent, intrusive questions, snooping questions, basic questions seeking alternately to confirm and deny the world and its raison d'être. Borne on this current of questions, Cybil Noland vowed to renounce glib pronouncements without however willingly forgoing the dangerous euphoria elicited by the fast, frenzied images of her century.

⁂

The light was now diffused throughout the room, a yellow morning light which in movies of yesteryear gave the dialogue a hopeful turn, for the simple reason that mornings in those days were slow with the natural slowness that suited the movements made by heroines when, upon awakening, they gracefully stretched their arms, raising arches of carnal triumph in the air.

The woman has moved her legs to change position, perhaps to leave the bed. Cybil Noland has raised her head then her body in such fashion as to hoist herself up to the level of the woman's face. The mattress is uncomfortable, with hollows and soft spots one's elbows and knees sink into.

Since meeting, the two have barely exchanged three sentences. The woman is a musician and young. *'But I'm not sixteen,'* she said with a smile in the elevator. Cybil Noland thereupon nicknamed her 'La Sixtine.' On arrival in the room, they undressed and the woman ordered, 'Eat me.'

Now that Cybil Noland has the woman's living face at eye level, her belly swells again rich with desire like a tempestuous wind. *Kiss me, kiss m'again.*[1] With fire and festivity in her eyes, the woman looks Cybil over,

---

1. Louise Labé: *Baise-moi, baise m'encore.*

caresses her, then thrusts her tongue between her lips. It might have been just a kiss, but what a way she has of breathing, of pearling each lip, tracing *abc* inside Cybil's mouth with the tiniest movements, impossible to separate the letters *abc*, to stop, demon delirium *abc* a constellation of flavours in her mouth. Then the wind surges, sweeping eyelashes, drying the perspiration about the neck, smoothing silken cheeks, closing eyelids, imprinting the outlines of faces deep in the pillow. The five sibyls of the Sixtine Chapel orbit the planet and the questions return. Cybil Noland opens her eyes. There are still traces of mascara on the woman's eyelashes. She too unseals her eyes. The look they give is laughing, languid, offering an intimacy glimpsable only in the strictest anonymity. Like a love-crazed thing all of a sudden, Cybil is aburn for this anonymous woman who had caught her eye in the bar of the Hotel Rafale. Something is exciting her, something about the anonymity of this woman encountered in the middle of a huge city, something that says, I don't know your name but I recognize the smooth curvaceous shape your body takes when navigating to the open sea. Soon I shall know where your tears, your savage words and anxious gestures hide, the things that will lead me to divine everything about you at one fell swoop. Thus does imagination take us beyond the visible, propelling us toward new faces that will set the wind asurge despite the barrier formed by vertical cities, despite the speed of life that drains our thoughts and leaves them indolent. The priceless eyes of desire are right to succumb to seduction so that one's familiar, everyday body may find joy in the thousands of anonymous others encountered along the way, bodies pursuing their destinies in cities saturated with feelings and emotions.

‡

The stranger gives off a scent of complex life which coils about Cybil Noland. City smells clinging to her hair like a social ego; fragrant, singularizing sandalwood, a trace of navel salt, the milky taste of her breasts. Everywhere an infiltration of life, aromatic, while the child in one does the rounds of all the smells, anonymously like a grown-up in a hurry to get thinking.

The air conditioner has stopped. There's silence. A surprising silence like the heady smell of lilac when the month of May reaches us at the exits of great, sense-deadening cages of glass and concrete. The silence draws out, palpable and appealing like La Sixtine's body. The alarm-clock dial on the bedside table is blinking. A power failure. Which means unbearable heat in exchange for a silence rare and more precious than gold and caviar. The silence is now diffused throughout the room. Surprising, devastating. An unreal silence that's terribly alive, as if imposing a kind of fiction by turning the eyes of the heart toward an unfathomable inner life.

The women lie side by side, legs entwined and each with an arm under the other's neck like sleepy reflex arcs. Suddenly Cybil Noland can stand no more of this new silence that has come and imposed itself on top of the first, which had been a silence tacitly agreed between them like a stylized modesty, an elegant discretion, a kind of meditative state capable of shutting out the sounds of civilization and creating a fictional time favourable to the appearance of each one's essential face.

⁜

Cybil Noland had brought the woman up to her room thinking of what she called each woman's essential face in her own destiny. Each time she had sex with a woman, this was what put heart into her desire. She was ready for anything, any kind of caress, any and all sexual scenarios, aware that you can never foresee exactly when, or for how long, an orgasm will recompose the lines of the mouth and chin, make the eyelids droop, dilate the pupils or keep the eyes shining. Most often the face would describe its own aura of ecstasy, beginning with the light filtering through the enigmatic slit between the eyelids when they hover half-closed halfway between life and pleasure. Then would come the split second that changed the iris into the shape of a crescent moon, before the white of the eye, whiter than the soul, proliferated multiples of the word imagery deep in her thoughts. This was how a woman who moments earlier had been a total stranger became a loved one capable of changing the course of time for the better.

All, thought Cybil Noland, so that the essential face that shows what women are really capable of may be seen, vulnerable and radiant, infinitely human, desperately disturbing. But for this to happen, the whole sea would have to flood into her mouth, and the wind flatten her hair to her skull, and fire ignite from fire, and she would have to consider everything very carefully at the speed of life and wait for the woman to possess her own silence, out of breath and beyond words in the midst of her present. In the well of her pleasure the woman would have to find her own space, a place of choice.

So when the air conditioner stopped, Cybil Noland felt she had been robbed of the rare and singular silence that had brought her so close to La Sixtine. As if she had suddenly realized that while the words *heat me vast*[2] were ringing with their thousand possibilities and her delicate tongue was separating the lips of La Sixtine's sex, civilization had nevertheless continued its headlong course.

Now the new silence is crowding the silence that accompanies one's most private thoughts. While groping for a comparison to explain this new silence, suddenly Cybil Noland can stand no more of it and wants to speak, will speak, but the woman comes close and reclines on top of her and with her warm belly and hair tickling Cybil's nose, and breasts brushing over Cybil's mouth, seems determined to turn Cybil's body into an object of pure erotic pleasure.

You'd say she was going. To say. Yes, she murmurs inarticulate sounds in Cybil's ear, rhythms, senseless words, catches her breath, plays on it momentarily, 'That good?' she breathes. 'That better?' Then over Cybil's body strews images and succulent words that burst in the mouth like berries. Now her sounds caress like violins. The names of constellations come suddenly to Cybil's mind: Draco the Dragon, Coma Berenices, Cassiopaeia, and Lyra for the Northern Hemisphere; Sculptor, Tucana, Apus the Bird of Paradise, Ara the Altar for the Southern. Then the whole sea spreads through her and La Sixtine relaxes her hold.

---

2. Nicole Brossard: *m'ange moi vaste.*

You'd say she was going to tell a story. Something with the word *joyous* in the sentence to go with her nakedness there in the middle of the room. Once she's in the shower the water runs hard. She sings. When she lifts her tongue the sounds crowd up from under, full of vim. Joyously her voice spews out, zigzags from one word to another, cheerily penetrating Cybil Noland's consciousness as she lies half asleep in the spacious bed.

'I'll tell you a story,' La Sixtine said, opening the window before getting in the shower. The window opens onto a fire escape. The curtain moves gently. Cybil Noland watches the movements of the fish, seaweed, and coral in the curtain's design. Life is a backdrop against which thoughts and memories overlap. Life moves ever so slightly, goes through static stages, skews off, brings its humanism to the midst of armed cities like a provocation, a paradox that makes you smile. In spite of yourself. The dark fish throw a shadow over the pinks and whites of the coral, Cybil Noland thinks before riding off again, a deep-sea wanderer aboard great incunabula.

⁛

The power's back on. The air conditioner's working. In the corridor, the chambermaids are bustling back and forth again.

When she got out of the shower La Sixtine turned on the radio. A sombre voice entered the room, spreading a smell of war and filth. The voice waded its way through 'today the authorities' and 'many bodies in front of the cathedral, some horribly mutilated. Fetuses were seen hanging from the gutted bellies of their mothers. In places the snow seemed coated with blood. Old women, open-mouthed and staring toward the cold infinity of the region leading to the sea, spoke of human limbs scattered about the ground. Other witnesses talked of hearing the cries of children although no children have been found. At present the authorities are unable to say what group the dead belong to since from their clothing one cannot tell whether they are from the north-east or the east-north.'

One after another the sentences fall to the room's pink carpet. Cybil Noland watches from the spacious bed. La Sixtine sits on the edge of the bed with a towel about her hips and seems to be breathing with difficulty. Then, as if tired of trying to find her breath, she turns and curls her body into Cybil's trembling nakedness. Her head weighs heavily. Her body is heavy. The present is a body. The body is a live, pure present that goes on forever between the electrical thrum of the air conditioner and the voice from the radio.

Cybil Noland thinks about the morning she spent in a Covent Garden café. Her head that morning was full of a woman who wants to write a novel. This woman lacks vocabulary to describe the volcano of violence erupting in cities. She is sitting in a large kitchen. While she spoons sugar into her teacup with a little silver spoon, her hair brushes over the sugar bowl. She is young and resolute, in contrast with the fact that she is still in pyjamas at this late morning hour. There is a dictionary on the table. With one hand she holds the silver spoon and with the other absentmindedly turns the pages of the dictionary. She gets up and goes to the window, where for a minute she leans on the sill. From here she can see the approaches to Hyde Park, the texture of the day and the fine rain of this weather that penetrates the very core of one. She gazes into the distance. At the far side of herself, she ponders a fictional life. She observes so meticulously that the pondering fits her head and thoughts like a helmet. A book by Samuel Beckett lies on the table. The sugar bowl looks like a volcano. The woman lives alone, surrounded by ferns and a wealth of other plants to which she will put no names so that in their green anonymity they will create a fine, rich tropical forest for her. The rain falls slowly. She lights a cigarette. Why would she write this violent book? She has no special gift for it, or vocabulary or experience. She puts a hand on the dictionary and draws it close. The hand stays resting on the cover as though she's about to take an oath. With the other hand she writes a list of violent words, words that turn one's stomach, turn one's head to suffering, to people and their progeny who thirst for vengeance. Beyond the window Hyde Park glows, adding to its mystery, offering its trees and green lawns as so many hypotheses that liven vertigo in contemplation of the future. Truth will never come without worry, nor will the illusion of truth. The woman pours herself another cup of tea. Her father's oak-panelled library is filled with women's books. Her father's books are stacked in the north corner of the kitchen. They stand there like three Towers of Babel. Three towers of leather-bound volumes showing their gold-leafed spines.

The fine rain keeps falling and the woman treasures those images of the north that make her homesick. It isn't memory that does it, it's this taste of happiness split in two by silence.

Baroque d'aube
1995, tr. 1997

SIXTH BEND

from *Green Night of Labyrinth Park*

tr. Lou Nelson

life is in the mouth that speaks

multiplying ideological anchors, escapes ahead, syntheses, feints, and perspectives, always seeking a mirror, drifting on a word, butting up against another, obsessive or distraught, thought remains the most modern of the language games that unleash desire. In one's mouth, thought is living proof that life is a statement that experiments with the truth of *je thème*.[1]

thus, the lesbian *I love you* that unleashes thought is a speaking that experiments with the value of words to the point of touch, stretching them out so that they can simultaneously caress their origin, their centre, and the extreme boundary of sense.

in the lesbian mouth that speaks, life discerns itself by the sounds pleasure makes as it rubs up against a speaking.

---

1. Translator's Note: *je thème*, translated literally, means 'I theme.' However, it is also pronounced the same as *je t'aime*, 'I love you.'

NINTH BEND

from *Green Night of Labyrinth Park*

tr. Lou Nelson

I am breathing in rhetoric

i am writing this text on several levels because reality is not sufficient, because beauty is demanding, because sensations are multiple, because putting a great deal of oneself into language does not eliminate the patriarchal horror, does not explain the composition of my subjectivity and all these images that move like a woman in orgasm. Energized by the raw material of desire, I write. Word matter, when it is too cold or too soft or so crazy that it is hard to contain in our thoughts, this matter that is eternally contemporary with our joys and energized bodies, murmurs and breathes, opens us to the bone and sews in wells and depths of astonishment. I exist in written language because it is there that I decide the thoughts that settle the questions and answers I give to reality. It is there that I signal assent in approving ecstasies and their configurations in the universe. I do not want to repeat what I already know of language. It is a fertile ground of vestiges and vertigo. Depository of illusions, of obsessions, of passions, of anger and *quoi encore* that obliges us to transpose reality. I am even more unwilling to retrace my steps since, in this very beautiful fragrant labyrinth of the solstice night, I owe it to myself to not erase the memory of my path, to not erase the strategies and rituals of writing that I had to invent in order to survive the customs and phallic events of life.

1992

THE AERIAL LETTER

from *The Aerial Letter*
tr. Marlene Wildeman

We concentrate avidly on the processes. Of writing, of desirous being, of ecstasy. We concentrate a great deal on the self. We exert ourselves, and in so doing we summon the other within ourselves to a reality that is transformed. Fiction seeks its own fictional subject and memory alone does not flinch. Memory makes itself plural, essential, like the version that foreshadows an aerial vision. Authentic as a first written draft. With each page, the necessary willingness to start over.

For each time I must enunciate everything, articulate an inexpressible attitude, one that wants to remake reality endlessly, in order not to founder in its fictive version nor be submerged in sociological anecdote.

On the one hand, taking on sociological reality by taking risks within. In order to dissolve its fictive character, in order to foil the impostures of the day-to-day anecdote. Here, a question: the text as ID card or identity as a science fiction of self in the practice of creating text? Those who have never been able to speak the reality of their perceptions, those for whom the conquest of personal emotional territory has been precluded politically and patriarchally, will grasp that identity is simultaneously a quest for and conquest of meaning. Desire slowly emanates from what is inadmissible in her project: transformation of the self, and the collectivity. Inadmissible will to change life, to change her life. Imperatives with regard to what in the environment appears intolerable. Identity turns into project when the border between what's tolerable and what's intolerable disintegrates or, one might say, when it no longer holds up. This is when words make themselves void of sense or take on another meaning, take a new turn in the sequence of thought's events. Words begin to turn round on themselves, inciting reflection, inciting thought toward new approaches to reality. And it is also when words begin to oscillate between derision and vitality, becoming, little by little, indispensable strategies for confronting reality's two slopes: the actual and the fictive.

On the other hand, tackling reality the way one takes on a project; so as to take by surprise equations, for they give to the surface of all skin its vitality, its reasoning, if you will. Bathing in the atmosphere of the senses and giving form to enigmas we imagine out of the white, while the certain body[1] refers us back to an implacable geometry: our feverish excitement, a fluidity of text seeking its source. Taking on reality in order that an aerial vision of all realities arises from the body and emotion of thought. Realities which, crossing over each other, form the matrix material of my writing. This text matter, like a fabulous mathematics, relates words to one another. All bodies carry within themselves a project of sensual high technology; writing is its hologram.

I

THE ORDEAL: THE TEST
AND/OR THE PROOF OF MODERNITY

The text, the notion of text, has been, as we well know, subjected in the past few decades to several transformations; most have been a response to the necessity for politico-sexual subversion. The textual site has become the repository for the body, sex, the city, and rupture, as well as the theory that it generates, which in turn regenerates text. Text has systematically proliferated, profaning the state of mind of both the petit- and the grand-bourgeois. The ordeal of modernity (Rimbaud's 'one absolutely must be modern') as initiation w/rite, has been succeeded by 'one must be resolutely modern' as political initiation project. The experience of text, understood as crossing through writing, will be transformed by experimentation, that is, by a strategy bound to disrupt.

Everything conspires to ensure that the writing 'I' speak desire and not its desire, keeping by this distancing its formal presence, its inherent prestige. In this there is a known principle of seduction whose function is both to excite and to incite. Seduction of what symbolically masters. Thus the textual 'I' will say: I will make you neutral, my I, so as to prevent you from

---

1. Cf. 'le corps certain.' Roland Barthes. *The Pleasure of the Text*, trans. Richard Miller (New York: Hill and Wang, 1975), p. 29.

letting your origins show, those which might be deemed ideologically suspect, your bourgeois, religious, or feminine origins. I condemn you therefore to anonymity, such that you cannot be co-opted or alienated, like all those little 'I's' that capitalism has reduced to marionettes but who, all things considered, can still express themselves – do nothing but, in fact. I intend to, that is, I will speak the 'I' that resolutely exists, I choose to speak out, I am subversion, I am transgression. If not, I do not exist. Theoretically.

Just as exposing oneself to everything seemed real to me, the 'I impose myself on everyone,' which followed in the modern texts of the sixties, seems to me fictive, like a seduction that has value only by virtue of a convention, a fiction.

It is here that writing begins, that I begin again.

I say that writing begins here between what's real and what's fictive, not between the knowledge we have of one and the intimate experience we have of the other, but between the words that we seek to conceive in their true relationship, so as to get to the bottom of the question, always integral, of thought and emotion, *motifs* and motivation.

We can imagine writing as a *rapprochement*, or as the concrete will to attract toward oneself the essential figures of thought/or even /to see one's desire come *as far as possible*, that is, closer: to the very edge, right to the limits – where it might very well falter. Balance or vertigo, when the 'exact expression' illustrates the thought of emotion, when what appears on the page seems like a *coincidence*: a perfect synchronization between explosion and mastery which breaks through to an opening. Each time it must be imagined; what would give *access* to.

I have just said 'imagine writing.' After all, maybe that is as far as we have come. Forced to drift in total lucidity into the imaginary world of words, tempted by an improbable literature and – since theoretically and ideologically improbable – displacing it toward what we would agree upon calling *fiction*.

But before coming to fiction, I would like to say more about text. I take as a given that the text-fetish, in the sense used by Roland Barthes, who wrote, 'the text is a fetish object, and this text desires me,'[2] has appropriated

---

2. Ibid., 27.

Literature, this practice of the written that consists of inscribing, among other things, the expressive part of a memory rooted in an environment at once geographic, social, and cultural, and that recalls the site of our origins as much as it does our first stimuli.

It is in order to avoid that these 'unmentionable' origins (ideologically speaking), like those 'unmentionables' (sexually speaking), be manifest in one's writing that little by little the writer becomes, according to his own formula, a 'technician' of writing.[3] For the same reasons, the text-fetish will reappropriate Literature (according to the old axiom), this having become prattle, too sentimental, and emotional (a bit too feminine, wouldn't you say!). One can at this stage, without answering immediately, inquire whether fiction, or that which I personally would call the fictive text, will in turn appropriate the text-fetish, which now has become too reductive.[4] (In chemistry, a 'reducing agent' is defined as being that which is apt to remove oxygen.)

Let us return once again to text.

To date, we have known a certain experience of text in which there is a vital practice of modernism, and several of these modernist texts are memento-screens testifying to the form emotion and thought have taken over the last thirty years. Emotion which, need I add, in Quebec is distinctly related to urban life. For the city concentrates energy; it calls for *fiction*, ellipsis, and theory, not to mention the politicization of texts. In some, the city stimulates *a modern spirit*; in others, it is responsible for modern *performances*.

I hold that this exciting experience of text that turns about itself, bearing and being borne by its own weight, simultaneously suggests excess, the circle, and the void. I say the circle, for it seems to me that in wanting to break the linearity, it is as if we have been forced into its opposite, to turn full circle, as if the text in this had come to its own end in itself, even were this to explode.

From excess, from the circle (as the sum of fragments accumulated from having been repeatedly shattered), and from the void, I would then

---

3. In the original, ' ... l'écrivain va devenir selon sa propre formule un écrivant.'
4. In the original, 'trop reducteur,' 'reducteur' meaning literally 'reducing agent' (47).

translate the results into the feminine by a shift in meaning going from excess to ecstasy, from circle to spiral, and from void to opening, as a solution for continuity.

But I would like to come back to this 'impression of void,' to which the practice of writing texts lends itself, for it is this *impression* that still motivates some of the lettered few (professors and critics, among others) to maintain the phobia of the text, an impression of a vacuum they preserve intact, in order to reach the conclusion that research and advances accomplished there are irrelevant.

If in Quebec the literary terrain is changing, this is not a result of criticism but rather because most of the textual few know how to re-read themselves in time. To this, I would add that the writing produced by women in the last ten years has considerably helped textual writers to re-read their work in time. For women have displaced the purpose of writing, the relevance of purpose. This may have been premature for some men, but for women, it came at precisely the right moment.

It is this very 'impression of void,' I might add, that will disturb and displace the very people who are given to text the way one gives oneself up to the immediacy of pleasure. I have said 'impression of void' because the text, we know very well, condenses; it sums itself up in certain words: city, sex, text, body, desire, script, the gaze (that of film, that of photography). The text is an ideogram. In a way, it is because the text condenses (it is not a chatterbox), that it does reduce (it takes the shortest route possible), that it gives this impression of running on empty, or of running wild[5] (something to do with its excessive vitality).

Thus, for those who write text, on the one hand, an improbable Literature (hiding one's roots), and on the other, an impossible text (an impression of void). But the desire to write survives. *Absolutely.*

Lucidity, the yearning for and of text, and for many, their very survival, will exact a new writing: one that drifts, that slips out from under; writing that eludes. Why not then submit proof of imagination by opening a breach: a spiral?

---

5. In the original, ' ... de faire le vide ou de faire le fou' (49).

To conclude my remarks about text, one last comment: it was not symbolically important to know who the actual author behind a text was, whether in the flesh, in memory, or in childhood, for text was precisely the formula that permitted the writer not to have to submit to *the test*.

II

**THE TEST AS SEEN FROM THE
FEMININE (ENTER FICTION)**

'Here and now I search in vain for fiction. This fiction, so keenly called for, is in a sense the opposite of utopia for it seeks to compose itself from all that anchors history.' – France Théoret

'And the Damned of the damned raise themselves up little by little out of imprecision and non-existence.' – Jovette Marchessault

Nothing is reassuring for a woman, if not herself, having gone and found herself among other women.

Women write, but at this point in time, they write more than ever with the conscious knowledge that they cannot write if they camouflage the essential, that is that they are women.

The female body will speak its reality, its images, the censure it has been subjected to, its body filled to bursting. Women are arriving in the public squares of Literature and Text. They are full of memories: anecdotal, mythic, real, and fictional. But above all women are filled with an original all-encompassing memory, a gyn/ecological memory. Rendered in words, its reality brought to the page, it becomes fiction theory.

Faced with text now impossible – because it denies the memory and the identity of its author, because it reduces the body to that of the neuter-masculine – how to, without reverting to a linear literature (that is, narrow and without perspective), how then to render what works at the female body on the inside and all over its surface? How to make use of words when, as Louky Bersianik points out: 'The symbolic is the place Man allotted to himself, though this was neither solicited nor called for. In so doing, he usurped the place of the other, that is, that of woman. Then he could say she doesn't exist.'[6]

What form could contemporary thought take exactly, giving to words an entirely new flair? For the body has its reasons. How to keep one's distance from words without, for all that, giving up one's place, without ending up neutered and neutralized in one's text, without losing sight of an image of self finally liberated from its negativity, without omitting that which reflects it (women and honour, as Adrienne Rich would say), and that which sense always transforms and extrapolates.

Writing sense/reading sense. A sixth sense is at work in the life of women. Repressed to the point of appearing non-existent, and by this same fact rendered inoperative in the patriarchal system, it seems to me that this sixth sense, for circumstantial reasons in the development of western civilization, is reaching maturity, and that it can, from this point forward, intervene in the reality and even in the fiction that it calls forth or represses. A sixth sense that might bring to mind the transformational role of a 'synthesizer' in music, which offers reality from diverse mobile angles, and then orchestrates their differences. A sense which excites/incites the desire to submit proof of imagination and which occasions a spatial shift: the imaginary. A sixth sense which calls into question the very notion of what we call intelligence; which, taken from its strictest dictionary sense, is 'the set of mental functions having as its object conceptual and rational knowledge (as opposed to sensation and intuition).'[7] The limits of this form of intelligence are quickly apprehended. More difficult to grasp is the form of intelligence presupposed by the existence of a sixth sense and the way it works in its role as gatherer of information generated and received by the body. Let us call this a system of perceptions or reality construct.

Women, conditioned not to take their perceptions into account (certain women do, of course, for their own personal stability, at times meeting patriarchal dictature head on), and conditioned never to speak about them, women are bound to see their perceptions as impressions. Through force of circumstance, they will go so far as to have impressions of

---

6. Louky Bersianik, *Le Pique-nique sur l'Acropole* (Montreal: Éditions VLB, 1979), p. 130.
7. Marlene Wildeman's translation, from the *Petit Robert*.

impressions, to the point where they have the impression that it is all in their head, made up, and that their perceptions are, after all, simply the fruit of their imagination.

This is why we can say, on the one hand, that until now reality has been for most women a fiction, that is, the fruit of an imagination that is not their own and to which they do not *actually* succeed in adapting. Let us name some of those fictions here: the military apparatus, the rise in the price of gold, the evening news, pornography, and so on. The man in power and the man on the street know what it's all about. It's their daily reality, or the 'how' of their self-realization. You know – life!

On the other hand, we can also say that women's reality has been perceived as fiction. Let us name some of those realities here: maternity; rape; prostitution; chronic fatigue; verbal, physical, and mental violence. Newspapers present these as *stories*, not fact. It is thus at the border between what's real and what's fictive, between what it seems possible to say, to write, but which often proves to be, at the moment of writing, unthinkable, and that which seems obvious but appears, at the last second, inexpressible, that this elusive derived writing, writing adrift, begins to make its mark. Desire of/for elusion and desire derived from.

Elusion desire: desire that deviates from the sense one would have expected to take – censure with respect to the text's primary intention, at times complete censure: silence.

Desire derived from: desire that originates from an internal certitude and that results therefore in writing that traverses a gynecological memory. Crossing over and crossed through by this memory, one can infer that a woman's writing de-rivets that which is firmly riveted in the patriarchal symbolic order. An approach, and a previously unheard-of knowledge (intellectually speaking), unfurls from this. It presupposes a form of contemplation and concentration for the woman who writes, which I call the thought of emotion and the emotion of thought. A mental space replete with possibilities stemming from a perspective that joyously initiates a shift in meaning. In the text all is moving, like woman's skin on woman's skin, and this occasions a pleasure that lights up intelligence and revitalizes all women who take part.

What is made here in this mental space is History. Without making a scene, biography and daily life are able to circulate so that the *test* (living/writing), and its deployment (thinking), are transformed.

To write in the feminine then perhaps means that women must work at making their own hope and history, in the one place where these can take shape, where there is *textual matter*.

III

THE AERIAL VISION

A) MEMORY PLURAL

I was moved at the beginning of this text to say: 'Fiction seeks its own fictional subject and memory alone does not flinch. Memory makes itself plural, essential, like the vertigo that foreshadows an aerial vision.' What should we make of this plural memory that would regale text to the point of transforming it into *fictive text*, that is, a real text, existing before our very eyes but about which we could still have doubts, as if it were unthinkable, even as we *force the spirit to think it,* with exactitude in its form and movement. Think it with the aid of this plural memory which now bathes in, now circulates from one brain to another, cortex and neo-cortex. Think it to the point where the pages, the underlying threads, and the pageantry of the species take on the appearance of live texture.

This body, which the text has fragmented the better to then recompose it as subversive virtue in the contemporary consciousness, this body thought (about) becomes body thinking at the speed of light. A while ago I might have believed it was this body Roland Barthes spoke of, 'this body which pursues its own ideas,'[8] but in order to continue writing I need to believe that this thinking body, whose complex texture is made up of infinite individual memories, active and industrious as if madly in love, is still somehow different from that known enraptured body we sometimes manage to touch upon with lines written in a feverish but nonetheless precise hand.

---

8. Barthes, p. 29.

But the body has its reasons, mine, its lesbian skin, its place in a historical context, its particular environment, and its polititical content. Under my very eyes, the lines come round on themselves: linearity and shattered fragments of linearity (those ruptures you've heard of) transform themselves into spirals. 'Beautiful muscular women in the grass, happy and ferocious, saw their body hair glisten with a thousand scintillae when the memory came to them that surfaces, deep down, gave birth to the consciousness of space (with them).'[9]

My body's plural memory also tells me that 'women's memory is torrential when it has to do with torture'[10] – systematic torture which, as Mary Daly shows in *Gyn/ecology*, has been camouflaged in the name of value systems and customs: Chinese foot-binding, the custom of suttee in India, clitoridectomy, gynecology, and contemporary psychiatry. The ravages are extensive. But memory comes back to the surface each time, as though to make a mental synthesis. It is from this synthesis that I take my point of departure, that I start over with each spire of the spiral in order to postulate the meaning of words otherwise – the dictionary has just one of the novel poses struck by these bodies with their memory, skin, cortex, anger, and tenderness.

Little by little, sight replaces the gaze, memory replaces recollection, sleep becomes a nocturnal siesta in summer's full light. And I haven't even begun to count the alpha waves!

These concrete acts, these skin signs, the words that go with them, combine to give birth to *yearning*, like an imperative aerial vision. This space is not at all a passive observation zone in thin air; on the contrary, it incites a capacity for synthesis that is made up of the living breathing body. It is then that words must prove themselves, that rhythm is transformed, that energy finds on the page the arrangement required if one is to succeed at taking on reality.

I am talking here about a certain angle of vision. To get there, I had to get up and move, in order that the opaque body of the patriarchy no longer obstruct my vision. Displaced, I am. And not like a girl who didn't quite make it but like someone they missed out on, someone they missed their

9. From *Amantes* (Montreal: Les Éditions Quinze, 1980), p. 49. MW's translation. ' ... (with them)' is '(avec elles)' in the original, meaning 'with them (these women).'
10. Ibid, p. 51. MW's translation.

shot on when they once had her in their sights, for the bead of a rifle will never have at its disposal the powers of a mirror. This displacement gives rise to all the others. Displacement of sense, not to be confused with disorder of the senses. Rather, it's a matter of what engenders the senses and what arranges them, a matter of all texture called upon to concentrate itself in text. This text I imagine each time, this text I bring about at the very moment when sureness of emotion engenders fictive fire in the breast, water and ardour giving meaning to the exploration. It happens therefore that I sometimes articulate *an abstraction.*

All memory works to reconstruct the skin and the hollows of childhood, even the colour of one's labia. All memory works in space to produce its form. Gertrude Stein wrote: 'It is hard not to while away the time. It is hard not to remember what this is.' This was in the context of 'Sentences and Paragraphs.'[11] And a few lines earlier, one could read: 'Analysis is a womanly word. It means that they discover there are laws.'[12] 'They,' these women, make me dream, remind me that knowledge, as we say, brings me back to the certain fictional aspect of things and emotions that nourish the body and impel it toward other senses and other meanings. Memory signals to me from the textual side of the continent of women.

B) URBAN WOMEN RADICALS

More and more women are writing and publishing. But who are these women who give me texts that make me think, a space I can take over and inhabit, a time for rebirth in each one? I call them urban radicals. Chance, the kind no throw of the dice will ever abolish,[13] has it that they are lesbians, by their skin and by their writing. That is to say that they conceive of reality the way they envisage themselves, in the process of becoming and of exploring pleasure, rapt, concentrated on the old landscape (to better comprehend), as attentive to knowledge as to their pupils.

---

11. Gertrude Stein, *How to Write* (1931; rpt. West Glover, Vermont: Something Else Press, 1973), p. 32.

12. Ibid, p. 32.

13. A line taken from Mallarmé's poem, 'un coup de dés jamais n'abolira le hasard.' My translation.

Women, urban radicals of writing in movement, change reality, call it back to the drawing board, the laboratory of thought. There, it is subjected to transformations essential to the survival of projects keeping us alive. Urban radicals cross cities and myths, meeting there all manner of women: ranging from the ancient neolithic Mother-Goddess all the way to today's little wife. Tchador and kitchen aprons. Amazons, witches, and learned women.

Text memory and risk memory. For the chances are great that while considering words one by one suddenly those multitudinous keys, which patriarchal oppression and its monstrous allure make manifest, will loom into view. Devoted to thought and to analysis, urban radicals shift the question of text to fiction and the imaginary. This brings to mind, by strange coincidence, several texts from Latin America, land of torture, land where everything that speaks intelligence and sharing is exterminated.

For urban radicals, words represent what is at stake every day in combat writing. In such a manner as to expand the mental space nourishing the body, causing us to redefine words as simple as: drowsiness, vertigo, memory, intelligence, experience.

The patriarchal universe has us all accustomed to exercising our faculties in linear fashion. Our reading of reality is conditioned throughout by the patriarchal tradition that itself constitutes reality. Our senses are trained to perceive reality through what is useful to its reproduction. Urban radicals unsettle the senses, thereby driven to a relentless exploration of sense.

Whether it is a matter of skin or a problem for linguistics, it seems to me that any meaning shift occasions a breach of reality, if only in the way we perceive this reality. If this breach is instantaneous, we can call it rupture. From one rupture to the next, we succeed in breaking linearity. But it can be newly reconstructed, as it was, as it is, fragment by fragment. In this, the work on the text will have perhaps only altered the chronological notion of writing without, for all that, having acted on its spatio-temporal relief.

When by contrast and contrariety a meaning shift produces a breach, and everything about it gives the impression that it has come to stay, the urban radical slips in the writing hand to take account of how sense breaks through to her senses. Then she slips her entire being in, concentrated on/in the opening, turns round on herself, until she discovers the curve that gives her to understand she has entered a spiral. She then applies herself to this reality, a previously unheard-of reality, difficult to believe, which becomes bit by bit fictive and then finally, fiction. Our most vital truths, do they not lie at the base of what seems obvious but what is in fact the fiction reality has moved so fast to make?

Urban radicals invent fictions that mirror them infinitely, like two and some thousand different raindrops. What they conclude about reality transforms itself into *a thinking perspective* that is the very texture of the texts they produce. Urban radicals project something resembling memory made plural, multifaceted mirrors reflected into real space.' Text experienced like a three-dimensional image, instantly available, like a new skin, a skin no longer imprinted with the anecdotal symbols invented by the terror-spreading patriarchal machine. What is unreadable, what is unlawful about urban radicals is only, all things taken into account, the plausible version of the energy of women in quest and in movement.

c) IMAGINE

One has the imagination of one's century, one's culture, one's generation, one's particular social class, one's decade, and the imagination of what one reads, but above all one has the imagination of one's body and of the sex that inhabits it. What could be more appealing to our imagination than the tenacious forms that haunt memory, mobile female forms that bring into play in us their own pulsating movement.

The imagination travels in language and through skin. The entire surface of the skin. This all begins very early, but it also takes place when the text shifts slowly between the lines, encountering en route the facets and versions that form fiction, suggesting that in reality it might actually be a new skin in the perspective of experience. When the body of the text shifts on its surface, it knows it can no longer escape its own constitution. It takes on a new posture, a posture initiated by newfound integrity. Thus does one traverse one's text, one's paper veil, as one comes through one's fictive woman in order to find there a real woman, sitting at her worktable, writing. New configuration. Words/knowledge/emotion: I foresee them simultaneously. And I come back to this.

In the present tense of the text, I imagine the emotion that relates it to its own intelligence. I intervene in my body's history, through its memory, its gathering activity: its reflection.

The female body, long frozen (besieged) in the ice of the interpretation system and in fantasies relentlessly repeated by patriarchal sex, today travels through, in its *rapprochement* to other women's bodies, previously unknown dimensions, which bring it back to its reality.

To a certain extent, it is because I am obliged by reality, and because I am initiated to what's real and its fictive version, that I shift toward the imaginary: but I bring along my text, this thought matter that serves as my inscription in the historical space to which I belong.

Imaginary and text: site of my ardour, what arouses me, what appeals to me. All this revolves around apparent meaning; what is unmistakable, and what actually manifests itself as essential to a writing project, where each coincidence of what's real and what's fictive prints on the public page the reality of this body: word still stuck in the throat. When the throat becomes valley, and the silence of valleys reaches my ear like a rumour that's true, then you have the imaginary.

Thus I inscribe: 'writing is an insurmountable fiction. An insurmountable fiction refers us back to writing. That is, back to a certain facsimile of self engaged in day-to-day life,' when, suspended over a major work, tuned to the timbre of voice, to local time, what unfurls is nothing other than one's raw material which, in a word, woman, burns with imagination in the same way one can be ablaze with beauty.

On all sides: thought. Enter this body coming from the continent of the imaginary, this body enraptured in space.

The imagination travels through skin. Skin is energy. Eros is at work in all writing. How then does it proceed in the feminine? Is there a suggestion of body? Which body does it propose as partner in order that from one complicitous moment to the next the desire of the woman who writes brings about her own authentic renewal? Is this a question of body or of mental space? Furthermore, is it a question of energy, intact energy as yet unspoiled by patriarchal propaganda?

If the question of text revolves around knowledge, the question of writing revolves around energy, like a spatio-temporal zone we must work our way into, be attendant to with brain and senses combined, rhythmic.

Writing is a privileged practice of the written word that permits the dreaming of text. I say one must dream one's text, like a living organism that multiplies the apprenticeship of the reason for all existence: ecstasy and thought. To borrow the title of one of Luce Irigaray's books, let us say that one doesn't move without the other.[14] We would agree then that this amounts to an enormous task in a civilization that works toward ensuring that neither one move.

IV

THE AERIAL LETTER

Everything I've written here leads me back to its beginning, that is, to an initial utterance, which is the aerial letter. To get there, I had to pass the test of text, the test in the feminine plural memory, my women's continent, and the imaginary. I am not concluding something here, rather, I affirm an initiation route. I examine the cartography of a set of realities which, having traversed me, initiate me to the idea of an aerial vision: a fiction-writing project that would co-respond to it like an echo. The fictive version of a few ideas, the passionate quest of form to render them real; that's what always ends up in my texts.

This capacity we have to live words in accordance with certain sensations in the perspective of all-inclusive thought, apt to renew desire and to see it take cultural and political form, sums up the overwhelming confrontation of the political and the personal. A question I feel I must approach by way of the aerial letter.

First of all, let us say that one enters the aerial letter just as one slips inside one's skin and into the writing that constitutes it and of which it is made. Under the influence of the aerial vision, certain zones known for their 'redundant opaque clarity' cloud over; others become nuanced or illuminated. Thus, at the heart of the aerial letter, certain zones appear clear, zones we would otherwise register with difficulty, given the political vision we have of beings and the activities they participate in.

---

14. Luce Irigaray, *Et l'une ne bouge pas sans l'autre* (Paris: Les Éditions de Minuit, 1979)

It is because the aerial vision never freezes its gaze on any one thing that it becomes possible to see the state of reality with incalculable precision. Something very precise is proposed to me here which I have to nonetheless discover then, on getting down to work, if you will. But one question still goes unanswered: in 1980, what inner resources do we have at our disposal for confronting a reality unremittingly altered to the point where it becomes logical to doubt it? For instance: What is a 'coup d'état'? What is the will of the people? Ronald Reagan, what's that? *Le Nouvel Observateur* asks – does it not – every two months: what does it mean to be French? And writers, what is literature? As if we were, one after the other, condemned to pirate the reality holographically projected onto the mental landscape of the eighties.

With which inner resources will we survive the civilization of man, that wasteland littered with patriarchal debris?

Meanwhile, as we make use of a sensual and cerebral capacity that lends itself to a form of original concentration, is it a fiction of history or a crisis in history, to bring its days to an end – and ours as well – in derision and the grotesque? Either way, we lose.

No matter how I look at the question, I am continually brought back to writing, not just any writing but that which I have to imagine in order to subsist, the way I dream an inexpressible reality, one that tests me, one I test and delve into deeply.

Writing is a fiction; that is why I imagine it assuming all sorts of forms inscribed in our biological rhythms, in the rhythms imposed by the environment, as well as those we choose. The aerial letter is what becomes of me (through the written word), when an emotion slowly sets to work, opening me to forms of existence other than those I have known through the anecdotes of political, cultural, sexual, or sensual mores.

The aerial letter is the fantasy that permits me to read and write in three dimensions; it is my laser. Space-time-mobility in History with this vision equipped for seeing History right down to the skin, in a manner that lets us distinguish those moments where we step out of it, moments where it is essential that, where possible, we reintegrate it, to change the course of it. To take leave of one's skin also means *to depart*, to make one's way slowly and with difficulty toward other fictions, toward that which in theory calibrates.

Writing then, as I conceive of it, with its aerial letters: is what permits me simultaneously to keep one eye on the historical anecdote (on which I depend, moreover), and one eye on the development of my global vision: cortex and skin of every gyn/ecological memory. Of every memory projected in the odyssey of mental space. From out in front, I correct the curve of my orbit, as one corrects one's text, for the sake of form.

The aerial letter literally constitutes my text, taken directly from a single and a multiple consciousness which insinuates that we are always like water and mirror, fire and matrix, like that which conquers even the principle of conquest, that is what captivates our senses and suggests the poem that makes me say that the chest holds the meaning of the breath we find there, as if each time it were a matter of writing: I carry on.

La Lettre aérienne
1985, tr. 1988

6 DECEMBER 1989
AMONG THE CENTURIES

from *Fluid Arguments*

tr. Marlene Wildeman

'I wouldn't go so far as to say they are all clowns
some accommodate the rest as they tumble in despair'

– Louky Bersianik

On this sixth of December in 1989, I am slowly drifting through blue luminous Paris, rue des Archives between the grey stones, rue des Blancs-Manteaux, and I am not thinking of what it's like in Montréal. I am on Paris time, no jet lag, and headed for a rendezvous with a Lebanese woman who is a student. She will be talking to me about a horror that is inconceivable to anyone who comes from such a peaceful place it is not yet called a country. Yes, I come from a place where the blood and clabbering noises made by humans in the pain of mass death haven't yet entered the site where words are formed.

That day I was walking slowly, following my usual habit of looking only at women as if to reassure myself about humanity. I walk in the full light of day. I have no reason to think of death. I have no intention of thinking of death. Paris is blue. Montréal is far away and covered with snow. I walk in absolute reality.

⸸

On December 7, 1989, I learn that a man has just killed fourteen women. The man, they say, separated the men and the women into two groups. The man called the women feminists; he voiced his hatred toward them. The man fired. The women dropped. The other men ran away. Suddenly,

>   *I/they are dead*
>   *felled by a*
>   *break in meaning.*

⸸

A WOMAN WHO IS CRYING OUT IN PAIN CAN SHE HEAR AT THE SAME TIME THE CRY OF ANOTHER WOMAN? THE CRY OF A WOMAN AND OF ANOTHER AND THE CRY OF ANOTHER WOMAN DO THEY COME TOGETHER COLLIDE IN SPACE AND TIME, THE DEEP CRY OF THE REBEL AND THE WAILING CRIES OF THE DOCILE DO THEY COME TOGETHER COLLIDE SO THAT IT WOULD SEEM ONE HEARS ONLY ONE IMMENSE LONG HORRIBLE SOUND?

§

DOUBT IN PARENTHESIS

The discourse, the analyses, and the commentaries that followed the massacre at the Polytechnique remind us that misogyny, phallocentrism, and ordinary sexism form such a cohesive politico-cultural whole that it is difficult to identify each man's actual participation in the oppression of women. The reasonable doubt each man benefits from has, as a consequence, the invalidation of every generalization that can be made about men's behaviour toward women, and thus it reinforces the presumed innocence of them all. In any case, given this 'innocence,' any well-intentioned liberal man can not only support feminist claims based on principles of equality and social justice but, all the while, discredit feminist research, analysis, and thought. Disturbing research that has discovered mass graves marking out the history of women; analysis that invalidates the foundations of patriarchal laws; creative thinking that, in the maze of paradoxes, contradictions, and hate metaphors of both fear and attraction employed by men to *domesticate the creature,* strives to understand the reasons why and the magnitude of men's hatred toward women – these work away at the very principle of life.

THE CONSISTENT HOSTILITY OF THE *INNOCENTS*

Misogyny, phallocentrism, sexism, and anti-feminism are four words that could seem to be easily interchangeable. It would be, however, a serious mistake to confuse one for another, for they play very specific but oh so complementary roles when it comes to the alienation, domination, and exploitation of women.

MISOGYNY

Misogyny, which is hatred or contempt for women, is so pervasive throughout both history and everyday life that even women hesitate to attest to the extent of it. It is so taken for granted that most of them see in it only traditions, mores, customs, harmless proverbs, good jokes; it is so commonly accepted that philosophers, novelists, and poets have been able to write the worst inanities about women without anyone asking them to justify what they wrote, the way no one asked Céline, Heidegger, and others to justify themselves with regard to anti-Semitism. All men are not active misogynists but they all carry the virus. The misogynist virus is particularly prone to activate itself when a man encounters one or more women who are recalcitrant, particularly with regard to sexism. Misogyny constitutes a semantic corpus to which every man experiencing a love crisis, or a lack of arguments to justify his privileges, sooner or later reverts. Misogyny allows women to be at once humiliated and dubbed inferior. Active misogyny nourishes the corpus; passive misogyny resorts to it, depending on the circumstances.

PHALLOCENTRISM

Opposite misogyny, which degrades women and dubs them inferior, phallocentrism enhances men's worth and deifies them, on the basis of the phallus fantasized as supreme signifier. Me ego phallus we are Man. Cultivated over thousands of years, phallocentrism provides justification for God, his emissaries, and all his representatives to be male. Phallocentrism explains why social organization is conceived and arranged according to the needs, fantasies, comfort, and sexuality of men (even those who are at the bottom of the scale). Phallocentrism reinforces in each man the certitude that each piece of power he holds by virtue of his maleness is *naturally* justified. Phallocentrism is a corpus to which all men avail themselves when the time comes to talk ontology, epistemology, ethics, and morality.

SEXISM

Sexism, which is a discriminatiory attitude and practice with regard to women, is so well integrated into our mores that we are able to refer to it as 'ordinary'. Indeed, sexism is always ordinary for it normalizes, makes the imaginary constructs 'misogyny' and 'phallocentrism' commonplace in our everyday life. Sexism is an instruction manual to which men refer in order to manage the unavoidable reality of the difference between the sexes, with regard to sexuality, reproduction, and work. Sexism is 'male politics,'[1] male management of personal and public life. Alongside the misogynist who consciously thinks and propagates his hatred for women and the phallocrat who fantasizes the superiority of the male, is the sexist, who profits from, protects, and perpetuates the privileges, honours, and advantages which for him are the equivalent of the pathological hatred and delusions of grandeur that respectively characterize the other two. Sexists are ordinary men that women recognize one at a time without ever being able to get an idea of their actual numbers.

ANTI-FEMINISM

Anti-feminism is the *political response* of men to the *political voice* of women, which has finally come into its own in the public sphere. Contrary to the ordinary sexism practiced generally by men in a relaxed manner, anti-feminism is a defensive reaction, which obliges men to make a fuss publicly and to flex the miso-phallo-sexist muscle that backs up their argument. It is rather interesting to note that, following the massacre at the Polytechnique, it took only a few feminists voicing their opinion for the majority of male commentators to manifest their hostile anti-feminism.

In summary, the events at the Polytechnique are there to remind us that from *male politics* (misogyny, phallocentrism, and ordinary sexism) to *men's political response* (anti-feminism), this is self-evident: men are just as hostile to women when they make no demands (women) as when they claim their rights (feminists), whether women pay attention to them (heterosexuals), or ignore them (lesbians).

---

1. The expression is borrowed from the French translation of Kate Millett's *Sexual Politics*, translated as *La Politique du mâle*.

YOUNG WOMEN AND VERTIGO

This permanent hostility men have toward women, this is what we forget about when the sky is blue, that is what those survivors – who were so quick to declare they weren't feminists – had forgotten. What, in fact, did they actually mean to say? Did they want to dissociate themselves from women who fight against unjust laws, against violence against women, against the degradation of women's image? Did they want to make it clear they were not lesbians, that they were not against men? Did they think, as the media would have us believe, that feminists are a category of undesirable women whose perspective is narrow and partisan, whose words are bitter and excessive, and whose bad will does enormous harm to the 'women's rights' the majoriry of women would be interested in? Did they think that feminists threaten the 'harmonious' relations between men and women? But what can a woman be thinking of when she says, 'I'm not a feminist'? What hasn't she thought of? Who hasn't she thought of?

SEXIST QUEBEC TRAGEDY?

The question is delicate, and nothing is less certain than our ability to answer it properly. Yet a large part of our incredulity, our stupor before the fact, and our shame at the Polytechnique massacre can be related to this question: how could such a thing happen in Québec? Are Québec men more sexist than the rest, do they feel more threatened, ripped off, or rejected by feminism? Has Québec feminism known such success that we must not speak of a 'suppressed' sexist misogyny? To these questions, I cannot respond. I can only note that in no other population with Roman Catholic traditions has feminism so rapidly influenced people's private lives and the social and cultural reality, in no other *French language* population has feminism been able to fight publicly, and with a certain success, sexism in language and advertising. But, it will be said, no doubt, men here are able to listen to what feminists say. Yes, it is true there is a certain audience, but what is more important is that Québec society has had to acquire in thirty years all the important currents of thought founded on principles of liberation (the ideology of decolonization, secularization, the counter-culture, Marxism, feminism), all the while educating itself in order to be transformed and to conquer its identity. In other words, Québec feminism was able to develop and take its place in the public sphere more easily because it was part of an immense liberation movement, because it happened at the strategic moment of Québec's arrival on the world scene as a modern *North American* society.

BRIEF EVIDENCE

The stream of remarks, attitudes, and reactions that followed the massacre remind us that:

- only feminist claims that are based on principles of equality and social justice can, in the end, be heard by liberal society

- despite certain social gains and the liberalism of some men, the solidarity of feminists, that is, of lesbians and women, still remains our only hope of changing reality

- women's lack of solidarity with feminists and lesbians attests to a symbolic split whose principal consequence is to reinforce the patriarchal clan in its ideology and its privileges

- feminists have nothing to gain by softening their intentions in order to give themselves a good media image

- the feminist movement must be visibly present all the time and not just during moments of crisis, such as the massacre at the Polytechnique and the Daigle-Tremblay affair[2]

---

2. Tremblay had a court injunction brought against his former partner, Chantal Daigle, because she wanted to procure an abortion. The case was brought to the Supreme Court of Canada, who decided in favour of Daigle.

• anti-feminists should be identified as political enemies

• whatever the complexity of human reality and motivations, nothing can excuse or justify sexist violence and discrimination. Furthermore, any biological or psychological explanation that aims to excuse men's violent behaviour toward women would be much more serious, for it would lead us to believe that men are incurable criminals.

'[La fusillade de Polytechnique]:
le tueur n'était pas un jeune homme,'
first published in *La Presse*
1989, tr. 1991

FROM SHADOW: SOFT AND SOIF

from *Ardour*
tr. Angela Carr

Today the air is opaque and clinking:
an erosion of symbols
the world in plain sight of our eyes.
Morning, I count
roses, insects. And solitude.
Hiding my sighs
I drown easily in the urban wind
verb tenses and your hair.
Feuillage dense d'origine.

°
°

outside the framework, joy in silhouette
i touch all *life follows its course*
a stone that endures, a child
a mirrored sound
and not necessarily a smile

°
°

in reality space thins
ardour draws its knots of presence
here and there in the city we live
on convictions yes and azure
we have dark hair
and our seductions vibrate valiant repetitions
in the gardens and parks take note
the words will soon come   there
to tear you from the simple present of the abyss

across the foliage of words
a few night syllables
let's watch
our dream muscles move
eyes outdistanced by nostalgia
we watch
tears, palms, and fists like thirst
and the idea that living is
necessarily all *à l'intérieur du langage*

§

since the wind sweeps across
both the horizon and breasts
in the rain sometimes there's no one
or a face in disorder
a mouth that exaggerates
all agape
at the end it's magnificent
night trembles like a fruit tree
a danger

§

some days a blow
of violence a blow of murmurs
the stories pile up
you observe the bodies
                   r
i repeat   o   n
we long to be t   from
the simple present of the abyss

§

it's yes: at nightfall
pain awakens carnivorous
rolls more nobly
quick under the tongue

§

yet there will be no portrait
of my mother, no etching or gesture
in language that flounders
there will be only a scene
still standing in the city and the wind
a beastly melancholy that dawn
will seize from speed and intensity

§

i won't write *wound*
and all the gestures that pool
at the end of the sentence

and don't complain
if shadow adds contour to reality
like at the cinema
if it's dark and hazy
between eyelashes and time

§

to be for a whole life in the changeable species
with this reflex that persists in wanting
to represent everything, euphoria, gestures
bites, rooms with their hollows
shadow and softness, worried foreheads
our fragility

of course, we are speechless with
every kiss

⁝

heat that whispers near the temples
fictions of dawn and the absolute
i like any night that moves the knees

i also noted this:
night inverts the horizon
but how does it become so silky
among the nebulæ without protection
entangled with the pain of the horizon
and softness that blazes in the voice

⁝

ideas of the fall and the labyrinth
as if at the tips of our arms
all that exists was
for a day made to move dawn
raise the curtain on the animal kingdom

so i keep watch
among knives and dust

⁝

i have not yet spoken of disappearance
before the pronouns
life makes decisions
under the skin
makes a dream wheel, hoops
math games and caskets

now here are the glaciers
some materials
from dawn and suffering

Ardeur
2008, tr. 2015

FEMME D'AUJOURD'HUI:
EXCERPT FROM A RADIO-CANADA INTERVIEW
BETWEEN FRANCE LABBÉ AND NICOLE BROSSARD,
16 MAY 1975

tr. Geneviève Robichaud

FRANCE LABBÉ (FL): You've written that through your writing you could establish a balancing act between yourself and your writing, and that you couldn't continue working within a masculine tradition.

NICOLE BROSSARD (NB): Yes, indeed, in the end the texts that I found nourishing for my writing were, in most cases, texts written by men, so ultimately I was following a masculine tradition, which acted as a kind of reference point. The texts I've written are valid, just the same, so I wouldn't dismiss them, but for me it becomes impossible at the moment to continue to write within the context of masculinity. I can still use those texts as tools, and I'm certainly not seeking to erase them. On the contrary, these are men who produced what I consider to be very good texts. Some of them even assumed part of their femininity despite the risk of madness, or by observing the lives of the women they loved. The texts that seem important and nourishing to me at the moment are most often by women, like the beautiful text *Nouvelles Lettres Portugaises* written by the three Marias or *A Room of One's Own* by Virginia Woolf, and all the texts that are being written presently because there has also been, in the last ten years, a release for a great deal of women who have begun to write and to rethink their writing in feminine terms.

FL: Do you think that there's a language that is specifically feminine – not simply at the level of the content, but at the level of the writing as well?

NB: I think there could be research done at the moment on the possibilities of language – language that has, in general, always been used the same way by men, and also reflects ... for instance, the French language registers quite well the dominance of the masculine over the feminine ... and there's also the question of word games, of linguistics ... and obviously on a thematic level, too, there's a whole affective network that's been unexplored in literature and that's been ignored by critics who have treated it as trivial because it was work by women, or because its themes dealt with women's experiences. For example, stories about childbirth or about the humdrum of women's daily lives at home have always been considered bland compared to what might happen in an office – the conflicts between a man...between a worker and his boss, for example. And there's an entire thematic dimension that's swept aside with a sleight of hand by critics who obviously have no interest in exploring the possibilities of the sensorial and emotional character of these realties.

Femme d'aujourd'hui
1975, tr. 2019

{ The City }

INTIMATE JOURNAL

from *Intimate Journal, or Here's a Manuscript*
tr. Barbara Godard

PARIS, 27 NOVEMBER 1975

Yesterday, the world needed to be remade again. Luce and I are continuing our work begun in New York. But this time, we're in an autumnal Paris. It's my birthday. In an hour, I interview Simone de Beauvoir about American feminists. Has the author whose *The Second Sex* was an illumination for the women who became radical feminists been inspired in turn by these women capable of smashing the patriarchal lie?

I was worried, because the day before I had seen an interview Simone de Beauvoir had granted to French television. I had been disappointed. Not by her words but by the dutiful daughter. No body; only a mouth that moved, and sometimes her hands approved, rising lightly, imperceptibly above her knees. Let's forget the body, I had thought in New York, but today I didn't want to forget anything.

Yesterday is so alive and present in Paris. Paris is yesterday at every street corner. We are walking, camera and sound recorder on our shoulders toward Montparnasse. Visual, sonorous, all the senses are kindled in a flash. We shoot. We ask questions. And then, one day, this footage, very short, disappeared as though it had all never existed. Disappeared how? Mystery at the National Film Board. Travelling shot in the corridors, in the cafeteria. No zoom-in prospect. Yesterday, a little while ago, soon no history.

19 MARCH 1983

Yesterday I thought that in a creative-writing workshop there ought to be at least one writing exercise with the words *window*, *drawer*, and *mirror*. After, we'll see! Yesterday 'maman died,' yesterday 'everything swallows me,' yesterday 'Cuba sinks in flames,' yesterday a text begins like this.

Yesterday, ante, haunted. The past haunts me in the intimacy of the journal. What exactly do you want from me? Literature that won't look like literature? Writing that will not be writing? <u>Do you want me to look cute?</u> Memoirs, autobiography, journal, fiction. O! of course, you need to differentiate them, but who is to do that?

20 MARCH 1983

Yesterday it would perhaps have been better for me not to go out. I went walking on Mount Royal. I should perhaps have gone to rue Saint-Denis where I could have met Yolande Villemaire, France Théoret, Pauline Harvey, or a girl from *La Vie en rose*. We would have begun by talking about the beautiful day, then about a coffee or beer to order, then about the book Sollers dared to title *Women* in the plural, or again, we would have returned to the subject in talking about the success of International Women's Day last March 8th. One of us would have said that the latest issue of *La Nouvelle barre du jour* was excellent, then little by little we would come to the point of showing each other some book bought just a while ago at the Librairie Androgyne. We would have smoked five cigarettes for one beer, ten for two, and a whole package with the fourth. Another woman would have bought a Perrier with lemon, and still another would have asked for news of Julie Capucine and I of Claude or Jean-Paul.

Yesterday, I'm not expecting anyone. Yesterday, is like an island. It's an island that disappears then re-appears. Yesterday is a sleeping volcano. At that time, it's like today, with a mountain slope transformed by fire. A slope of the lunar landscape after having spit out fire. And the other slope, the untouched side? And the other slope?

It would have been better for me not to go walking on Mount Royal. But all that, the walk and the reverie, I only did that in order to write. It's a closed circuit: I don't go out because I must write and I'll have nothing to write if I don't go out. I need to go to the gynecologist, the dentist, to the department stores, I must go to Radio-Canada for an interview, I have to make an appointment for lunch at the Café Laurier, and I should call my mother, I must pick Julie up after her ballet lessons. It's so beautiful outside, such good weather. Just the same I'm not going to begin to write down everything that's running through my head. I no longer recognize myself.

I feel as though I am going to end up saying everything and the Id, it's not very interesting. At any rate, one can never say everything. There are gaps, spaces. Blanks are inevitable. In painting, in music, in writing, the white space is de rigueur. The blank space is inseparable from fiction and from reality. Through the white space we engage the circumstances of writing as if entering into the invisibility of our thoughts. Others call white the void we need to fill in order to get to know society. Or again white, the vibrant luminosity that is eventually separated into the vividness of anecdotal colours. Blank of absence, white of full presence. One always has to begin again, like a particular day we'll observe, a holiday, when the world is unravelled all around us.

Journal intime, ou voilà donc un manuscrit
1984, tr. 2004

WORN ALONG THE FOLD

from *Surfaces of Sense*
tr. Fiona Strachan

See: fold.

as with matter, erosion, the wear and tear of the double sex / doubled up
over reality, searching for the yielding sinews, the uterine walls – inner,
outer, and real – a fold in the linen, a wrinkled brow

....

fold page in two (horizontal line)

one cannot fully conceive the extent to which a brown comb, on the brown
chest of drawers, in Adrienne's white bedroom, has something of the
abstract about it.

I imagined something abstract wandering freely through the house, the kitchen, the table, the pencil: a utopian symbol, which I could use to represent reality, together with everything going on inside my head.

Adrienne alluded continually to the utopian dreams burning inside her. Something abstract, which I could only imagine, filtered through her, as if to incite her more strongly toward reality; as if to bring her into closer contact with the odour of bodies, the cold, the blue metal.

It was essential that we play an active role in this City, or there was a huge danger of disappearance: incarceration, incineration, annihilation.

Rusty metal in the grass. Also, that heap of tires over in a corner.

Fictions, strategems of reality. From a separate vantage point, each woman's eyes, seeing and seen as the fires in the City. Each was a witness. The female witness in the cycle of experience. One legitimate form in the patterns of existence breathing down on the City, ultimately producing unremitting desire, mobile and ravenous in the lace-work labyrinth.

The witness: *she* knew how to focus on images of water, self, and desire, in order to assuage her fevered body.

However, each one was witness to the hunger outside the window. The oval window in each face was sensitive to the full spectrum of vibrations.

Adrienne: her mouth half-open as if she had something further to say.

Can one construct *a flaming structure* by asking a series of questions? I imagined it was possible on certain days when desire penetrates through several zones, several states of being. So that finally it is condensed materially to such an extent that I can no longer look the book in the face and my thoughts are somewhere else, attempting to integrate with exactitude the emotional shocks (and the silences) assailing the body.

I was thinking of Adrienne's messages, received several days ago, informing me of *the death of Gertrude* like a declaration which spoke of immortality among the frescoes of the city.

Ordinary, everyday thoughts, invigorating, enabling me to cope until the next day; on that day, I concentrated on keeping them alive, like a vivid memory, until they reached the critical moment.

Dazzling light. Leaves. Dampness. Squinting. A feeling of accomplishment. Something plausible has crept into my book, which has become a legitimate expression of reality, at all levels of perception.

At the foot of the cliff. I imagined myself being unable to answer, a sentence left hanging: has it happened.

Madly, I had thought up a great love story for I wanted to write a book, no matter what. But in such a way that this foolish temptation would not be exaggerated; this foolish episode which, unknown to me, runs up and down my spine, which makes me write down *all these things:* tell me, Adrienne, just what could I have told you that night, what could I have confessed to you, apart from dying embers?

Yes, the writing process (admittedly) scarcely resolves the question, does not resolve it. Rather, feeds the problem, even anticipates it, so that it delays the impact of the structure.

From one story to the fiction devours devoured surfaces of sense this delirium devouring the story the broken surface. Fiction slumbers in the cavities on the surface cavities of childhood very real for the fire the cliff.

....

all the versions

Le Sens apparent
1980, tr. 1989

SCREEN SKIN UTOPIA

from *Picture Theory*

tr. Barbara Godard

By beginning with the word *woman* in connection with Utopia, M. V. had chosen to concentrate on an abstraction of which she had an inkling. From the moment when M. V. had used <u>the generic body</u> as expression, I knew that behind her the screen would be lowered and she would be projected into my universe.

She would have no other choice but to agree. *Agree* is visibly the only verb that can allow verisimilitude here, the transparency of utopian silk/self (in my universe, Utopia would be a fiction from which would be born the generic body of the thinking woman). I would not have to make another woman be born from a first woman. I would have in mind only <u>the idea</u> that she might be the woman through whom everything could happen. In writing it, I would have everything for imagining an abstract woman who would slip into my text, carrying the fiction so far that from afar, this woman participant in words, must be seen coming, virtual to infinity, form-elle in every dimension of understanding, method and memory. I would not have to invent her in the fiction. The fiction would be the finishing line of the thought. The precise term.

Itinerant and so much a woman. Brain——————————————
memory. Night, numbers, and letters. At the ultimate equation. I would loom into view.

⁂

Time becomes process in the ultra-violet. I am the thought of a woman who embodies me and whom I think integral. **SKIN (UTOPIA)** gesture is going to come. Gravitate serial and engrave the banks with suspended islands. I shall then be tempted by reality like a verbal vision that alternates my senses while another woman conquers the horizon at work.

Utopia integral woman

Gesture is going to come: a sign I'd trace, a letter that would reflect me in two different voices I would be radically thinking like a ray of light, irrigating the root, absolute reality. The generic body would become the expression of woman and woman would have wings above all, she'd make (a) sign. Plunged into the centre of the city, I would dream of raising my eyes. FEMME SKIN TRAJECTOIRE. *Donna lesbiana* dome of knowledge and helix, already I'd have entered into a spiral and my being of air aerial urban would reproduce itself in the glass city like an origin. I'd see this manifestly formal woman then inscribe reality, ecosystem.

⁑

From there, I'd begin, the woman in me like a centre of attraction. Surely life if life has a term death would be another, concentrated like a neuron, still it would normally be a sign. I am on the side of life if I die *in* slow motion, I occupy space in Utopia. **I can push death away like a mother and a future.** Brilliancy, amazement today that energy the lively affirmation of mental territory is a space at the turning point of cosmic breasts. J'ÉVOQUE. JE CERTIFIE MON ESPOIR. **SKIN** utopia slow vertigo. I work on the context of the already written of our bodies' fluorescence, I perform the rite and temptation of certainty so that it ramifies. I would see a formal woman opening up to sense because I know that each image of woman is vital in the thinking organism——————————
gyno-cortex. At the end of patriarchal night the body anticipates on the horizon I have in front of me on the screen of skin, mine, whose resonance endures in what weaves the text/ure t/issue the light when under my mouth the reason of the world streams down. M. V. agreed. In her eyes, it was epidermic this will for serial circulation of spatial gestures which the letter had initiated. **Skin.**

⁑

The mother came back sometimes without knowledge of words, to tell everything and also that it would be for a last time, asserting as a hypothesis that she would give up her right to speak to M.V. whom I had never so much watched writing what she felt straightening up her body in front of the Sphinx, invested by the enigma word by word progressing (on her face, in slow motion, everything from the fiction became visible in each cell and la peau travaille **skin I win the double glory of** ses seins sont miens et grammatrice **look at the double you** of the state we formulate fair tide in the city. **My** *m*ind **is a** *w*oman.

It wasn't possible then to lose sight of <u>hope in the hologram</u> over what had never been a detail. In the waters of Curaçao, Anna Gravidas swam with long movements her arms alternating in the water. Sitting on a deck chair, I saw a head come out of the sea, distracted and lost rediscovered rising out of the waves: the sun was wiping out the anecdotal cards of the casino. To like one's project, repeat it, fuse with it, cite it Claire Dérive had said one day at the seaside. I should die of shame for having heard only the word *citation*.

⁂

The dictionary was lying beside the bed, Recto-verso. Hundreds of definitions. Who defines? I lean over to pick it up. It weighs heavily at arm's length sort of agitated animal. A the impression. The hyper-realism of words transforms the body/the body unfolds D N A. The long spiral dissolves time. Each second is no more than an image. I open the book. Sequence of the instant: sidereal day. I see her coming. Between the minute when she entered the Hôtel de l'Institut and the one when the woman came out, undoubtedly that night she focused on the very precise idea of the verb <u>define</u> which led her to question all definitions concerning women. Continuous surface, waves come in relays, is said also about sensations and sentiments.

She said wave it's a matter of an ordered sequence of terms sitting in the middle of the room in the however of real things. At arm's length: body/dictionary. The circuit of abbreviated sentences. Cortex spiral. The woman utters some invisible words 'it's reality point blank' or hackneyed words at the same place to break off suddenly. Short-circuiting emotion, idea, concept. Hope according to the curve of crystalline lens; from where I draw on the (f)actuality of words.

⁝

At grips with the book, baroquing. Sweat beads. Resort to the window to track down sonorities, poetry passes through the millennial quotidian in order to come back to the idea of her I have been following well beyond my natural inclination, she who pre-occupied thought has seen words come like foreseeable attacks and changed their course. She is the one who inhabits me and who familiarizes me with the universe. Scintillates in me. All the subjectivity in the world.

Utopia shines in my eyes. Langu age is feverish like a polysemic resource. The point of no return for all amorous affirmation is reached. I am there where 'the magical appearance' begins, the coherence of wor(l)ds, perforated by invisible spirals that quicken it. I slip outside the place named carried away by the thought of a woman converging. Anatomical slice of the imaginary: to be cut off from linear cities to undertake my dream in duration, helmetted, virtual like the woman who gathers up her understandings for a book.

M.V. had straightened herself up, slowly turned her head her gaze caught between the window ledge and the horizon. Le poème hurlait **opening the mind**

Picture Theory
1982, tr. 1991

JUST ONCE

from *French Kiss*

tr. Patricia Claxton

In which the text slows down in Camomille's mouth, salivating letters and words of love the better to … suck on fragments of fiction. With all the energy of irrigations and convergences. Membranes that meet and meet some more till the last contractions, to exhaustion. The ultimate dilation. Ecstatic perfusion in Camomille's mouth. An exile throughout the long lingual journey over those plausible surfaces and mucous membranes connexting in her mouth. As if in a muffled world filled with liquid symptoms, concentric desires, capsules within to be opened and discovered, little scaly pink fish of that 'miraculous catch' whose stirring and harmonious lilt we feel in the merest reflex. Lick at those walls. Prolong the desires with the telling, the narration of a long uninterrupted kiss. How hard it is to articulate or devise compromise. The kiss, a ball of fire. Life's serum restored with undulant and penetrating movement, a reliving of the taste and smell of birth for a tongue consumed in dance beneath Camomille's palatal dome, Camomille whom I love with all my power of intervention. A wish: to abolish walls between mouths. Mm-mmm the taste of it.

Luckily keeps flowing in the text and on my tongue, erotic substitutes, and luckily that tipsy feeling in the dark, inside beside a cheek so just enjoy, rejoice in the juice, turn and return to that first excitement. What is excitement? Encouragement to do what you feel like doing when seen by someone else / the reader in company with Lucy, Georges, or Alexandre, or Elle; being used to spinning out one's dreams by muddling one's own reflection in the mirror so marvellously that paradoxes come to life and whatever the cost force a retake of the sentences, the caresses that started the excitement (what did we say it was?), stimulated spine and breasts dandled in a hand, a phallus emerged invitation to oblivion, to the feel of rhythmic shudder, loins more titillating than some corny happy-ever-after tale, pelvic basins the pornographic mudholes of one's imagination. Narrator fem./masc. Pelvic basins liquid base. Stop and ruminate a moment near the pond, the basin in Lafontaine Park with its little boats going just fast enough to the music of the band on a Sunday made for sunning in a park with sunning playing fountains. The water basin changes shape to triangle or rectangle. Like imagining Versailles made avant-garde. But how old and worn the film, how grotesque, like some faded foreign boulevardier ... then, as if from one exploration to the next, a long hop to Chambly Basin, immersion there in unmuddied waters fed by springs, our origins, a running brook of words rippling-aroused tracing a thighline like a hand, retracing the story line the better to write it down. From that point on it's ink and blotter and quill by power of suggestion. Confusion springs.

Again, Camomille, your mouth, that's good, you get me off!

When the text lets Lucy move, we'll make her arms stir just barely round him / her, her partner, for Lucy's seductiveness is bounded only by the italics in a sentence and italics become her like any pleasurable and prettifying artifice, disguising her almost. So seeing them together we, in the guise of narrator, end up flitting deliciously from one image of them half naked to the next as in some threatening text, brandishing blackmail photos before pale frightened eyes, above a man undone, stuck dumb – a movie *Caligari* lurking round the background. And those corridors. Tongues slipping through. Chew in ardour and get chewed. Reptiles about to shed a too tight skin. Mimes of fiction in the tender realm of Camomille's mouth and mine, I reaching for the limit of how / where to pass beyond and leave you to whatever, Camomille, or persuade you to cross with Lucy to pleasure's realms, with Georges to pleasure's realms.

The moment of the kiss comes at the moment traffic sounds cross Saint-Denis Street from one side to the other, on the heels of pedestrians, getting stuck between the wheels of buses, caught like a sound in an ear in a baseball glove. Traffic / circulation in the heartbeat's private mutterings. *Lakes* had taken shape in Camomille's eyes I recall – though her lids were closed – hunting and fishing lakes in spring at dawn when the mists don't rise, don't rise even for eyes asleep and gently moving, shadowy reflections of signs left over from the night before, and spun of dreams, sufferings, self-completion when the body's smit with lovely images, in fluid mood.

Camomille, it's good inside your mouth. You (I) send me bats completely bats.

CRACKPOT. Carnival mood. Twentieth century the way I like it. Vibes, brainwaves yow-wow-wow which … listen … Begin again: on Camomille's lips a kiss, rather chaste. Nibbled lips. Pain / relaxation. Pleasure, lips licked, left wet. I slip through the slot the text provides and enter Lucy's homosexual fantasies, seductive Lucy in total control of herself. The slot, parted lips, saliva. Like victims in a racy murder mystery, the membranes yield oh so gently to my tongue probing deeper DEEPER INTO THEM. OOF.

Shudders and muffled sound. In the city ramifications undulate on no specific course but round construction sites. Geography of reliefs, tongue against your teeth, in cheek, tickles hee hee – comes on like an electric train or a loving toothbrush jiggling with joy, rubbing, tickling gums – those gaping holes downtown, sprawling ranks of cars parked all humpy rounded bumps. The city in relief beyond the moment of right na-ow. Visionary and vulnerable – emerging from the Hippolyte Lafontaine Tunnel eyes blinking harder than those far-off yellow lights. Emerging from an analogy as from the analogy of tunnel and urethra, along a long straight line. Canal / communication. Oil on the tarmac, a few reflections on the surface of the road. The moment of the kiss, you realize, coincides with Marielle's arrival at Saint-Denis Street, where she enters a busy bar-restaurant, crowd ahum and rhythmic, panting and expectant. There fiction takes on / loses all its sense. Let it melt into what's real – there's not much sense to any of this if not *this* pleasure, *this* sense, I mean to say this play inside a mouth which, apart from choking her, offers her a thousand ways of composing pleasure on a tongue.

She spots her brother, Lexa dahling. Melts in his arms, that old delicious fantasy. He lights a joint for her. All's serenity while David Bowie beats his breast, with rhythm to the rafters and round the chairs, revelry in the smoke as it escapes and circulates like a French kiss urge. Camomille's left leg pressed against Lucy's.

The right one sweet against Georges's.

People coming in and others going / passing out: a minor neighbourhood event. The barroom door keeps swinging like a body wavering between two river banks, rivals.

Five around a nondescript table. Surface and smear of beer. Ashes. Insufficiently appreciated posters take revenge on eyes. Colours explode on retinas, corneas pop. Puffed-up bags. Uncontrollable bags and pipes, music, organ-word resemblance – stare very openly past Alexandre's knees, inside his BVDs. Detached we float above the tables, evidences dangling in mirth. Taste of peppers and pepperoni. Camomille eats a bit of everything, tastes everything when mouths open and breaths crisscross, exchange. Breath. Bit of chicken stuck in your teeth? What you been eating anyway? Oh, never mind! Into your mouth with my tongue, teasing like a lure to a fish to make you come. A fish swimming with the sperm's current, a pouring sweat of panicky words as the page turns laboured breathing. Must make sure the phantasms get to us from over the horizon. In the slippery occidental night whose existence Lucy's trying to deny. Abort the premonitory signs of fear. Realize that the city won't ever be reproduced to suit privileged eyes and ears like ours plugged into all forbidden things.

Lucy and Camomille drift with the music from cut to cut, side 1 the funny side, side 2 the head-spinner of the platter, drift at the speed of the water's flow and ... the bed's a vast surface where birds come pecking in the sere of autumn. Dead fish.

The *language of the birds* speaks for itself. The 'verbal alchemy' of analogies and phonetic equivalents. A prayer of joy heard through the other's wisdom teeth, whence, with saliva, flow into Camomille powerful intuitions of movement perpetual and circular – around gyrating hips and waist hula-hoop on the sidewalk after supper before dark, try again, can't do it, how you ever going to learn to dance? – inclusive hoop.

Each mouth leaves its colour its copy on the other. Each endures the other like a wintry cold, lips trapped in ice. Exceeds its bounds, a circus of two, two educated animals alone occupying sweetly all the surfaces of desire. The tongue's like a cutting word, a flicking whip, Camomille, arch your tongue – the way you do your back – a whip that flicks until it bites your tender flesh. My sanity's a hemisphere.

> Words get confused
> so hotly used
> phonemes
> celebration

The language of the birds speaks for itself

and what follows flows saliva lips scars spoken aloud over which to linger a long expectant moment, to dream as it were or to make mirrors talk back to us, ambiguously and resonating on our eardrums. The city, the fragile clink of glasses raised then put down on tables. The curious lapping sound of tongues before they find each other in the dark spaces over Adam's apples that bob as if in warning. Mouths touch and salivate beyond control, venture blindly toward each other. Toward the dark. Each to lose itself inside the other's geography. Camomille regains her breath, the other's breath, its difference marking her deeper than the fingernail she's digging into Georges's arm. An assault by a ramifying thing irradiating all its surface, epidermis – her desire.

Her tongue folds, unfolds, folds again, sucks at the other tongue, triggers, lubricious and circumstantial metamorphosis under the palate's / palace dome – under the verandah, pull down your pants, I won't tell (gustatory memory: popsicles, pink jujubes, popcorn, licorice, tootsie rolls, rock chocolate, peanuts) – like a deposed queen, her tongue yields to the other weakly with tenderness, disengages, drifts, a multiform body sought. On a wave of vagueness.

A detail on vagueness: Camomille agrees to make mirrors and shadows and incongruous details talk. Nuclear love. Brings a lump to my throat. Almost makes me think I'll always love you. Time to catch anoth-other breath.

This morning everything was wet. Sometimes I think I'm sinking inside you. Downtime for Camomille.

bullet bitten, bit in teeth, she squints and her eyes itemize, recompose like a kaleidoscope, detail by detail, one petal at a time, one shape and then another, a text of successive surprises; a city where lanes become streets. Elle in a nutshell, animated by all possible pulsations, varying the spaces, invention at play. Emcee for herself and for lines of force – prospects in mouths duplicated – a tracing.

Now to put her tongue in the other's mouth. Her desire in the city and geography. The other's house / garden path.

The city revives in their breath, their speech; perks up a bit. Because of names of buildings they must drop, streets they used to take to get to work, smells they discover to have clung to their hair during the day. Georges obliges, lifting a lock of hair to his nose. Asks Lucy too to bear witness to those curious and many smells that stick to a scalp any day of the week.

Almost a demonstration; wild enthusiasm (suddenly) for the smells of other people's hair. May go over by a hair's breadth if hair's not one's bag. Alexandre extends his train of thought as far as the station whence he walked to Marielle's one day. The city emerged at the moment he did from the Queen Elizabeth (Station Exit) and, polluted, grafted onto him. Profiles of men and buildings. The streets ramify anonymous, juxtaposed, and bring him back to now.

His/her tongue in the other's mouth, a subterranean passage where/during which he / she slips some information by body language to the other, a narrator burdened with decisions, optical letters in colour; two ends to choose and make meet in the text – let doubt take over, narrator (fem.) astonished by Camomille's transparency, her real facial / fictional traits, fleeting as when one loses oneself or maybe the other when making critical decisions from which one really doesn't hope to gain a thing, just store away each smile and each caress. At times of loss we dare to wish death on things. Flow and let flow like self-destructing ink over pages and pages of entreaty. Object: to exert loss of control over whoever / whatever and wherever on the globe. Ocular exertion / reading. The dimensions lost in the assembly line. The object decomposes. Forbidden zone of decomposition / decomperdition. *You the deaf*, look to your ears! Perdition. The tongues get hungrier, leechlike, draw bigger huffs and puffs. One stronger puff fired red-hot to bring forth amorous penchants for other inclinations. An oblique tongue, silent like a detail. Which suddenly I like.

Friday squeezed between one's legs like an animal that won't calm down. Near excess. Teeth and nails unrestrained the better to gnaw through the tie that binds, that holds back the body's shudderings, joyous rhythms gr/ um/p 1, such endearing ways; upside-down syringes in our heads. Not battered but disoriented heads, *wingover weather vane, I learn from all this as always what's best and what's not so bad in our forbidden bents cocking snooks toward the north.*

Ramified belly and text. Coincidence. Georges tilts and rocks his chair.

On Fridays all cats are grey.
Marielle's back from Lanoraie.
Another week begins.
Pim(p)s at the bar.
First choice.
Bully boys with sidewhiskers.
Bread and dough.
Dark décor in purples.
Traffic around the tables.

Movie house: moustache, black and white on May Irwin's white upper lip; one's first kiss which wasn't quite, a PECK almost but not exactly on the mouth.

unbutton the text and prod it to get rid of inhibitions in a narrator who changes them to make them fit a personal desire for prolonging pleasure, keeping a few forbidden things, a few mad impulses; when bodies are to be disguised, convey their attitude with lots of lascivious posturing.

Friday like an animal to grab by the scruff.

move along the circumstance, the other's lips while tongues travel each seeking to suppress, annihilate the other from a vantage point of mastery when one yields, gives ground, salivates beyond control, gives up its energy to the other whose power of domination it becomes.

upside-down syringes in our heads squirting dense dramatic scenes and fantasies upward to the sky into the blue. Disconnected speech, the world upside down in our veins, adrift … incense-perfumed super super neurons injecting upward, high above our heads and higher still, images of strange wild beasts astride other beasts galloping, galloping unrestrained, suspended like undecided meanings beyond the blue, super she-monsters, witches, Corriveaus uncaged assuaged in the grey of cumulous.

on Fridays cats chase round the neighbourhood lanes, through yards where little girls play with dolls to pass the time, like that old aborted dream of trucks and planes you can play with and get away with. As for dreams, even pimps once believed in them. Anyway with so much talk those dreams got to sound like fairy tales, bedtime stories for putting us to sleep ... once upon a time ... story cut short. Brutally by a speedy bouncer. Lost his head and fired into the pack, finished off the lot almost. Orgiastic violence.

catapults syringes cats and little girls so long long ago don't remember nuttin' no more nohow nowhere. Collective loss. Blank sleepless night and guns not loaded up enough. Blank, blur, ble, back to childhood.

FRENCH KISS

On with the kiss, so dense it strangulates articulations; pleasure moans. Weep talk laugh pleasure suffocates and makes tears well up in eyes and trickle back down over rounded cheeks. Lucy undulant amoeba, a fellow traveller cell while crossing arid desert zones. Remote seductress, imbibed in the text and gentle curves of love, she gazes round her, faraway like a Garbo idolatrized, makes heads turn. Fix on her. A mixture of words mixed with sensations. Real forms – a tourniquet.

Fix my lips like leeches onto yours, a sense to be got across to you. An Iroquois dream: lipstick, the other's dancing teeth, tongue around a red-hot cold sore – hurts! Firm tip of tongue (as in a picture in a doctor's waiting room), forked diabolical tongue of a torturer drawing near his victim, thirst aflame.

At this point we'll have made lines, nerves, and avenues cross, retraced the broad outline and motifs. <u>But let's cut out the trite intrigues.</u>

Imprint of fleshy lips on other lips in footloose festive mood. The city. Beat-up lanes and snack bar at the corner; display Camomille's lips and desire as urgent functions to fulfill; a level crossing bristling with risks and danger of getting stuck ... of not being able to move along to town, to the red-hot resources of a zone seething, bursting with activity, exhausting.

Mordant thought.

Ramify all inclinations till the sense and fleshy parts and functions are transformed. Turn on the spotlights to set the scene. In the darkened hall, the silent kiss is seen on the silent screen ———— FRENCH KISS, lapping sounds, the kiss as bite on film, nuns and vampires, *Nazarin, Mourir de plaisir*. You see, Camomille, taking my time this way, my teeth forget themselves against your neck, feel like priceless smuggled diamonds. My delinquency.

Felonious narrator, mutterings, dark seething waters and every imaginable succession of words. An un / lashing of ties / to get our teeth in / to / as well as grasses and jackasses amid the city's density. Population – Papa see the traps open and close, rise, flood the scene. Fog, smog. Rot and ruins.

Noisily, Georges stirs words and things in his head. Pulling objects behind him on the floor, like interdictions. Inter / dict, int / eradicate the words in speech, unsew their fabrics, pantsleg hems, having one's highwaters on feeds the millrace of desire. Room for everyone. Morning firewater, sorta. Behind the curtain, the rain puts strain on sentences. Parasitic words under one's tongue, and jawbone moving curiously.

A raccoon raid on the narrator's apple orchard. Apple peels inspire a smooth tenderness that's effective on your belly. The softness of teddy bears and love.

All of which just gets the lips apart, gaping like hungry traps inviting flies into the ink, there to sleep and sleep some more while I get back to the text and Camomille's lips.

Concentration on / under the roof of the other's mouth, a moving staircase escalating toward the dark, the uvula, and the phrase *palat(i)al roof and gardens*. Poetically falling rain. Rain, city, ————spiral stairways on

Saint-Denis Street; and the roofs – roofs are over heads and minds, control of consciousness, soon brings an urge 'to escape from our individual consciousness, break up and out through the roof of a mouth or house.' Transmutation in mouths. One struggles without voice to forge a voice the way a wrought-iron balcony suddenly gives access to the city's far-off sounds when you step out round midnight to breathe the air and stymie sleep awhile.

Essentially, the exploratory fabric woven from your characters' saliva takes the turn determined by a concentration of energy which you let explode at ir- or regular intervals.

We know beforehand that the kiss must end. As surely as the population density diminishes once Marielle has crossed the intersection of Sherbrooke and Bleury streets. The kiss can't cover the whole city. It's bound to the ghettos of our mouths. Same way love was bound when I wrote *perhaps forever* speaking of nuclear love in a dialectic of possession. A code and palpitation's trap.

Camomille *brushes on* strategy, with curling tongue and penetrating movements in the other's mouth. Funnel shape and spiral. Water-fall, fall of bodies.

It's getting dense and hot because people are coming in in droves for the lunchtime special spaghetti and beer. The shady morning guys have gone. Now it's ordinary people we're being jostled by. Terribly like boredom.

A glass of water, tomato juice. A MOLY. Camomille is still several intuitions ahead of Georges and Alexandre. In her forced imagination they laugh like shutters flapping against a wall 'be-cuz be-cuz' of a wind which always bears off something of the images behind them to areas of so-so ambiance, like vacant lots. Mucky spaces, li'l tin cans, ol' tin lizzies, everybody's discarded fridge. Coke-bottle view of the horizon. Green shards not sward. Yellow autumn grass. Rain, rain. A glass of water.

Elle and Lexa talk in stage whispers, cheek to cheek – prelude to a tango of licentious love, brother, sister dear – tenderness. A *motherly MaryE*lle for the nonce.

Sketches, plans. Maps of the city, abstract but also real. Asphalt and billboards. Destroy all solid, tangible things, build crazy objects, towering and scary ones like suicides.

Mother, my tongue's hooked on your snares. Lexa's gambled and is terrified. I tell you, mother, all this stuff about contractions, *expulsion* and desire's like wheels spinning in nothing, we're in the age of mutation. Incisors in your hide betide … Why can't she take our liquid discharges, once and for all! Complete the cycle (tri) / (try). Descent of bodies in a ring; gold, sun, orbit. Then disappear over the horizon like an orange. An odyssey.

Two MOLYs. The bubbly brew sticks blond to Georges's mustachios.

Lick at the sides, suck at the bits of food dangling from between the teeth – tendrils of celery, vines for dauntless Tarzans to swing by, by and by – transverse line of the tongue like a fiddlestick drawn across the strings, vocal cords by which you can hang with the ponderance of all those muscles and of fountain water playing over music playing in a park, hang from her neck like a sapphic semantic charm, taut like a lesson; pressure on the larynx, strong medicine that constricts your memory and wind. One capsule, one tight encirclement.

And yet, Camomille, all this proof that your mouth gets to me gets me.

Runs over my whole body like a car or truck travelling along Sherbrooke Street past rooms to rent and paunchy bombé wrought-iron balconies. And beyond. Through a fuzzy fleece of lanes, busy blocks of busybodies, back fences and clotheslines – Cree creepers for swinging across pitfalls from one side / from the other, pretending to be Indigenous, growing up aware and passionate.

Georges draws away from Camomille but soon is back, enticed. It's as though the kiss is riddled through from stem to stern with flying laughs. Laugh. And stalk your words, slipping in and out between your teeth, wind on the rise, that old signal warning you of bursts of laughter. Fragments. You'll hunch your shoulders, bend your head the better to find them, read them, hidden points, darts leaping to darting eyes, moving targets.

Fragments plastered against your gums. Write at least to make your mouth open and close. On silence. Once it did on sleep, I recall. Open the space up wide inside but don't rush – water, rain, saliva. Threads of drool stretch from word to word, spread ramiflorous inside / outside your throat / your lips. On the verge. The sentence is undone, dishevelled like a trumped-up tired old film effect showing a woman. Just having come.

And this recalls a certain 'neurological fidelity' between Camomille and Lucy, between couples and this three-cornered, two-faced text. As though, without realizing, both characters and narrators had dropped their masks, plunging on despite the risk of surfacing in historical or future baroque style; undone and re-done by an oblique, penetrating laser that leaves us where its beam has been, heads bent, suppliant.

Between Camomille and Lucy and … Marielle, the city and its structure. A concrete jungle in which a writing looks for cracks and openings, telltale breaths of air, hoping for a passage through. If writing dies, so will the city and its harlots. Will wrap about itself like a grieving young widow's luxuriant neurosis. A microscopic serpent in the testicles of steel contracting males, stainless to be sure. Rouses then goes all soft again … to which one doesn't feel like reacting anymore.

Montréal transpires; a sweaty sign, proof to be worked out, that your desires are not my realities. Your mouth open to mine. Heresy. Breath of both compressed. Breathed in. Lower belly twitches like moist felt wings aflutter. Must drop anchor. Then sling some ink, take off with palpitating pen. Lucy's tongue turns like a wild propeller in Georges's mouth, clips electric snips from the blue of others' eyes, crammed with cross-references. For signals.

To set my mouth in motion against yours. Get to the point of a tongue. Head off those symptoms that make you tighten up, pick out semantic fields that are booby trapped – pressure of a finger on a ... blackhead. Black on surface, blank in sense. Put teeth in the sense of a vertical desire. Bared. Bare flesh and decomposing word for word in the sense that's lost.

Eager, perspicacious Camomille.

'Man locks himself in his own eye.' Alone decides to be born, to take that wild turn one does when possessed by the optical illusions one pins to reality.

Fiction.

The inside of the bar-restaurant begins to feel like a uterus. The rush hour's over and the customers who stay stay because it's warm and comfy there, on no account allowing the alcohol count in them to drop. Cheerfully shadows take on shapes, busy movements, stick together in the semi-dark, stand out like beauty spots, fine figures, dark baroque gems unperiwigged. Jawing to beat the band. Just now it's fat thighs and cellulite. Flabby stomachs. Paunches and heart attacks. Each a grey manner of airing the matter. Feces, farces, phrases, bile and aching head —————————

————————— Montréal by feel, forward, back, upright or crouched, Montréal fractured on its east-end surface of cultural crap. A crack across. The balconies crack and rot. The body's anatomy suddenly resolves into another, the urban anatomy of layouts and corridors. Tattoo on its skull, *no* entry, parking, U-turn, left turn, right. With illustrations of the right way to proceed.

Ramifications and contractile profanities. Inspiration / expiration. The lungs' alveoli move, suck in air. In the breast an appetite for life swells, puffs up, tortures desires. Then decomposes, seeping creature smells intriguing to the nose. Which reacts. Result: in the breast, the architecture dallies mid blissful scenery. But the cement is cracking and the rest keeps seeping as though secretion instinctively begets rebellion. Demerits like a dose of radiation.

Train my narrative intentions directly on your questions. Wait.

Slow myself down.

Bum around the neighbourhood. Watch one's time by one's watch. Bluff, hang loose and jocular. A crazy way to levitate ....
.... above the city, a huge map with dotted lines from edge to edge. Islandwise. Collage-montage of neighbourhoods in jigsaw puzzles round the mountain. Suckling through the soles of one's feet from the vegetation, water ... *current* ...

At the island's tip, bridges like deletions for cutting in the text. Trace clear-cut autoroutes with maniacal cloverleaves full of twists ... in your mouth, seven tongue twists before speaking, to say exactly what? To say one doesn't want to talk at all. Camomille comes loose in the kiss like a sentence in your mouth that's tried too long to take a pause. And destroys itself. Other sentences get lost. Some get into books. Sentences a mouth spits out, parasites on its membranes, bugs killing themselves with green relish. From your mouth to mine, having a ball and all. Touching, exploring you, disseminating me. Textually so.

Thing is that part of the body might come loose and take off on the wind, like dust / depart. So in a zone once well defined which threatens to come loose at every other line, improvise. Space for discourse. The time for checking things out comes after the words have rarified.

I'm not confusing things, I haven't even pressed the manic button, the right one for fishy sides and metal rods and coloured spellings on lighted billboards along the Metropolitan Boulevard. Tigers in tanks. I turn on and over the traffic conditions, about the possible potlatch on the blank page. String come undone, necklace of teeth falling, fall, fa, f. Low gear in your mouth, finger poked all the way to your Adam's apple. Heaps of cheek.

no limit no way on the sentences being turned   mouth (fragile paper tiger mouth) spaced out jagged crack   an opening to make you talk lick you like an asshole improvise around an anus

I'm not confusing things.
Lipstick. Vaseline.

Shiny table surface. Alexandre bends his head a touch. Concentrates on a smear of spaghetti sauce. Scratches with a fingernail, graphics graffiti in the texture.

Sponge, wipe, water. Pores / arborite. Absorb the liquid. Drink like a fish out of water, in a vital space, a void. Not a water hole an empty hole in a consciousness crammed with ambiguities. Weary, Camomille gives her hide a little stretch. Points her breasts skyward and takes a deep breath. Smiles. Thinks feel okay like a fan spread but in no hurry to cool a whole room. Sponge rubber sponge, the waiter's hand, wrist, sleeve. He brushes against the table. Scratches his cheek. Clears the table. Glasses.

So we're afloat between two generations of drinkers ———————————

———a floating city, Montgolfier's balloon, up and up to touch the blue and dizzy turns, turning upside down; puffy clouds race by, dip and scud against the rocks, the river below. The plunge. Yes we've turned upside down.

Head downward and plenty of concepts stirring there, concentrating denser and denser in a single meditative strategy.

Not much noise in this joint at this hour of the afternoon.

Titubating tongue.

On cheek close to lips, on brow beside the eyes, she moistens, turns —— —————————————————— soft, dissolves faces.

Gives me visions of ramifying cells, others coming loose under the mouth's roof, green ones with yellow nuclei, blue ones following closely in the text your mouth   the city full of shadow creatures with the fall of night; pinball machines, juke box, bar, grill. All the other side of the coin too of course; the kitchen and a game of patience, the TV, the bedroom – won't sleep much between now and tomorrow morning.

Or else, so anxious to nullify oneself, one explodes in the other's mouth. Point blank.

So the kiss will have been a rerunning of the gauntlet before a mirror, a puckering of lips, a total opening, an uncontrollable plunge. If twisting your wrists to make you open your mouth and getting me inside helps to ventilate some fantasies, it's because the text itself begs for a possible intrusion and abuse of use that you'd fritter away some other way anyway;

Camomille, you've got to swallow / spit out the other. Exclude the too too obvious from your mouth in any case. Tongue oblique / over / the other tongue, make it circulate one way then the other, a whirligig of duplication, complicity.

BYE-BYE FRENCH KISS, GO DRAG YOUR STUFF SOMEPLACE ELSE: the thought hangs on the tip of my tongue like a saliva drop, a checkered blob of false reality. Impression that your teeth are blowing on the window panes, that snow is falling, that fragments are breaking into silly little flakes, molecules and desire and also eager laughable snickering narrator, off her rocker in mirth. Literally infinitely fibs

flip-flops

brandishing suspended meanings. Which fall into place as fictional / real —————————— the other's mouth; Camomille disrobes in almost classic style, dress falling circular on the floor. Key. Click. Pale chic lipstick plastered everywhere blotting the landscape, the scenery. Special effects.

Such a kiss it will have been that neither the desire nor the saliva could have been more meticulously, tremblingly strewn inside your mouth, wherein to do the tour, idle round your mouthhole in the lower reaches of the city.

French Kiss
1974, tr. 1986

CHAPTER TWO

from *Turn of a Pang*
tr. Patricia Claxton

Any fictional form but factual sequence too. Thus April 22, 1942, five days before the plebiscite, 20,000 persons are assembled at the Atwater market. Intrigue is rife. Nothing new but fiction and rattling of bones; chance signs, mysteries, high drama brewed to taste as if to shape a composition from time / on / time holding back the straw that could break the camel's back.

Heads move constantly. The moment is adrift in the folds of cloth coats rubbing together this <u>wartime</u> evening in the unspoken urgency of electing each his special permanent place in the land. Jigging heads (their number creates a <u>state</u> of unsuspected euphoria the very moment of treachery) wartime shell-shaped heads, swelling ears ... jarred by rumbling screeching endless empty Montréal Tramways cars – bane of the French-speaking orators.[1]

Skirmish and ... arms reach out and fall violently on heads ... the sidewalk and horse crap. Ellipse, hustle roughly prodded 'think I passed out getting in the police wagon. I think.' And that's the end of it ... diversion, curiosity, military convoy to be watched parading intestine style or nooselike in the market square . . . . right beside the police station and the bowling alley. Men are recruited there during the little town's descriptive game: situated less than twenty miles from Montréal, the town of Beauharnois boasts two major industries ...

ENTRANCE, a bowling alley and its fury of senseless noise around balls rolling endlessly toward teetering pins. 'There's the soldiers, two cream sodas, Evalinda. Betcha a game it's yer Momo's turn next week.' 'Don't gimme that' pronounced across the countertop. Conversation all around the alleys ... the words crumble: the bowling alley is a huge deserted beach where scenes of reality brew and composites of potential images take form, in infinite variations around the alley and the <u>grill</u> an infamous place in Albina's <u>pious</u> old mind out there on the second range just beyond the village; between the alley and the grill the paths are beaten wide 'cause you gotta look like what you are: cattle and beef <u>meat and grill cannon fodder blast between the eyes meat and too much such cannon grill.</u>

EXIT, 'that way if ya finished yer game.' The main street by the park; from there you can see the river and the islands, tranquil nature undisturbed by fishing boats or tankers, islands not far off. Khaki tents in the market square, officers with officious airs barking the word ORDER all over the place 'like goddamn loonies.'

Standing and watching the word river, and the islands not far off.

Maurice's truck comes by at last, on the way to Ville Lasalle with tomato plants.

---

1. On the evening of the protest meeting that took place on February 11, 1942, at the Jean Talon Market, attended by 10,000 people, a constant stream of empty Montreal Tramways streetcars passed not far from the meeting to prevent the speakers from being heard by the crowd.

The redhead sitting on the sofa, arms and hands and fingers cramped, studies an ashtray in front of her, crystal iridescent flower, contemplates the equivalences of colours. Between the eye and the object, a distance travelled at one's risk and peril of surreptitious rumblings foreign to the ear, of the left hand for example moving suddenly. She says, 'I'm not shaking, it's my whole body vibrating.' Excitement fills her with chills with fire, floats her far from reality like seaweed tossed by a frenzied sea like hair of dantesque red (mane-horse-gallop-fury-wild-freedom) necessary process for sustaining unripe images like Gleason's, king of spades with predatory eye, magnificently sodomising the redhead laid on tulip stems on flowered sheet.

⁰₀

Network of thighs about as delicate as muscular projected in the copulatory act, like a twosome of trapeze artists, she writes about the word network so as to give the story continuity. 'Pure madness' – we learn to read together after all – an attempt at corruption, word for word, executed as the occasion arises, hands and fingers skilled in the pleasure of effect confronting the networks (from red to mauve) esoteric ramifications of the lines of the hand, folds that move on the stomach in the languid aftermath, undulatory traces of that same white substance slipping gently toward the permanent reality of death.

⁰₀

Now in '42 all that stood the test of time and orgasm. Such giddy sensations, with in mind the focus contours of a life to live out to its end, kept returning astonishing the character played by a woman of thirty.

Now as then behind the PRODUCTION factories, the men roll themselves a 'good' cigarette, thinking: bam crack oof uh grrr, thoughtfully. Above their heads the letters crowd together caught in a threatening loop. COMIC STRIP.

⁰₀

A celebration of imagery or ... apathy for output and production stirs in their eyes; imagery coloured by thoughts churning in bodies male and female at coffee breaks and the ends of working days, to the shrill tune of the factory whistle spewed above the factory a trace almost locomotive smoke in the wind, longing to get out of there and not come back.

Insistence on electrocuting perforating thoughts of the insane abyss of pleasure. That's what arouses attention: material good for <u>orgiastic</u> consumption (EXCESSIVE USE OF WHAT ONE LIKES) gnawing presence pervading in the neck.

§

The redhead takes in the presence of sketches and outlines littering the work table. The illusion is perfect; the paper dims, numerical production from zero to vertical one bent in, say, eight other ways so as to proceed with the precise calculation of data which would justify the improvisation.

Self-generated mathematical delirium focus of imagination, of productive effusions also awe-inspiring prospects because I bring them to bear on the ineffable world of conquest.

§

Fear of looking closely at the one who (as can be seen by looking in the mirror) is engaged in writing. Stare at her face until she notices <u>something</u> and enters bodily into an embarrassing complicity in which seconds are prolonged without one's knowing whether this EVENT satisfies the desire or renews it cumbersome like an unusable weapon.

§

At this point I should perhaps tell a story of I you he we and other plurals recounting one by one all the phases of the enchantment, reconstructing the play of words and of gestures and their consequences in the quebec microcosm; all the phases in the destruction of the he's and she's, braving each reprieve until the narration finally and surely comes to an end. Time and collective animation, and their recording, pursue their course.

⁂

GRAFFITI (plural) GRAFFITO (sing).

One or other on the rotting wood fence, on the piss-green doors of toilet cubicles.

MANGE D'LA MARDE   Hostie

invocation of excrement, the eating of   and sacraments always
enigmatic and also   representation

CUL CROSSÉ PAR EN AVANT PAR EN ARRIÈRE
fuck you

to be inscribed out of context on paper when words of that ilk ought to be scratched in hard opaque surfaces so that no one could (or even think they could) extract the letters one by one as if to remove them from decent view, from the obscene hand which might linger caressing the little damp gashes laid bare there for all to see who care

VA CHIER P'TITE PLOTTE A JOHNNY

an invitation to a little slut to go shit. Everyday humdrum overthrowing order and distinction established in four walls, and elsewhere than on the wall the handwriting shows in broad slaps of paint across a politician's mouth

Le QUÉBEC AUX QUÉBECOIS

on his eye *TRAÎTRE* between his teeth, the phallic Indepen-
dence I lifting (an impression) the black freshly daubed moustache.

⁑

The crowd because without it nothing is justifiable. Frenzy, confrontation.
Response. Back to square one and all that must go to stem the spate of
disharmonies in the age-old habit of writing like we talk.

The crowd (how many are there?) before always BEFORE the something
to confront with oneself among others with others before City Hall before
parliament or neon Seven-Ups or the barricades yet.

Text because the references are too easy to manipulate. Places of encounter
'bring on the drinks'. . . . .
Something to get across the textual allusions, primary source quotations
from line one and face to face defying the phony wooden muscles
outstretched brandished here there and everywhere.

Questions of references: for the moment these those in the mêlée on both
sides in the sense that words get to be no more than slogans snarled
between teeth, crusted on lips.

Sold Out
1973, tr. 1976

HARMONIOUS MATTER
STILL MANOEUVRES

from *Typhon Dru*
tr. Caroline Bergvall

I presume day rises in different points and since this thought occurs to me
in the midst of reality, its unnameable poses, I do, to bear witness of time
languages mobile, take stock of the notion that nothing is too slow nor too
brief for the universe

§

I know that all isn't said because my body settles with a certain joy into
such a thought and somewhere in the inexplicable jolt presses words on,
water running as much thirst, I can, by joining vowels and the hump of
thoughts, eyes slant fascinated, get closer to death and its opposite

§

at this late hour where a suppleness of gaze is at its height and life turns
returns between the blue and the startling law of highlighted cities, at this
late hour where words clasp their chest as in operas, and images look out
for the jumpy tracks of fever and the future, my eyes lowered low over
humanity are troubled at the root of eyes desire

§

all isn't said, I do know, since it's absolutely that I love in tongues, coral
shells of meaning, the diligent structures that graft rapture and torrential
stuff on to the centre of the voice its stance, secret matter, matter more
round, matter like your sighs and other liquids yet

§

today I know that the most blue sea-structure closes in on our cells and on the suffering untouchable just as life does three times a round our childhood never really touches on it since we're close up to reality and matter can't let down without a warning strand us there skin hesitating between philosophies and dawn, too halved, forever in torment, in the major complication of beauty

⁂

all isn't said since the body's punctual and there remains, read: passion, rare gestures, an incredible synchrony of the senses, while thought, such well-placed alliance ensures a retake in the mind, the setting the old portraits, their imagined symmetry with childhood, lines that give us rest while we burrow the universe with our shoulders, and tiny fantasized lips would be working ceaselessly for the living making up world and cosmos to the measure of our hands whenever their caress is fine, indistinct of voice and palm, on a human body has breasts

⁂

at this late hour I know that life can confirm silence set fire to commendations trace up circular tears breed dust, and I like that it's so since I've learnt to watch July to October all fires, immerse myself in the strong smell of nakedness its splendour mauves, the facades and peculiar sonnets that gesture across language like we do dreaming at night not to die without voice

⁂

all isn't said it's here I dash toward, my skin full of cyprin of echo feel like smiling physical and thinking, inseparable from a nature's long breath, so when I watch stable objects when time reverses in my chest splits the thought with a jump clarifies death I know that all isn't said because my heart's rucked up

§

at this late hour where memory's wary of its jumps and nerves in the midst of desire are rich with answers I know that all isn't said I know when light fractures shadow revives my consideration of shadow and light I know that, brimming air energy, the living which is mine takes me far to breathe closer to hand the long images of necessity and of sentiment are gorgeous cracks against a backdrop of dreaming and identity

§

at this late hour where to name is still a function of the dream of the hope, where poetry splits daybreak from great gushes of daylight, and women will walk a number of times, invisible carnal into the storylines, I know that all isn't said, between urban conversation and tradition it's cold in vertigo, and sometimes in the volatile matter of tears a peculiar sweat of true settles as if life could touch its metaphors

La matière harmonieuse manoeuvre encore
1997, tr. 1997

SOFT LINK 1

from *Notebook of Roses and Civilization*

tr. Robert Majzels and Erín Moure

It's fears slow and fascinating that enter life each morning at coffee time while she wonders if tomorrow there'll be war and brusquely as she does each morning slices bread and cheese. It's gestures of uncontrollable avidity that proliferate in the throng and its worldly febrility, its parquet fever on the trading floor and stage. It's hesitations, heart cries that crisscross broad avenues full of shade and dust that attract and make us think of our legs and elbows, our knees too when desire bumps and bounces words and feelings upward, it's simple things with prefixes like cyber or bio that hold thoughts fast, float them a moment till we believe them aquatic and marvellous. It's certainties that in tiny increments of dust and light are soon mixed with our tears. It's inexplicable feelings made of small hurts strung over long years and vast horizons, it's blues ideas that settle in where the happiness of existing threatens to take the breath away or to lodge itself in the throat like an instrument of fervour. It's glimmers of intoxications impossible to look at for long, thoughts so precise that engage us beyond shade and wind, far beyond crude words, so noisy so terribly close to silence that the world all around seems suddenly engulfed in high seas and continual rustling like the music in our heads that in one stroke of the bow dislodges all that resists torment. It's underlined passages, fragments of happiness that traverse the body and raise bridges all around because elsewhere and in the wild blue yonder they say there's euphoria. It's written down with bruises, abundance of life burst to fullness in a world and its niches of worn paths that lick at the shadow of bones.

Cahier de roses et de civilisation

2003, tr. 2007

SMOOTH HORIZON OF THE VERB LOVE

from *Notebook of Roses and Civilization*
tr. Robert Majzels and Erín Moure

1

an urban image from the eighties
when we hung out at Chez Madame Arthur
and at the back of the room
women wrapped their arms around
nights of ink and dawn

2

calendar of murmurs
vague caresses about the planet and its water
we could have confused words
but there were doors open
confetti in the midst of darkness
gentle ways
to swoon in a corner with she who
put her tongue in my mouth

3

focus on yes, on the woman's
eyelids
caress not silence not word
focus beyond. Hold me back

Cahier de roses et de civilisation
2003, tr. 2007

EVERY ARDOUR

from *Notebook of Roses and Civilization*
tr. Robert Majzels and Erín Moure

1

beware of words that blur
of summer heat that unfurls
like an ocean over the species

2

thus we'll leave
without remembering
verbs in their time
that brought us closer
to mirrors and rapture

3

since immensity seeks
to take on another form
imagine the speed of the murmur
the noisy surging of old intentions
this great yes risen
from the depth of memory

4

if the whole body is bent over
what respite if the body
kneels breaks surface
at the hour of bedsheets or ink

Cahier de roses et de civilisation
2003, tr. 2007

THEORY, A CITY

Introduction to *Theory, A Sunday*

written by Lisa Robertson

The feminist writers of Montréal have altered their city irrevocably. When women write about and from the cities they live in, they are transforming the material city into a web of possibility and risk. The description of the city bends back on itself – it not only represents, it opens up a site for the political imagination. Through the fictive and theoretical act, the city is re-inscribed as a space for radical otherness. Montréal is more than its official civic history. In this volume, it figures as a character, a velocity – its streets and cafes and bars are exerting forcefields. it's a gathering of urgencies, errancies, overflowing critiques, pausing to make in the movement of women's language what the political economy has disallowed.

The feminist consciousness that Nicole Brossard recognized in the writers she invited to the Sunday theory group in 1983 – what supported it, what permitted it to develop? Why do certain cities at certain times become the stages for intense social and cultural transformation? I think of early twentieth-century Paris, the city that was a home for so many of the women expatriate writers who have become the crucial figures of modernist literary and intellectual culture – Gertrude Stein, Djuna Barnes, Mina Loy, Mary Butts, Sylvia Beach, Nathalie Barney. From my admiring distance, and across the duration of many friendships, Montréal feels to me to be a place of comparable intellectual generosity and intensity. What generates and supports the networks of friendship, argument, and intellec-tual collaboration that have caused twentieth-century women's writing to consistently develop and strengthen as an urban, cultural, and political force in Montréal and elsewhere? Thinking about and reading the work of these Montréal women now, twenty-five years later, I am brought to the realization that feminism is one of the scintillating companions of the culture of cities. Feminist culture, discourse, and resistance has shaped contemporary urban experience and urban space. Certain writers have claimed the city for feminism, to insist that any city is the vibrant space inflected by women's voices. There is no city without our voices.

For the young feminist writers of 1980s Vancouver, where I then lived, the Montréal women's writing scene was mythic and galvanizing. Reading the translated Québécoise texts emerging from The Women's Press and Coach House Press, and in journals such as *Writing, Raddle Moon, Room of One's Own,* and *Tessera,* we relished the presence of a vigorous, complex, avant-garde feminist context. We didn't need to invent feminist writing entirely on our own – it was already happening, and it was welcoming our desires, our political passions, our experiments, and our transformations. Brossard's 1985 book of essays *The Aerial Letter,* translated into English in 1988, and Gail Scott's *Heroine* (1987) and *Spaces Like Stairs* (1989) forged a discourse that was as insistent on women's solidarity as it was on our ecstatic experience of language as embodiment. That politics could be ecstatic, that feminism could make a world where the particularity of our language, our friendships, our love, and our bodies could continue to transform our relationships to the institutions of history and culture: our early exposure to Québécoise feminism brought this wildness home to us. Montréal's was a desiring feminism in every sense of the phrase.

So Montréal, as spoken and written here, also transformed the speculative potentials of other cities into sites of feminist becoming. This was so in Toronto, where the late Barbara Godard, translator, theorist, and founder of *Tessera* magazine, lived and translated the works of Brossard. It was true in Calgary, where scholars like Susan Rudy and Pauline Butling opened a feminist discourse for their students and their communities. It was true in Winnipeg, in Victoria – across the country this work was received by feminist writers with intelligence and passion. The women of Montréal, by living, writing, and discussing through their own specificity, altered the cities of their readers. Through their texts, all cities became the potentially charged, vibrating matrices of self-realizing female speech and text, the cusps of a long series of embodied realizations. The space of the city, the space of language, the space of the imaginary, the space of ethics: each of these, separately and together, is in the *Theory, A Sunday* texts a female space, a feminist space, which is to say, in Louise Dupré's words, 'a territory in motion, open, polymorphous. A movement.'

If Dupré's terms suggest a Deleuzian sensibility, they invite us to recall that the formative texts of twentieth-century French structuralist and post-structuralist theory, philosophy, and psychoanalysis arrived on the North American continent by at least two very different means: one was the familiar embrace by American universities of the translated and academically mediated texts of structuralism and deconstruction as specialized discourses. But the Québécois had a different cultural and linguistic access to European French theory, a differently mediated relationship to the texts whose readings have, in the Anglophone world, been largely removed from the social and political movements that inflected French writing in the 60s and 70s. In France, we can identify the radical presence of Occupation Resistance politics, the war in Algeria, and the accompanying militarization of French Algerian life within France, the French war in Indo-China, and the events of the May '68 student and worker uprising as being crucial to the discursive decentring and politicization of philosophy and criticism. As these events unfolded in France, parallel yet independent social and political transformations were taking place in Québec.

The Quiet Revolution, the term Anglophone media used to describe the period from 1960 until 1966 in Québec politics, named a period of intense change at every level of society. The secularization of a previously highly traditional, church-dominated social and family structure, the turn from a largely rural, agricultural economy to state-supported urbanism, the flourishing of demands for civil and linguistic rights, as well as women's rights within and outside the family – this period completely changed the face of Québécois social experience. In 1964, the liberal government passed Bill 16, 'which abolished a married woman's judicial handicap by which her legal status was that of a minor.'[1] This period also saw the formation of a decolonialist, Québécois, nationalist, separatist politics most forcefully articulated by the Front de Libération du Québéc. The FLQ was an armed separatist faction whose demands for Québec's political, cultural, and linguistic sovereignty were expressed by a chain of violent actions beginning with bombings of military barracks in 1961, continuing to a bombing attack on the Montréal Stock Exchange in 1969, and escalating to the 1970

---

1. Durocher, René. 'Quiet Revolution.' The Canadian Encyclopedia. Historica-Dominion, 2012. Web. June 6, 2013. http://www.thecanadianencyclopedia.com/articles/quiet-revolution.

kidnappings of a member of the British Consulate, James Cross, then the provincial Minister of Labour, Pierre Laporte, who was ultimately murdered. In response, Prime Minister Pierre Trudeau instituted the War Measures Act in October 1970, essentially suspending all civil rights and transforming Québec into a military zone. Under the power of the War Measures Act and subsequent, related punitive federal regulations, in less than a year, hundreds of people were arrested and detained, and thousands were searched, without charges or warrants, nor recourse to legal counsel.[2] This political crisis had a momentous effect in Québécois and Canadian history, serving to foreground and stimulate the organization of groups, actions, and discourses around civil liberties issues, freedom of speech, and rights to autonomous political action by citizens, arguably intensifying the separatist movement rather than curtailing it. Indeed, since this galvanizing period in Québec history, we have seen Québec as a centre of popular self-determination and resistance. During the summer of 1990 in the town of Oka, outside of Montréal, a coalition of Indigenous peoples defended a Mohawk burial ground that was under threat of redevelopment into a golf course for luxury condominiums.

An eighty-seven-day armed standoff between the native Mohawk people and their supporters, and the Canadian armed forces occurred. The uprising was eventually successful, and the proposed development was withdrawn. Also, at least contingently successful, was the recent Printemps érable, the Spring and Summer 2012 student strike and mass protest against the increase of tuition fees, a protest that inspired a solidarity movement among both students and worker groups, as well as across the country. The struggle to defend the French language against the ahistorical Anglicization of culture in Québec is ongoing.

I point to this vital, popular, historical presence of political resistance movements in Québec for several reasons. In the context of the publication of *Theory, A Sunday* in the USA, it seems essential to indicate the political history specific to Québec, a history that both conditioned and surrounded the feminist community in Montréal, and served to politicize

---

2. Clement, Dominique. 'October Crisis.' Canada's Human Rights History. Web. June 6, 2013. http://www.historyofrights.com/events/flq.html.

many of us elsewhere in Canada. That this Québécois political history is underrepresented in the North American Anglophone context is undeniable. But I also want to indicate the relationship of Québec's political history to that of France, in order to suggest that the reception of French theoretical texts in Québec, as well as their influence by Québec, bore a meaning utterly different than it did in broader North American contexts. In France and in Québec, theory was not only an institutional discourse but a manual and testing ground for political revolution. It responded to conditions in real time. For example, Deleuze and Guattari's 1975 book *Kafka: Toward a Minor Literature*, a text that so cogently articulated the political positioning of minor or colonized languages, showing such languages to be rife with covert agency and transformational potential, essentially describes the long-existent complex situation of Québécois writing and language. Québécois French, an isolated language community within the dominant Anglophone political economy of Canada and the USA, a minor, underrecognized, and often patronized language in relation to European French linguistic and cultural history, a language always under assault by the tedious and ubiquitous hegemonies and entertainment products of capital, has had to find and organize within itself a strong current of resistance, by means of which its identity has been consolidated, and its agency radicalized. (Here I will indicate in passing the important presence of historical micro-communities of French speakers across Canada – in Northern Ontario, for example, in the Métis communities of Manitoba, in the Acadian areas of the Maritime provinces, and in northern Alberta.) The writers of *Theory, A Sunday* are, in this sense, multiply marginalized as writers who are Québécois French speaking and feminist. That their recourse to French theory, from de Beauvoir to Lacan to Irigaray to Wittig to Barthes to Meschonnic, has been one of the tactics toward survival, rather than an embellishment or diversification of the vocabularies of academic speech, is central to their vision of what theory is, what theory performs.

Just what is this Sunday activity, *theory*? First, we can surmise that it is a collective activity. Six women theorize together, which is not to negate the solitude of theory either. In Fourier's terms (referring here to Barthes' 1978 course 'How to Live Together,' at the Collège de France), solitude and being together are not contradictory states when they take place in or via the utopian imaginary. This feels like an essential recognition, here within the experimental terrain of feminist theory. Collectivity does not negate singularity, but complements or even enables it. Next, as well as being collective and singular, theory is punctual, regularly practiced. Part of what makes theory *theory* is that it is returned to with rigour and openness. On Sundays, for example. This punctual revisiting is what transforms thought into theory, or a point of view. Theory is the space made by returning, in order to have a position from which to view the world. The space is collective and solitary: mutual. So the looking that theory performs is situated and multiple. As such, theory is political. it's not different or separate than the ongoing questions about how living together happens and what living together means, or could mean. Theory doesn't necessarily or exclusively happen in academic institutions. In fact, academia was emphatically not the site for a feminist invention of theory in 1980s Québec, as Louky Bersianik emphasizes: there feminism met with only a demeaning misogynist refusal of its claims, terms, and necessity. When theory happens outside of academia, it means something different. It's more mobile, edgy, responsive to experienced conditions. When theory happens at home, right where life is most concentrated and messy, it's bound to disrupt the banal and gendered dualism of public and private language. Its space is symbolic, not institutional. So theory is also transformational: 'Theory, a story I tell so that the world changes in my favour, so that it swerves toward my own eyes,' says Louise Cotnoir, who goes on to discuss how theory changes 'the registers and forms of the real. To invent the language of a knowledge based on decategorized emotion.' So the work of theory is a work *of* and *upon* the imaginary, which is to say that it creates new, necessary situations and emotions. In this sense, theory is not a second order language; it doesn't only speak about *something else*, it generates knowledge on its own terms. Theory is an agent, and it is a resistance. And here, on a Sunday, the knowledge that theory generates is this: how to create a female subject, a *subjecte*. It's the way, France Théoret beautifully insists, that we tell the story of our female lives each day. Theory is our city.

2013

YESTERDAY

from *Yesterday, at the Hotel Clarendon*

tr. Susanne de Lotbinière-Harwood

While others march gaily toward madness in order to stay alive in a sterile world, I strive for preservation. I cling to objects, their descriptions, to the memory of landscapes lying fully drawn in the folds of things around me. Every moment requires me, my gaze or sensation. I become attached to objects. I don't readily let go of days by banishing them to the blank book of memory. Certain words ignite me. I take the time to look around. Some mornings, I yield to the full-bodied pleasure of navigating among seconds. I then lose my voice. This doesn't bother me. I take the opportunity to lend an ear to ambient life with an eagerness I never suspected. The idea of remaining calm doesn't displease me. Some days I make sure everything is grey, like in November, or sombre, for I like storms.

It doesn't take much to upset me. I read a lot. I've a sharp eye for misfortune. I rarely talk about misery. I grew up surrounded by the beauty of white winters; every summer for years, I drowned in the unsettling heat of July, buried body and soul in the noble and frivolous green of vegetation lightly tousled by the wind coming off the river. In town, we lived across from a park. Stray seagulls often performed great landing manoeuvres in front of the house before softly, softly wedding their sleek wings to the dawn's fresh dew. This gave me pleasure and I concluded that I was a happy child.

I rarely talk about my little fears. I don't know how to explain a mother's love for her children. I own no weapons, like the folks to the south do. Little nothings don't shake me up. When the ice storm plunged us into the cold, I read four essays on antiquity under the most tragic lighting. I'm easily influenced, and it upsets me to realize I'm at the mercy of a statistic, of a proverb, of three chapters I suspect were written under the force of the tidewaters of violence or of deepest despair.

Yesterday, I walked for a long time. First day of May. People were making their presence felt throughout the city. I folded myself into a group of workers in blue aprons singing with their throats fully open like flags unfurled atop a ship's main mast. After leaving their vocal ensemble I felt lost. I no longer knew where I was. I thought about the wandering children seen in war movies, about their mothers, their crazed eyes when they've just grasped the fact that they will never see them again. I often think about war, but the way one thinks about eating a soda cracker. I mean I quickly forget I've just been thinking about war.

I don't know much about pain but I'm convinced that, in order to write, one must at least once in life have gone through a devastating, an almost agonal energy. I don't much like using the word *agony*. Since Mother's death, I know it means to gasp for breath, the self enclosed in tiny blue veins like butterflies about to fly off far away. Agony: I see it's about the eye, an inward turning of the eye even though the pupil is working very hard to say good-bye, to ask about the weather, to let the light in, ever so little, ever so little.

Words ignite me. This is very recent. Actually, I believe it's since I've been working at the Museum of Civilization, on Dalhousie Street. I've been assigned the job of preparing notices to describe, date, and geograph-ically situate the provenance of the objects exhibited. I take notes. I'm the one who composes. I enjoy pronouncing the words out loud as I write them: callipygian statuettes, Celtic brooches, porcelain dolls, antique pistols, ritual knives made of gold. I occasionally accept short contracts with contemporary art galleries in Montréal. Yesterday, for example, it was odd writing 2000 without adding BC.

§

Yesterday, during the vernissage: I'm looking around at people. I recognize the astonishment in their eyes due to the simple, almost nonchalant fear leading them unhurriedly from one urn to another. It's hot. Men mop their foreheads. Women pat the top part of their bosoms where the flesh is soft and inviting.

Fabrice Lacoste comes and goes in the large exhibition hall. Smiling, welcoming, he offers advice, information, sometimes a few words, which, instead of enlightening the visitor about the exhibition, make it even more mysterious and thus more desirable. To those enquiring about the location of White Room Number 1, he has a strange way of answering with his hand closed, thumb vertical, index finger pointing in the right direction.

Time glistens in time.

It's been a month already since Simone Lambert gathered the entire staff around the crates that had arrived that day. She talked at length about the exhibition, about its importance and our good fortune in producing it. She went into detail about the little gestures and precautions to be taken, then discussed the strange sense of well-being we would experience once committed to the exhibition. She warned us about the vertigo followed by a certain vulnerability we were sure to feel during the first weeks after the opening of Centuries So Far. 'We must be responsible before history, not let it pull us into oblivion.'

It had taken three years of negotiation, four trips to the Middle East, the patience of a saint, and a woman's iron will to overcome all the pitfalls and red tape that had come up, cultural misunderstandings and sexist pettiness, border bureaucracy and tricky transportation, to end up on this gorgeous warm spring today. Now time rushes straight at Simone Lambert, straight at her body, her life, her future. It winds around her genes like the serpent around the Tree of Knowledge. Time manufactures time using her skin, her bones, her way of walking, of addressing people who, having noticed her leaning against the rail of the mezzanine, come over to congratulate her.

Down below, Fabrice Lacoste is talking with a handsome, feline, well-read man. One hand in his jacket pocket, the other twirling to the same rhythm as the words issuing from his mouth. He is having a grand time. No doubt he is going to charm the stranger. He knows. Has always known. He does well with any subject; usually he sticks to ecology, nationalism, and archaeology. He aims for the heart of the matter, then skirts around it so as to talk about art as long as possible without being interrupted. He usually begins with a historical fact to which he gives inordinate importance in order to segue into a full-fledged argument, allowing him to slot that same fact back into the proper place in the collective memory and, from there, to launch into a vigorous and sensual description of the passion that the sight of the artifacts should elicit in any genuine lover of art and civilization. He talks, smiles. Soon he'll notice that his interlocutor's breathing has accelerated slightly.

Surprising, though, that the same man who has such difficulty breathing in his own culture has the gift of inspiring comfort and excitement in culture-seeking museum guests. Had he not once confided to Simone just how much living here disgusted him? 'Listen, Simone, I love history, but I hate this city.' Simone had turned cold. Nobody working in this museum had the right to talk that way, especially not in her presence. Lacoste would have liked to crumple up his words and toss them in the wastebasket like a bad draft. He had merely added, 'What is this strange passion of ours? Are we interested only in tombs, urns and masks? I know, love what's around you. At least understand it. But aren't we headed for our own demise with all these fragments of mourning haunting us in the name of civilization? We've been living among collections of arrows, crucifixes, rosary beads, ciboria, rocking chairs, for fifteen years. It drives me crazy.'

That day, Lacoste had gone back to his office without closing the door behind him. Simone had overheard him asking his secretary to put him in touch with the director of the Uffizi Galleries, then, lost in thought, Simone turned toward the window. In her head, spring was stirring faraway landscapes that had haunted her since the day of her very first dig. For months everything had been blue as if God existed, then every emotion had become tinged with white, for a sweet forever-lasting folly had gripped the stone-and-bone landscape. For months she'd shared the most precious moments of her life with Alice Dumont. They'd gone from site to site in search of a future and of words that would make of their love a reality.

⚬

Since Mother's death, I've started saying what I think to imaginary people. I voice my ill humour, my thoughts, my fears. I also try to imagine the answers when things are cracking up in my mind. Saying everything doesn't necessarily make me happy and, indeed, I don't know why there's such emphasis on all and sundry telling their story, and what's more, doing it live. As of yesterday, it's as if I'd become a better person, sparked by some flame that sets me dreaming in a world where no one dreams of dreaming anymore. Misfortunes multiply like beasts amid technological knowledge. Knowledge spreads like misery. My imagination seems to work too quickly; its volume doubles with the heart's every intention. Without end, the images violently interpenetrate, changeable and indescribable. I go to the theatre often. All forms of dialogue arouse my curiosity. I'd like to understand what gives dialogue its nobility and what makes it a high art for those of us who live wrapped around solitude like harmless boas. What is the value of a question in a dialogue? How important are the answers?

Yesterday, on my way back from the museum: my head is full of images of storms. A boundless sea of paintings and photographs. Other storms I build like a backdrop, with sombre and anonymous characters, impossible to identify. I remain thus all evening, pressed up against the existence of a storm without feeling threatened. Waiting. After a while I become, I am, the storm, the disruption, the precipitation, the agitation that puts reality in peril.

⁍

Sitting in front of the big window of her river-view apartment, Simone Lambert is reading the correspondence of Marie de l'Incarnation for the fourth time in twenty years. Every five years she immerses herself in ordinary life as it was lived in New France around this woman who captivates her more than anything. With every rereading she tries to sort out what belongs to the woman, to France, to the seventeenth century, to the random circumstances of a life, such as the freedom this woman recovered barely two years after marrying. Simone Lambert has always enjoyed autobiographies, enjoyed reading the correspondence of the world's great men and of the women who make up its core. She knows that people's worth ably reveals itself through the long-lasting words that can be elicited only by love and friendship. She likes standing silently in the dailiness of women and men who knew how to talk about the wind on their skin, about the fire in their bellies, and about every possible storm containing high levels of historical violence.

With every reading she discovers unsuspected landscapes, unknown aspects of Marie Guyart's personality, simple anecdotes that give her a better idea of daily life in the land. She carefully scans for any information likely to justify new digs in the city. Still today, the mere hint of a rumour making plausible the possibility of a new find is all it takes for her to decide to go and probe the streets of the capital. She imagines herself discovering precious objects or mysterious bones overlooked by previous archaeological forays – just as, at the time, while walking along the Seine, Alice liked to fancy that fate would guide her hand to the first edition of a major work or a manuscript thought to be lost forever.

The telephone rings. It's Fabrice. He retells, verbally transcribes, the praise for the exhibition circulating on the Web. All are enthralled with the lion, the Venus of Prussia, and the back of the silver mirror in Niche Number 7.

The call has extracted Simone from her bubble of harmony and melancholy. She decides to go and indulge her pleasure and solitude on the Plains of Abraham. From Rue de Bernières it's only a three-minute walk on fresh grass before she reaches the green bench where she often comes to gaze at the great river running to the sea. On the opposite shore, Irving Oil's reservoirs and tall chimney stacks whose smoke always ends up merging with the clouds and their graffiti over Lévis.

⁚

For each index card I invent a caption through which I relive part of the life of the object as if my own story depended on it. It's my only way of penetrating the core of the artifact, of spending some time there mentally so as to breathe in the climate of the period attached to it, of entering its landscape with my contemporary sorrow. Yesterday, I hadn't realized its magnitude. No sorrow's ever a waste. On the contrary, it's intensely alive, nourished by ever greater disasters, deliberately fostered, it would appear, to create new industrial waste sites where one and all can dump their grief. Sorrow is constant. Everything around it disappears: parents, friendships, buildings surrounded by the most golden olden days and yesteryears like so many friezes and church squares.

Contemporary sorrow doesn't enter all objects the same way. Some resist grief better than others, be it collective, like that of war, or intimate, like the ache of a broken heart. Collections of radios, cameras, and pens are those that most easily absorb the sadness, the nostalgia, the enormity of the sorrow mutely at work, making us die of anxiety when confronted with the obvious fact of the short term.

I don't usually entertain such thoughts. Sorrow flows naturally into the object and the object naturally regains its small-object lustre while I assign it a name, an age, a function. The impression of secrecy, of rarity, and of fragility emanating from small objects, even if they were once thousand-bladed weapons that caused death and spread terror, has always fascinated me. They are like roots gorged with sap, pierced through with meaningful arrows, making them akin to the trees of Life and of Knowledge. At the museum, I have the rare privilege of being able to touch them and love them in their every aspect, to detect just the right angle that will enhance them in the dark
and in the light.

Yesterday, an eighteenth-century mirror in my hands: the object is smooth, it slides through my fingers and by some miracle I manage to catch it. I hurt myself in doing so. I think about the word *speculum*, about all the centuries assembled in our eye, so curious and enthralled with faraway stars.

Hier
2001, tr. 2006

Translations,
Retranslations,
Transcollaborations

MAUVE

from *À tout regard*
written with Daphne Marlatt

La réalité est un sursis au-delà
et du réel lorsqu'on observe
en l'apparence virtuelle, courbes
de ceci qui ressemble combien de fois
les images : la bouche au féminin
dose de sens émotion dorsale

Real that of the under-bent
curves of the virtual we take for real
a gap   delayed that-over-there   re
semblance the images repeat
mouth in the feminine, dos(e)
of sense making a dorsal
commotion

les liens autour de l'évidence
graphies, bouches modulées mentales
et
du corps pour ancrer la réalité
for real

chained leans on the evidence
on hand/writing   mouths
changing key, mental
or out to sea and
of the body's anchoring reality
for (the) real

les avalanches et le bord de page

au bord : vitesse/équation

• il y a des pierres au bord de la mer, des risques d'erreur et l'encombrement du bruit des vagues. il y a quand je pense «dississit» langage qui reflue dans mes yeux comme un horizon, bord de pensée : réalité des bouches

avalanche and page edge

bordering on : speed/equation

(carried over)

take some stones at the seabord, hazards of miscalculation, blockage of wave noise. take my thinking 'say'd beasayingsays' language ebbs in my eyes horizonlike, thought's border : mouth's reality

la peau et preuves à l'appui
penser que parfois
écrire leur ressemble
en des traits indécidables
fiction culture cortex
M   A   U   V   E

skin and its evidents

to think to write
sometimes resembles in
undecidable features

fiction culture cortex
M   A   U   V   E

M A U V E
cortex fiction culture

stains the other
mew   maiwa   mauve
malva rose core text
fiction rings round
skin immersed in
resemblance takes
the stain, sense
roseblue in tissue re-
membering

Mauve
from *La Nouvelle barre du jour*
1985

POLYNÉSIE DES YEUX/
POLYNESYA OF THE EYES

from *À tout regard*
tr. Nicole Brossard

POLYNÉSIE DES YEUX

c'est un long parcours afin que l'œil
y trouve son ambiance. Mauve tangible
en équilibre la présence
la collision du jour et de l'oxygène
la permanence que nous faisons
de l'usage devant l'océan perplexe
des choses réfléchies

POLYNESYA OF THE EYES

it is a long voyage so that the eyes
feel the ambiance. Tangible mauve
equilibrium of one's presence in
the collision of daylight and oxygen
the way we render permanent
the personal use we make
in front of the puzzling ocean
of reflected things

tout à contempler l'attrait
de la lumière
la transcription et la lenteur imprévue
là-bas là ou l'eau se fait écho
de la conversation le reflet sérié
le silence intact
qui nous plonge en l'attrait initial

contemplating the abstract attractive
light
transcription and unexpected slowness
there where water echoes
the conversation its serial gleam
the unbroken silence
which plunges us into the initial attraction

il faut des verbes pour inverser
l'horizon, la lumière crue, indécidable.
Qui engloutit hibiscus et plumera
la touche magique du verbe
pour la lecture
des corps qui obsèdent
et que tombe la nuit
comme un timbre de voix
bleu bascule

it takes verbs to reverse
the horizon, the bright light, indecisiveness.
Which swallows up hibiscus and plumera
the magic touch of the verb
in order to read
the obsessive meaning of the body
so night can fall
like a tone of voice
blue tilts up

Et le jour. Le regard atténue
le climat
les couleurs brèves dans leur différence
point de repère
dans leur différence. Les mots
qui me 'marquèrent profondément.'
De brèves indications, écailles

Hence the day. The gaze tones down
the climate
brief colours among their differences
no reference mark
in their difference. Words
who 'influenced me deeply.'
Brief indications, scales

me voici. C'était donc recommencer
la place du corps
dans la marge lointaine
la précision
des yeux polysémiques

here I am. So it means to start again
making space for the body
in the distant margin
the precision
of the polysemous eyes

Voilà. me voici c'était
tendre le corps
balayant des yeux la réponse
'le merveilleux sourire' de la mer
interrogeant. Le sens. Alors vint
la nuit pacifique une pluie fine
mobile comme une hypothèse
le long des reins. L'immensité

So it was. here I am it was
a tendency toward tenderness
a stretch of the body
a sweeping glance on the answer
'the marvellous smile' of the sea
questioning. The meaning. Then came
the pacific night a fine rain
mobile as an hypothesis
along the small of the back. The vastness

la permanence calquée dans l'œil
corail calligraphe. Le calme
'loin de tout' me venait australe
la certitude versatile, les yeux doux
point vernal
la permanence au-delà des transcriptions.
Voici le jour, la lumière crue
qui efface l'horizon. Le tableau

permanence copied in the eyes
coral calligraph. The calm
'far from everything' versatile
certitude would come to me, austral
vernal point
permanence beyond transcriptions.
Here cornes the day, the bright light
painting out the horizon. The scene

loin de tout, les yeux travaillent
les contours. Les yeux cernent
les planètes et l'or souvenu
de la règle, l'attention soutenue
le visage est incompatible alors
les yeux prononcent 'la démence
et l'horizon' les orchidées.
Le silence

far from everything, the eyes work out
outlines. The eyes ring
planets and the golden rule
occured in the mind, attention is sustained
one's face is then incompatible
so the eyes pronounce 'insanity
and horizon.' The orchids.
silence

oriente

points out orient

les choses réfléchies
de l'usage devant l'océan perplexe
la permanence du jour et de l'oxygène
en équilibre la présence
y trouve son ambiance. Mauve tangible
c'est un long parcours afin que l'oeil.

of reflected things
on the puzzling ocean
the personal use we make
of permanence
the collision of daylight and oxygen
equilibrium of one's presence
tangible mauve finds its atmosphere
in the long course of the eyes

Notus
collected in *À tout regard*
1989

POLYNESIAN DAYS

With Strings
a homophonic translation by Charles Bernstein

this is a long parquet fashioned with oil
where drove her ambiance. Mauve tangible
in equilibrium the presence
or collision of day and of the oxygen –
permanence that we fashion
with the usage deviant of ocean perplexed
choices enmeshed

all to contemplate the attraction
of the lamination
the transcription and limping improvidence
under where the 'o' makes itself echo
of the conversation reflected in series
silence intact
where plunge in traction initial

it floats verbs to invert
the horizon, the lamination cruel, undecidable.
Who engluts hibiscus & plumera
the touch vatic of slurs
pours the lectern
of corpses obsidian
& entombs the flight
combing a timbre of voice-
bled basilicas

& the lure. The regard attenuated
by climate
less colours (brief in their difference)

point of repair
indifferent. The motes
cue me 'marked profusely.'
Debriefed indications, echoes.

me voiced. Sitting dunked recommencing
the places of lapses
in the merged ointment
the prosceniums
of yoked polysemics

Voilà. Me voice it was
tender, the corpse-
belly, eyes, response –
'marvellous souvenir' of the mar
interrogates. The scent. Allures vent
louis pacific a plot we find
mobile like an hypothesis
longing for reigns. The incumbency

permanence clacking in the oil
(corralled calligraphy). The calm
'loin of two' me vents: australopithecine
certitude. Versatile, yolked deuce
point venal.
Permanence of the deluge of transcriptions.
voicing the jaw, the lamentation crude
who efface the horizon. The table low ...

loin of two, the yokes of burden
lax contours. The yoke ascertains
the planets & the ore soothing
of the (regalia), the attention southern
the visage & incompatible allure

the yokes pronounce 'demented
horizon' – orbits. Lake
Seance.

orient

the choices inflected
of the usage deviant of motion vexed
the earnestness that we fashion
collusion of day & of the oxygen
in equilibrium the reticence
where drove his ambivalence. Mauve tangible
this is a long arcade refashioned with oil

1989

IF YES SEISMAL/SI SISMAL

first published in *Absinthe*
a transcreation by Fred Wah

SI SISMAL

si aboyer ou noyer la voix
parmi les images et les mots
éveille un peu de crainte
abrite alors la figure choisie
le bord renversé de vivre
labelle spacieux

si quelque tissu de soie persiste
sur les lèvres et trop excite
respire d'un air naturel
même si demain va vite
dans l'anatomie
cherche d'autres récits

si à petits coups de langue
d'expression la tension continue
rapproche les mots crus
l'horizon s'il le faut
jusqu'en la bouche

si le timbre de la voix
se transforme et que trop de chaos
ou que mélancolie s'installe
combine la variété des réponses
la théâtralité de parler

IF YES SEISMAL

if above the clysmic bark heaves
noise the voice detonates images and
words for life a little crazy we
think but all right before the actual
figures choose choice the border
labels space in you

if any persistent tissue bristles pitapat
on the heart's much too excited lip
could be the air's too rare
naturally some same body
remembers too late
to search for another wave

if a small cup of language
soups intention with a continued
expression against word crust
until the horizon of approach
whose fault whose lips

if the forest of the voice
transforms into the trop of chaos
or melancholy installs itself
in the parlour of surprise plant
variety re-speak pond

si ça recommence et qu'il fait chaud   if the see-saw bounces back hot to trot
trop chaud encore dans les jointures   trembling shows up again late cell
appuie partout sur le quotidien   synapse applied part out on
il reste de grands trous   a day of rest great truth
des saveurs inexplicables   a vague smack of the lips
baies, corail, littorines   gulfs, coral, littoral

si, tu trembles, tu vois bien   if, you tremble, you should see
forcément il y a du blanc   inevitably there is some white
c'est vrai et forcément   it is true and of course
tu trembles   you tremble

À tout regard
1989, tr. 1992

L'AVIVA / AVIVA

L'Aviva/Aviva
tr. Anne-Marie Wheeler

AVIVA

l'aviva son visage et les relais
de connivence l'ampleur des images
toute penchée sur l'attrait, sa bouche
or les lèvres il y a normalement mots
au bord de l'émoi une phrase reliée
tapie et à l'insu carassée
tout en longeant les bras d'excitation
s'appliquer, l'idée tenait tenace
car lier

L'EN SUITE TRADUITE

l'anima l'image et les effets
d'alliance teneur du visage
toute pensée sur les traits se couche
or les livres singulièrement toi d'aloi
au loin l'émoi qui s'écrie
à l'infinie d'utopie l'ainsi caresse
d'excitation longe le geste au comble
langue sujet vorace s'appliquer ignée
ç'allier

AVIVA

aviva a face and the relaying
of complicity, ample images
leaning toward the lure, her mouth
now the looks there are normally words
on the edge of emotion a phrase related
hidden and unknowingly caressed
while running the length of her arms in excitation
applied, the idea tenable tenacious
for linking

THE LATEST TRANSLATED

anima image and effects
of affinity facial formation
all learning on her traits laid down
now the books singularly, you: virtue
in the distance, emotion emotes
in the infinite utopia thus caress
in excitation running the height of the gesture
tongue voracious subject applied igneous
liaising

AVIVA

ainsi l'aura penchée sur elle
pendant que la figure guette
l'émoi et l'(ensuite) humide, très
en prenant entre les cuisses, le temps
et des verbes rencontrés en plein séjour

L'EN SUITE TRADUITE

ainsi d'elle l'élan et l'aura
d'harmonie pendant que figure leste
ensuite c'est certain décide
entre les mots, suffit ce qui plaît
les détours plein verbe ombré

AVIVA

thus the aura leaning toward her
while the figure keeps watch
emotion and the (latest) humid, very
between the thighs taking, the time
and some verbs encountered mid-stay

THE LATEST TRANSLATED

thus from her the *élan* and aura
of harmony while the freed figure
later be certain decide
between the words, what pleases is plenty
the detours mid-verb full shade

AVIVA

pendant que c'est tout à l'endroit
la main glisse et pâlit ô exactement
dans l'évidence, et la paupière
lente et léchée comme un énoncé
le corps les vagues et le lierre du lien
la probabilité d'une manière de
tenir compte et prononcer l'attiser

L'EN SUITE TRADUITE

des signes à tout moment l'endroit
maintes mains au fond c'est lien lisse
un énoncé parfois paupière sans
dans le vague un corps pour la manière
et tenir à tout en place, l'évidence alors vient
la manière déplacée des probabilités
et tout à fait la voir venir ignée

AVIVA

while all is right in place
the hand slides and fades o exactly
in the evidence and the eyelid
slow and licked like a statement
the body the waves and the ivied ties
the probability of a manner of
taking account and pronounce stir her

THE LATEST TRANSLATED

signs at any time and place
sleight of hands just a tie that glides
a statement sometimes eyelid naught
wave away a body in the manner
and hold to, all in place, the evidence so comes
the displaced manner of probabilities
and absolutely see her come ignite

La Nouvelle barre du jour
1985, tr . 2008

SILK FONT 1

an anagrammatic translation of 'Soft Link 1'

published in *Asymptote*

tr. Bronwyn Haslam

SOFT LINK 1

Ce sont des peurs lentes et fascinantes qui entrent le matin dans une vie à l'heure du café pendant qu'elle se demande si demain il y aura la guerre et que d'un coup sec comme tous les matins elle tranche le pain, le fromage. Ce sont des gestes d'avidité incontrôlable qui se multiplient dans la foule et sa fébrilité mondaine, sa fièvre de parquet de bourse et de spectacle. Ce sont des hésitations, des cris du cœur qui sillonnent de grandes avenues pleines d'ombre et de poussière qui attirent et font penser à nos jambes et à nos coudes, à nos genoux aussi quand le désir happe et relance vers le haut des mots et du sentiment, ce sont des choses simples avec des préfixes comme cyber ou bio qui collent au pensées, les font flotter un instant de sorte qu'on les croit aquatiques et qu'alors elles nous émerveillent. Ce sont des certitudes que d'infimes doses de poussière et de lumière ont tôt fait de mêler à nos larmes. Ce sont des sentiments inexplicables faits de petites douleurs étalées sur de longues années et de vastes horizons, ce sont des idées de blues qui vont se loger là où le bonheur d'exister menace de couper le souffle ou de se déployer dans la gorge comme un instrument de ferveur. Ce sont des lueurs des ivresses impossibles à soutenir du regard, des pensées pleines de précision qui engagent au-delà de l'ombre et du vent, bien au-delà des mots crus, si bruyants si terriblement proches du silence que le monde tout autour semble soudain marée de haute mer et bruissement continu à la manière des musiques qui dans nos têtes déplacent d'un seul coup d'archet tout ce qui résiste au tourment. Ce sont des passages soulignés, des fragments de bonheur qui traversent le corps et dressent tout autour des ponts car ailleurs et au grand vent dit-on il y a allégresse. Ce sont des écritures avec leurs meurtrissures, l'abondance de la vie éclatée à sa mesure dans un monde et ses niches de vieux parcours qui lèchent l'ombre des os.

It's fears dense and mesmeric that creep into a life at reveille, cereal time, as she questions conflict to come and as all mornings, in an unequalled queenly snap, slices baguette and brie. It's pendent upended movements pullulate, teem in esplanade's febrile melee, its fevered parquets of trade center and stage. It's a queued coiled duo, tense idem, a clone rule, a tenuous noise. It's hesitations, corecries that cross sombre avenues of fluent suede, shade and dust, attract and recall our legs, feet, tendons, joints, as desire needles, quoils up to top verbs, sentiments, sense, it's simplicities prefixed, cell— , nano— or cyber—, glue to our pensées, float our neurons a moment so ideas seem aquatic and marvel us. Certainties that pelletised doses, pulverent, luminous, soon mix in our tears. Sequels steepened, sequence equaled, seeded minute quipu nodes educe reels of quoted sequin code to nestle Québec's metered scene. It's eerie unsettled sentiments composed of sores unreeled across deepened years and immense orisonts, it's peeled elegies, blues ideas set up in the lieu mere being emotes, menaces to sever our breath from our throats or reeve out in fever. It's duelled oneness, a ruled pun, deciduous tongues quoted, untied, united. It's ebullience's seamless glimmers one peers at, squints, but can't focus on, concepts so punctuated exuded above breeze and umbrage, above crude seeded sentences so strident and so unpiteously quiet all seems exceeded, muted in a sudden tidal squall, in a susurrus segues, queued, sequential as music in our cerebrum releases in a pulsed arched shot all repelling torment. It's underlined passages, pieces of happiness that course a torso, erect bridges all around as out in squares, museums and neon marquees elan murmurs, a relearned reverse elegy. It's letters and sentences' bruises, existence sluiced, deluged, scattered across oceans and rivulets, curled old routes that tongue bones' velvet coves.

'Soft Link 1' in *Cahier de roses et de civilisation*, 2003
'Silk Font 1,' tr. 2016

A BOOK

from *A Book*
tr. Katia Grubisic

2 1

Words too many, words that linger without ever really being written down safely, appropriately. Superfluous words, piled up outside the text. There are characters in the text, but they're far removed, they exist only as a pretext. The text must keep moving, with no ambition but to recount its own genesis as life unfolds. A strange narrative. Not implausible.

O. R., sitting at her desk, is writing an open letter to the newspaper. On the topic of open letters. It's a way to engage in some public act in a literary way. O. R., curled over the whiteness of the paper, the page, the almost-letter. A gratifying gesture: to write. O. R., who is obviously in Dominique's sights. He is drawn. The moment she finishes writing and signs the letter.

2 2

The text is disjointed, echoes the disjointed life of the mind, of gesture. A way to be and to speak that rarely stops to take stock. A mechanism that leaves little time to understand the spaces, the gaps, the hollow, revealing intervals.

So O. R. and the others are narrated arbitrarily, here and there, as words trade their lettered selves for images.

O. R., Dominique, and Mathieu are alert, their fingers deep in the popcorn. New-Age visionaries. In the dark, the theatre is half empty, half full. There is a mood. Up on the screen, other characters are filling in, full colour.

23

On the lawn, at the C.s' place. Dominique is stretched out on the grass between O. R. and Dominique C. It's about eight o'clock at night. All three of them are very calm. Their stillness is plant-like, more than just chilling out: they are in a state. Pressed into the earth, the three of them lie there. Nape of the neck against the ground, eyes closed.

Could also be.

O. R. and Dominique C. surround Dominique. Green all around. Private property. The C.s' lawn. Around eight. Lying on the ground. Three bodies smiling.

And lovers, much later in the night.

24

O. R. is about feeling something different for once. Dominique is an experiment, an experience. O. R.: feeling something, acquiring a broader knowledge, skills. O. R. on page 659 of the dictionary. Dominique in the kitchen is cooking an egg: ongoing. O. R. facing words. Face to face. Word by word. A matter of words. The tone is set, half-spoken on the hot July afternoon.

25

On every new page, something new takes up all the space, finally born so that the gleaming, inordinate lines of the manuscript can emerge again, once more. Stepping immediately into the realm of reading, and swept away by what will come.

But on the same page, O. R., between two aisles, is choosing cans of food.

Air conditioning. O. R., a grocery list between her fingers. The metal of the shopping cart is cold to the touch. Cold hands. Goosebumps. The grocery list: simple words.

The cashier, the employee. Daily life: complicated words.

26

In the kitchen, O. R., Dominique C., Mathieu, Dominique, and Henri. Together for the first time since that night, the whole night spent drinking and talking. They sit around the table in front of a large platter filled with fresh fruit. Elbows on the table. Looking at each other in silence. Laughing.

The others are somewhere else.

The five of them. Brought together by a word, a number. There is a unity that weighs in each of their lives. The night goes on, makes its way through their words, or the story meanders into metaphor: INSERT TITLE HERE. The story itself. Told through its title. The night, slowly.

They stay up in the white light of the kitchen, around the table, around the coffee pot.

27

They sit up all night. All night they stay close. Awake but relaxed. Henri recites Miron. Starts the same poems over and over. Henri's voice. The hum of a fly caught in the door screen. The text is read. The night expands, white and wakeful. And so it goes, until dawn. They retire. O. R. and Dominique stay, alone. The rain starts to fall.

28

Writing the present passage. A passage that opens on nothing more than the position of the hand and the eye against the sheet of paper. The passage from words desired to words written. A gesture that pulls focus and condenses it into a few sentences, hoping for new ways to direct the gaze.

Everything that's not essential can be written in this passage. Everything that is said and that speaks of something within can be written down, left as a witness to the whims of time. Anything that can be wanted can be written. Only the obvious, which doesn't have to be translated into the curvature of language, is an exception to the rule of words. What's obvious isn't what's literary.

So writing and continuing to create this text implies a bias for literature, and for repetition.

29

The thing written.

'They don't have much to say to each other. Not much to write...'

Often the thing becomes significant in the text. Thing as a general term to designate either a truth that's hard to articulate, a circumstance, a tautology.

Deep down

O. R. and Dominique are asleep. The phone rings. Rain on the roof. Street noise. The phone rings.

Things happen by themselves
one way or another, a warning that it's time to wake up.

O. R. is sitting on the edge of the bed. Dominique is asleep in the damp sheets.

30

The turned page. Cover to cover: 1. The space reserved for O. R. and the rest. 2. The space required to execute the text.

The page turns and the eye awaits the next chapter. The text goes on, the same characters, a few variations now and again. In the text as elsewhere.

O. R. and Dominique got up early this morning. The rain heralds a new day. Different day.

31

The execution of a text.

It's not much different from what came before, but it is unique, unlike any other. A single page, written in a slipstream of composition that recalls others; groundwork.

One thing is put to death to make room for another. The text faced with the strangeness of the text. Words that explain words in relation to other words at the expense of characters, outlines of men and women that will remain as such. Henri seems a stranger to these moments lived by Mathieu, Dominique, O. R., and Dominique C. And yet. Henri is in the text on the same level as the others. A character.

32

Henri in a space.

The text: Henri alone, Henri in the crowd. Himself a variance among the others. On Saint-Denis. At four o'clock in the afternoon, in the rain. Grey day. A passerby like the others. Distinct because he is named and written in a text.

The life of the text. Life through a text. A different kind of real, because it becomes the focus, the attention is on this man, his private life.

33

The private life of Henri.

Henri alone in his room. Listening. Music. His private life, for the moment unfolding in a vacuum. He wants for nothing. There is an intimacy with the objects, he is intimate in his skin. Aware. Henri in the present. Selfish and in love at the same time.

Private life: because others exaggerate and slowly cover over the space (in cubic feet) required to carry out the most intimate movements. Life… deprived of others, their words, personalities, pretensions. Their tenderness too.

Henri in the intimacy of his room. Eyes wide open. There is no comparison. Wide open, seeing, a seer.

34

Henri's words.

They are few but heavy with consequence. Political. Words within reach for everyone. Clear, precise. They uncover corruption, they cause a stir, for better and worse. Henri is beyond these troublesome words, he's involved in the story, embedded in a trajectory of the excessive.

Words that have nothing to do with this text: necessary words, prerequisites that require continual repetition.

Henri's words are at the top of everybody's blacklist. Action words, made scathing by repetition. Incendiary words; invaluable. Henri and words down in the Maurice Richard arena on this twelfth night of July. The heat, the sweat. Somewhere other than in the text.

35

Henri in the text, between the words. A character who shows up after several pages of writing but is right there from the very first line of the book.

Note.

Henri at the flower shop. Surrounded by flowers, stems, ferns. The smell of death, they say. An easy death, probably a happy death. At the flower shop. Air conditioning. Flowers in the cold anoint the air. Henri, his hand on the green of the stem of the rose that smells like a rose and distracts him. Smells like a rose and makes him happy. At the shop the rose is not yet a rose. Red rose: the folie des grandeurs (aesthetics, the colour), unmistakable in these words.

36

The night is as long as a comparison that keeps writing itself, born and reborn in the sentence.

The ritual of black coffee sipped slowly. Rare words. The night is long in the yellow light of the kitchen. At O. R. and Dominique's. All five of them sitting around the table. Exhausted. Persistent, though.

Words accumulate outside the text. The overwhelming impression of living beyond objects and words, a disproportionate existence.

Henri, a book under his arm, at dawn, in Parc La Fontaine. His palms moist. Eyes full of tears. Henri through the park despite the fatigue and the joy. Henri who remembers nothing about anything anymore, only the water he is looking at in this instant.

37

Same day. About five hours later. Henri lying on a bench in Parc La Fontaine. Eyes open. He is covered in sweat. He wants to move, to be even hotter. Henri running down Sherbrooke.

Ten minutes.

Henri in the shower. The rush of water smoothes the hair on his body, the water is invasive over the body. Under the running water, pleasure. The phone rings.

The text hovering behind this excerpt shows Henri among the objects. The text is overcome by what's going on. Catches up, begins again to anticipate the painful exaggerations that will develop in its frame, that are tucked within any form of speaking.

38

Henri's room. O. R. and Dominique C. are pressed up against each other. Henri kneels over their bodies. Dominique C., her lips. O. R.'s open legs. Hands move. The body moves, its wet, gleaming core. Out of breath, life. Henri. The smell of the two women. Their caresses multiply. Their beauty. Henri is euphoric.

The flesh sinks into the wasteland of the unsaid, of knowledge. To write is to bear witness. Spectator. To watch is to stand outside. Superfluous (cf. words too many, page 196).

The text without variant. The text has been postponed within its own writing. It is unlikely now to be read.

Wait for the words to come out on top.

39

On the bus. A Sunday afternoon in July. Variants are rare. A few, here and there, sweating, flopped on the green leather seats. It's all about the ambiance: Henri at four that same afternoon at the corner of Bleury and Sherbrooke. The colour of the buildings. Living things, attractive. Life, beyond any doubt. Reduced to its simplest expression but in the text it is complex, obscured by words, always elsewhere. Unreal. Subject to impossible desire. It is always in the future, and better.

Henri in the text is ineffectual, an acolyte.

40

The book today: touched, considered. A trinket. The written object, a fictional epitome that civilization holds shimmering awkwardly before the inattentive but compliant gaze of the illiterate masses. The written object is dead. The power of death, that vertiginous power. It seeps in because there's nothing, no one to resist the charm of the written object, dead thing.

Words circling words.

Henri is sound asleep in his bed. Under the sheets. Covered from his feet to his shoulders. Henri in the eyes of another. Looked at. Touched. Caressed by Dominique C.

41

The book is becoming concrete.

Pages come together, make a rectangle (10" x 8"). A quarter inch of space and letters. Book-to-be. Manuscript, Book.

O. R. and Dominique look at each other, narcissizing each other up. On the rug. Cross-legged. Hairy buddhas. They breathe in the polluted air of the city. They feel good anyway. O. R. smiles. Dominique keeps watching her without moving a single muscle in his face. Still, immobile. Dead happy. O. R. is restless, tries to distract him as best she can, dances around. The glitter and clang of costume jewellery. With one hand, Dominique pulls O. R. down beside him. Why the violence? Because: the rules of an old game.

42

Still July. O. R., Dominique, and Mathieu come over. Graveyard. Flowers on the graves. Gravestones. Names. Names written to signify regret.

They see things but do not think them. Death is elsewhere. Their presence in this lush place called Côte-des-Neiges cemetery. Words.

43

Words happen. On a surface, in a specific time. An atmosphere. They understudy the main characters, mask reality... and the mask slowly becomes reality. The only thing is the book, clasped. Reality a mood purchased at any cost when the time comes to forget a little.

Words consumed
The words are valued at $2.00 per page, more depending on the demand. Monetized words. Wealth. It's reassuring, as all wealth is.

TABLE: A FEW WORDS

Quiet Revolution	1962	Liberals
dialogue	1965	Catholics
Progressive Conservatives	1969	Conservatives
corporate commando	1969	Union nationale
silent majority	1969	Republicans
runaway revolution	1970	Union nationale

Under the chart, Dominique C. jots a few notes before getting back to work.

Un Livre
1970, tr. 2019

FIGURE:
THE DISINTEGRATING CHAPTER

from *These Our Mothers, or: The Disintegrating Chapter*
tr. Barbara Godard

FIGURE

The figure is real like a political intent to subject her to the plural before our eyes, or, singularly, to power. The realistic figure is thus the most submissive there is. Quite simply, she agrees. She can be reduced then to the general (to the house) by using the singular: woman or image of milk women, lait figures. So the figure turns, two-faced, accelerates, bores into the eyes, the incidents, again, in a final struggle against blindness: apprehend her. Now the figure is in motion. At full speed the figure is unrecognizable. Intense unreadable. Sequence. The figure is migratory.

FIGURATION

She breaks the contract binding her to figuration. In the theatre of the past full of countless nostalgias, she alone, along with all women, creates the entire body of impressions. Not mythical like the double bodies sacrificed during scenes. The body-shock or nerve-impulse that prepares for action without alibi, a body where one is alone, in this case. The body of one cut off from retreat. Girl's body manifested in the precise sense of conflict. Arch, rising delirium: did anybody notice that during the scene passion riddled the eyes like the insertion of a woman into an inverted context. That's because in her interpretation of figuration, of apparent form, visibly, she modified the dream.

DISFIGURE

Tracks to de-face or make unrecognizable. Because after remoteness or open-mouthed privation how can you undertake a word-by-word within the figure: meaning: in the state of nature civilized like a deviation or multiple marginals. In transforming laughter. It must be written down that hate cannot be written or death like a political anxiety: in children's stories, the ogre's life explodes breaking food, bodies into pieces; girls come out of the houses as from the context. In the forest, heads will be bounced on pensive knees. The abyss or into the gulf thrusting them aside. Distancing as for a fiction.

GEOMETRICAL

Issue of gorges circles sphere spirals: butterflies or the result of emotion. The figures tumble about: on the surfaces, refracted, intimate pauses. To attempt the delay of space without line without writing only the war of limbs of frantic arms of tepid hands. Projected: an illusion of gills of water of tresses – eyes become feeble in space intentionally, from acting with fresh perception. Let them close like watertight mouths in an optical slow motion of premonitory cats on a full mid-season day.

ON INTENTION

She has multiple intentions but one of them is always much too hidden: her body like a paradox of matter seeing that she has patiently waited ovaries of several intensive centuries of intension-survival at the frontier of the eyes, day after day the tracing. The beginning again. The rings circling the eyes get bigger. So in contrast the figure (or like a reflex) designates a new configuration fit for inflecting the common meaning. In a hurry to attain a dimension other than symbolic. But the figure reaches its fullness: steps over the taboo or the transient buttocks of a male. Beyond terrorism. The other passions brave the trajectory, pressed in their materiality, that other form of fold.

TAKEN FIGURATIVELY

In the flow to deliver meaning or to utter with concision – who is she depicted manners and propitious as presumed victim, who is she, knows it, ellipsis or sometimes when she bears, that displaces the shadow and the effect of long nights begins to make itself felt on the surface or intensely. Her thirst like playing tricks on the desert, inevitably: grasping the figurative and proliferation. When the profiles move getting ready to speak. It's the shivering or perhaps the rustling of paper. Is an apple on the work bench enough to make sense? Or to turn the stomach?

THE FIGURINE

Hunted to earth but in my hand can she stop my death what is she doing on my grave (on horseback) ochre terra cotta, the stone, her breasts where's her mouth then let her put new life into the disintegrated part of the body. There you have millennium and silence. Would have been put in a museum, large-hipped Venus. Sometimes any intention whatsoever ... but slowing down often makes me converge on the fountainhead. It's her belly. How fruitful she was with her castrating sex. The figurine, it's through the eyes, from time to time the mouth, that a distant reign, in my hand, salt, breast.

HAS FIGURE(D)

Say what: reality – collar halter stall – we've seen them, tied down, bound daily or white bitches in the morning. Reality doesn't exist. Go see five o'clock come. It doesn't exist, it's ·still light. It's somewhere else. Don't talk to me about reality. Nor appearance. It remains to be foreseen. But to have access. Or to begin again. That doesn't exist. Where is your Utopia in the drawer in Mummy's room? Reality, that's life and it's an illusion. White arms in the snow. For sure that doesn't exist. Long before I tremble. Great fear that it doesn't exist. Or else on the sea the wave inside the hollows, softness. In fact all it is is the intense body far from his eyes well positioned *to know*. That has nothing to do with it. But know the alert figure, stature, and history. In hereality.

FIGURE | 209

PREFIGURE

To support muscle like a business, domestic. Agitated figure, of arms of fragments of vaginas within her always to be changed into bread or breast. Fictive that she be ideal because I have a terrible time grasping it's filled with junk like an attic. Shifting so that her body coincides with a few familiar sentences. The symptoms went away to her mo(u)rning mate oppressing him. In fact, she feels better without allergy. The figure is really a girl watching her childhoods, supposed to be a woman, but in fact, a girl. Always: overcome what obstructs the synthesis. About her passing through her own fiction, ourle hurle houache illico, hem howl wake then and there.

FREE FIGURE

Constrained, remember: there is a clandestine space where every law is subordinate to the imaginary or if infiltrating it like a reality they make them rescind themselves. Cloudy water in appearance but interior tissues knowing the only way to go. All in all, it's a question of practice. The slope of that other passion. The same. Or it could be said when imagination catches fire, it ends up a fuse and political. One fecund and suffering trajectory of the body. One last ghostly vision in reality. No belly, no breast with no head lying attached to it, to remember.

from *L'Amèr, ou Le chapitre effrité*
1977, tr. 1983

RECONFIGURATION

from *SeaMother: The Bitteroded Chapter*, published in *Asymptote*
a retranslation by Robert Majzels and Erín Moure

Now the struggle. The book. Fiction begins suspended mobile between words and the body plausible as mother devouring and devoured.

Fiction theory: only in the final embrace will words have been of use. The first word lips and gummy slobber on her breasts. Theory starts the moment either breast or child is held at bay. Strategic wound or sense suspended.

FIGURE

The figure is as real as politics intent on making her submit to the plural in front of everyone's eyes, or singularly power. The realist figure is thus the most submissive face there is. She grammatically agrees, end of story. That's why she's generalized in the singular (in the home): woman or image of wet-nurse. The figure turns, her double-face speeding up, lunges into the eyes, these acts, once more, a last-ditch effort against being struck blind: grab hold of her. But the figure is on the move. At full speed the figure is unrecognizable. Intense unreadable. In sequence. The figure is migratory.

FIGURATION

She dissolves the contract that binds her to figuration. In ancient theatre where nostalgias are rampant, she is simultaneously alone and with all women in producing the effect of the body. Not mythic as in the doubled bodies sacrificed on the stage. Shock-body or body of the nerve impulse that girds itself for action without alibi, a body that turns out to be alone. Body cut off from retreat. Girl-body manifest precisely in the sense of conflict. The arc, out of delirium: did anyone note how passion riddled the eyes during the scene, like the insertion of woman in a context dislodged? It's just that in her interpretation of figuration, of tangible form, she visibly altered the dream.

DISFIGURE

A few clues to undoing or rendering unrecognizable. Because if distant or in drop-jawed deprivation how to proceed word by word in the figure: which is to say: in a state of nature civilized like a gap or multiple marginals. In transformative laughter. Write it down so well that hatred can't be written, or death, like a politics of anguish: in the stories of children the ogre's life explodes fragmenting food, bodies; girls leave home as if abandoning the context. In the forest, heads will be bounced on pensive knees. The abyss or in the chasm by pulling them apart. Creating distance as if for fiction.

GEOMETRICS

Out from throats circles spheres spirals: butterflies or the effect of emotion. Figures stir: over surfaces, refracted, pauses of intimacy. Attempt to give space a reprieve unlined unwritten but for the struggle of limbs of wild arms or damp hands. Projected: a fantasy of gill-slits of water of tresses – in space the eyes are meant to falter, acting on fresh perceptions. Let them close shut like mouths sealed all day at the height of the season in the languid view of premonitory pusses.

OF INTENTION

Among her many intentions, there's one more that's always veiled: her body like a paradox of substance seeing as she's waited patiently with ovaries over many intensive centuries of survivalintension at the corner of her eye, day after day the replica. The replay. The shadow widens. It's in contrast then that the figure (or like a reflex) draws a new configuration expressly able to alter the usual meaning. Pressed to end up in a dimension other than the symbolic. But the figure fulfills itself: pushes through the forbidden or a male's transitory hip. Beyond terrorism. Along the way, holding fast to their materiality, the other passions dare this different form of fold.

CAUGHT IN THE FIGURATIVE

In the flow that carries meaning or utters concisely – who is she as represented morals and suitable as if presumed victim, who is she, knows it, ellipse or sometimes when she creates, it displaces shadow and the effect of long nights begins to make itself felt on her surface or intensely. Her thirst like trying to outwit the desert, inevitably: caught in the figurative and proliferation. When profiles shift gathering themselves to speak. It's the shiver or maybe rustle of paper. Is an apple on the desk enough to provide meaning. Or to turn the stomach.

THE FIGURINE

Stalked steps but in my hand can she stop me dying what business of hers is my tomb (astride) ochre terra cotta, stone, her breasts where is her mouth then let her revive that eroded part of the body. Here they are, millennium and silence. Will have been consigned to the museum, callipygous. No matter how I try...but slowing down often makes me converge on the source. It's her belly. How fecund she was and trenchant sex. It's via the eyes of the figurine, her mouth occasionally, that a distant realm, in my hand, the salt, the breast.

UNE FIGURE

Just say it: reality collar halter harness – we've seen it all, tied down, held all day every day, or white she-dogs in the morning. Reality? It doesn't exist. Try waiting for five o'clock. It doesn't exist, it's still light. It's elsewhere. Reality? I don't believe it. Same goes for appearance. It's to be expected. But to have access. Or start again. It doesn't exist. Did you find your Utopia in the drawer in Mommy's room? It's just a fact of life, reality's an illusion. White arms in the snow. Once and for all it doesn't exist. Long before I tremble. Afraid it just doesn't exist. Or how about at sea the wave within the folds the troughs. In fact what's real is the intense body far from her eyes in the right spot for knowledge. Nothing to do with it. But check out the figure alert, upright, and in history. In shereality.

PREFIGURE

To underpin muscle like an enterprise, domestic. Nervous figure, of arms of fragments of vaginas within her always transforming bread or breast. Fictive, let her be an ideal because the dust I can't seem to grasp is as cluttered as a junk room. Moving so that her body coincides with a few familiar phrases. Her symptoms then moved on to weigh on morning. Fact is, she feels much better with the allergy gone. The figure really is a girl who examines her childhoods, supposedly a woman, but in fact, a girl. At all times: overcoming all obstacles to synthesis. To her living her own fiction hem holler heave ho pronto.

GO FIGURE

She's constrained, remember: that clandestine space in which all laws are subject to the imagination or if infiltrating it like a reality are just nullified. Water murky on the surface but below it the tissues know where to go figure. All in all, it's a question of practice. The flowing of that other passion. The same. To put it another way: when the imagination catches fire, it ends up in cahoots and political. A trajectory of the body, fertile and suffering. A last fantasy in reality. Womb-less, torso-less so no head's involved, so as to remember.

Note on Translation

Subtitled 'a theory-fiction' in its 1988 re-edition, Nicole Brossard's ninth book, *L'Amèr ou Le chapitre effrité* (1977) takes up concerns of language and the mother, of mothering and the difficulties that face a woman who wants to write. The book's title bears the scars of struggle: in *L'Amèr* we read the bitter, *l'amer*, the mother, *la mère*, and also the sea, *la mer*. *Effrité* means 'eroded' or 'crumbled away'; an external force grates at the chapter the woman is trying to write. To capture such resonances is a challenge. In French the 'bitter' looms large, partly effacing 'mother.' To keep 'bitter' present, we created a Celanian portmanteau word, *Bitteroded*, to modify *Chapter*. Brossard doesn't use portmaneau words, particularly, though she does bend words and syntax, so our invention sticks out, yet allows the *bitter* a presence. *SeaMother* is more Brossard-like. It brings out *seam* (and *seem*), *mother*, *other*, and – again in ghostly fashion, as a tip of the hat to Barbara Godard, the book's first translator – *smother*.

Our translation is neither a correction nor an improvement to Barbara Godard's, whose work appeared as *These Our Mothers, or The Disintegrating Chapter* (1983) at the cusp of the 1980s during the effervescence of discovery in English in Canada of French feminist thought via its effect on Québécoise writing in French. Of course, translation occurs through a body or bodies contemporary to their time. Every translation reflects not just an original text, but also a reading. We chose to translate the 'figural' series of poems from *SeaMother: The Bitteroded Chapter* to see what voice and tenor would arise from a reading of these texts in 2019, an era without the same effervescence (a fear at the planet's struggle casts a long shadow) but still: at the cusp of a new century's Roaring Twenties.

from *L'Amèr, ou Le chapitre effrité*
1977, retr. 2019

TYPHON DRU

from *Typhon Dru*
tr. Caroline Bergvall

et c'est l'envol vagues typhon dru
comme un coude dans la nuit
rai de moeurs
le monde est vite obscur

partout où la bouche est excentrique
il neige et quelque chose est chaud
sous la langue, le moi s'enroule émoi
plane ruban de joie
paupières harmoniques

car le monde est vite obscur
et la nuit me rend avide
de partout frôle tant
que la langue avec son sel
un à un les verbes les troue
de silence, typhon dru

en plein vol si j'ouvre les bras
mes cheveux sont lents dans l'oxygène
je pretends qu'il y a de vastes lois
au-delà des villes et des sépultures
ruban de voix, lame des yeux

ce soir si tu rapproches ton visage
et que la civilisation s'étire
au bout de tes bras, ce soir
si en plein vol tu rattrapes mon image
dis que c'était au loin
comme un dé dans la nuit

and this is lift-off breakers typhondru
like an elbow in the night
slit of ways
the world drops quickly

every where mouth is eccentric
it snows something's warm
under tongue the self coils anticipation
glides joy ribbon
eyelid harmonics

because the world drops
quickly and night makes me crave
through and through brushes so
that the tongue its salt
one by one riddles
verbs with silence, typhondru

in full flight if I open my arms
my hair is slow with oxygen
I pretend there are vast laws
beyond cities and sepulchres
voice ribbon, eye current

tonight if you bring your face in
and civilization stretches
out to your arms end tonight
if in full flight you pull my image up
say in the distance there was
like a dice in the night

et pendant que mon sexe songe à l'aurore
mouille muqueuses heureuses
il neige et la proximité encore
je prétends que c'est l'aura
ou l'image asymétrique
de l'image brève en plein vol

lame de fond, cérémonie de l'image
mon coeur est agile
l'émotion entre nous
matière du rire, matière c'est vrai
et ma voix qui craque
dans le froid rose des galaxies

je prétends veiller en silence
dans le froid rose des galaxies
je prétends que si l'oeil est noir
il ne peut pas veiller

partout où la bouche rieuse virtuelle
d'énergie dévore l'aube déverse son oui
elle crie du mieux qu'elle jouit
tympan, mauves sonores
vastes lois qui lèchent
au loin le fond de l'air

au matin e plane haut
et les rivières sont longues
sous ma peau d'autant de parcours
à saveur de femme et de lucidité
au matin, la rivière est haute
quand je te touche
face à face dans l'affirmation

and while my sex thinks of daybreak
soaks mucously beaming
it snows and proximity still
I pretend it's the aura
or the asymmetric image
of a briefly imaged in full flight

undercurrent, ceremony of the imaged
my heart is agile
this emotion between us
materializes laughter, material indeed
and my voice snaps
in the galaxies' cold coral

I pretend to be watching in silence
in the galaxies' cold coral
I pretend that if the eye is dark
it cannot keep watch

every where a teasing mouth of virtual ener
gy devours dawn discharges yes
cries out for better she comes
eardrum resonant mauves
vast laws that lick
a far the air drum

by morning her glides high
and rivers are long
under my skin they're many routes
cream of woman and of lucidity
by morning the river's high
when I touch you face
to face in affirmation

Typhon dru
1989, tr. 1997

TYPHOON THRUM

a retranslation of 'Typhon dru'
from *Museum of Bone and Water*
tr. Robert Majzels and Erín Moure

and it takes flight whitecaps typhoon thrum
like an elbow in the night
ray of mores
the world is swiftly dark

everywhere where the mouth is eccentric
it's snowing: and yet this heat long
beneath the tongue, the me curls up emotion
glides ribbon of joy
harmonic eyelids

as the world is swiftly dark
and night turns me avid
from everywhere so much brushes up
that the tongue with its salt
pierces one by one the words
with silence, typhoon thrum

in full flight if I spread my arms
my hair slow in the oxygen
I claim there are vast laws
beyond cities and sepultures
voice ribbon, eyes' blade

tonight if you lean your face close
and civilization stretches out
at the end of your arms, tonight

if in full flight you catch my image
say it was from afar
like a die in the night

and while my sex dreams of daybreak
engorges ecstatic epitheliums
it's snowing and again proximity
I claim it's the aura
or the image asymmetric
of the image in brief full flight

groundswell, image ceremony
my heart is agile
emotion between us
matter of laughter matter too true
and my voice that cracks
in the cold of galaxies

I claim I keep watch in silence
in the rose cold of galaxies
I claim that if the eye is black
it cannot keep watch

everywhere where the laughing virtual mouth
of energy devours dawn disgorges its yes
she cries out as wildly as she comes
tympanum, sonorous mauve
vast laws that lick
the air's depth from afar

in the morning the she glides high
and rivers beneath my skin
are long from so many windings

savoury with women and lucidity
in the morning the river surges swept away
when I touch you
face-to-face in affirmation

Musée de l'os et de l'eau
1999, retr. 2003

INSTALLATIONS

from *Installations (With or Without Pronouns)*
tr. Robert Majzels and Erín Moure

SITE

each time I settle
into a pronoun other than the absolute *I*
I remove myself from anxiety
pointing a finger
at the changing shape of relations
but the final distress comes from the image
far away
a fatal *I* delirious in impersonal beauty

KNOWLEDGE

my darling, I'm writing so you'll show me
your sex in a fine mood
and your accent in my ears
and your little gender in my mouth
to dream matter and its thresholds
the best of arguments and choice partitions
I want all your music, your areolar colour
and so to understand the world

ENCORE

it's never enough
each time
you roll hope around in your mouth

to appease too many ideas their opposite lit
a taste for curves and for everywhere at once
with the option of crying out
should death and utopia start
to collide

REDUNDANCY

come on I must say come on
if I want being together to imagine
history and the winged contour of language
upends the senses
come on there's no redundancy
when chest and breasts girl or woman
lips and labials touch
when summer's hot
there's no redundancy
when living's
at eye-level

REPETITION

maybe there are too many words
like right now
going off to think in a poem
the idea that it's sometimes easy
right now I can't
say half aye, half life
and stay intact
supposing right now
I could hear the deepest whisper of the voice
the back that cracks under great ambition
right now going off to live in a poem

can't be confused with exile or sojourn
right now I can't
imagine what life resembles
if in a few words I had to
get through the night and repeat to myself
like right now with a desire to
speak directly in our thoughts
of eternity and recapitulate everything

TOMORROW

for the body is supple
I like it on your skin
next year I still exist
July and such embraces because I listen
to words and answer all at once
my lips are intransigent
I check off lively words
I don't let go the embrace
full of terrible conclusions
I stand watch beneath the stars
unmoveable in the oxygen
fervour for ages

Installations (avec et sans pronoms)
1989, tr. 2000

THE MARGINAL WAY

from *Nicole Brossard: Selections*
tr. Jennifer Moxley

the rare and difficult emotions
can they be taken off guard
like a double the sea, surrounding and well-defined
if she is re-engaging with the project
if writing knows because it is real
or facing the landscape (*au-delà*)
thought is ingratiating, then spatial
the will without option this is
desire, freeing or fictive the history
of the word *esprit* when she writes
ever more so for those born fluid

already the body trembles in the atmosphere
of beech trees, glass, the compelling echo
– There is no good likeness of me
on the beach/*sur la plage* –
the equivalence, still vague (wave) and bright range
is this not being, precisely

likely modernity in the rain
affinity assured

unexpectedly giving reality the slip
light slits the eyes
who then will recognize again
the primal version around the lips which
I will evoke three-dimensionally before
the echo the flight my body is vague (a wave)
an elision moving through several chapters

and still you want to transform *le sombre des villes*
again, on the beach, stretched out
. . . .
the feeling devastatingly the certainty
bur first she is at the heights
translucent against the outline of lawns
the gestures were subliminal consequence
so I took the landscape in her
for granted *double sea binding*
the body in the warmth
nor far from the sound of games
the continents succeed each other
in the shadows you think about passion

existence juxtaposed with vision
abridging the surfaces
you construct the day around
a certainty before the sea
the body burns in cerebral
proximity (marks its outline
at the burn horizon) of a line
as follows: the amazon

the intention extreme beauty
you add the landscape to the light
of inclination
the hour is plausible *au-delà de la réalité*
the cosmic body comes from afar
voie marginale, in a flagrant way

poetry is perfect in the place
of transmission, the multiple faces mapped
such an idea in the atmosphere *petite baie rocheuse*
by means of pleasure the cliff, the equivalence
the resonance of the water

on this body or twofold way
devastatingly wave (vague)
DO THE READING AND I'LL FOCUS

memory fashions with hope
on the cliff the erosion the dictionary
you chose the language the contrast
so emerge in the bright affirmation
proceeding with your prior gaze
keeping the holographic walk
for fiction

the cliff is not familiar
in shadow
borders harm the gaze
yet I say being circumvents the echo

airborne in the overhead equation
of seas, this syllable here is hope
mon esprit upsets the in*her*ent

she begins at the heart of the spiral
at·the centre of a planetary
burn, she trembles consequence
and future
for whomever is born fluid devours the tides

if in the shadows I think of passion
at the back of fragments in complete tranquility
it's a feature of reading
a position taken in order to see
the matter at borders split the eyes
I broadcast my existence live

I obstinately stretch out my profile
at the end of the century one day
inflamed in the entity; at the horizon
the abstraction splits the cliff
it reminds me of her to find myself
facing the landscape *au-delà du noir*
chapter finished she touches you at
infinity's last possible step
spinning the written

Double impression
1984, tr. 2010

FIELD OF ACTION
FOR NEW FORMS

from *Daydream Mechanics*

tr. Larry Shouldice

IT'S UNDERSTANDABLE SHE LACKS IMAGINATION

assailed by ideas of this and that how could she avoid them with the increased number of worlds such as consumed taken for granted in the freezing the orbit watching hastened by the forms by *labels* the name of these things stirring about her going almost without saying coded *lurking* reference point coupled red / sky taming symbol sign memorized for centuries TO EXORCISE new memory for new perception to communicate

⁂

THUS ADOPTING A NEW LANGUAGE

to say new blank memory contradictorily for ancestral memory in the fox-holed skin and I going to amuse learned memories

to perceive are born the versions the VIRTUAL an other memory generates language EXPLOITS it: unheard-of gestures are imminent and running underground like an atmosphere being transmitted code to body code to – unravelled still unclear – code with message to be completed in silence aloud so as to perceive the difference

⁂

so that the game will develop cancel out and progress: lettering printing surface: the memory impress recalling right to the image a motion of exchange that fiction effloresces and colours with *fancy* names

HER LACKING IMAGINATION MAKES HER SUSPECT

illegible but to be verified what is involved the information circulates and has the effect of a rumour she remains subject to credibility to communication but to read how if the name of this game is not written? doubtless reverberated and paled existed answer like the frequency of the looks linked to complicity

⁚

AN ACCOMPLICE AND SHE COMMUNICATES

two under the treat of suspicion transmitting on another the premonitory signs of a new involvement of eye and ear, of an other secretion of images and spoken gestures

through a code almost a quality in itself a determinism of the look the slow process preparing the similarity multiple identity / / DEVIATION

NOW IN THIS GAME OF WRITING TO DETERMINE THE REASONS FOR DEVIANCE AND TO EMPHASIZE IT SINCE SOURCE OF KNOWLEDGE

⁚

quotation however
'once past a certain level of tolerance, the variant's distance from the system is such that the former loses all significance and no longer communicates anything but "its own excentricity"' mysterious circumstance suggested in sub-title

TO SUPPRESS EXCENTRICITY
WOULD BE   TO ABSTAIN

and so to widen the field of tolerance through the frequency of marginal actions until they are perceived *signified* in the order of transformations – their *raison d'être* validated by the collective eye

CIRCULAR LANGUAGE

to reduce tension by the repeated use of everyday terms in perspective – which would for example seek the presence of a third party thus concealing the reality of the initial project

SINCE IT ASSERTS THE
OPPOSITE

to make possible the gaps between what exists and what lives at the level of differentiated dissonant language thus anticipating complicity in the interruption

⚬

IN ORDER BETTER TO EXPRESS HER
SELF   SHE   COMMENTS

the attempts to confuse her with the message who the latter makes her necessarily implied like an invasion into the very heart of the images that new memory is no longer able to transcribe to project onto vision overwhelming nocturnal vampire images when she is resting and that she slowly breathes in without remembering

BUT AWAKENED SHE   LACKS
IMAGINATION

and multiplies attempts at aggression against the obstacle the opacity which prevents reading – to see it clearly – opaque cutting off the field of vision of communication the imagination lacking DIURNAL 'The surest sign of the prohibition against certain ideas or certain objects is to be found in the existence of metaphors' the· gesture she makes – this is her way of attempting despite the *sovereign* prohibitions to find again a place to reflect open space favourable for calligraphy with marvellous drawings with numberous incursions (infractions) accomplished as such with arrogance then following the course of what is written fount of apprenticeship to pleasure and density – process of composition (vertically the pieces of chalk on the black board!) which she justifies field of action for new forms in the realm of consciousness

⁂

SHE LENGTHENS THE NIGHT
THROUGH
HER LACK OF IMAGINATION

night hidden like a chosen term between the intervals of this adaptation she is preparing proposed liaison under the sign of an impression which emerges from the whole before sinking into the desert-like silence or spreading the rumour bothers messages all turned upside down IN THE FRENZY before the dead centre signifies AND THIS LIVED THROUGH WITHOUT FURTHER DIZZINESS

⁂

resorting to action words towards the multiplication of reciprocities NOW POSTERED confronting titles verbs even more the information network in the sequence of imprints
link: HOW COULD SHE HAVE
IMAGINATION
with all the slogans she taken with BIG BLACK lettering already extensible language which shrinks in the eye which gigantic when flown above the crowd or she alone taken with posters for THIS the zenith of her lack of imagination would justify perhaps her running away or would let herself stray to consume for the glance the form of words *foreign*

§

THE INFINITE NUMBER OF
CONINCIDENCES
SUBSTITUTED FOR THE IMAGINATION

to transmit the substitutions at the same rhythm as the surrounding messages take *form* the agreed to suggestive memory in the profusion of images THAT SHE IMAGINES to be able to transmit again from one end of the line to the other if necessary coming down on the black lettering

COMMUNICATION BLANK

dividing before the eyes carnal coincidence the code rhythm of execution fusing together in her body THUS SHE GIVES HERSELF UP TO THE IMAGINATION

Méchanique jongleuse
1973, tr. 1980

THE MOST PRECIOUS THINGS IN THE
FUTURE WILL BE WATER, SILENCE,
AND A HUMAN VOICE

from *Fluid Arguments*
written in English by Nicole Brossard

'Language cannot do everything.'	–Adrienne Rich
'We need a silence multiplied by silence.'	– Roberto Juarroz

Good afternoon. It is a real pleasure to be here and a privilege to give this inaugural lecture. Thank you for inviting me. I wrote this speech in English and because of that I will ask for your indulgence if by mistake I come up with unorthodox sentences or expressions.

It is a great pleasure to be back at the University of Western Ontario. The first time I was in London was in 1989 on the occasion of a conference titled: Discours féminin dans la littérature post-moderne du Québec. The second time was to receive an honorary doctorate, which made me very proud. As usual, those visits would start with silent moments at the airport and then on the plane. My face close to the window or leaning over a book and a notebook, I would let my thoughts move their way toward poetry and I would, as sometimes poets do, let my imagination follow its course so I could encounter Laura Secord making her way through the forest or see Margaret Atwood canoeing on an Ontario lake or have a drink with Margaret Laurence in Lakefield.

I don't know if it is by contrast but knowing that the topic of this conference is on silent moments and ill-communication activates in me the desire to recall and honour the opposite: the brilliant and exciting moments of conversation and communication that I have been experiencing within the feminist and the literary communities of Canada: at the Dialogue Conference/Colloque Dialogue in Toronto (1981), at Women and Words in Vancouver (1983), at the Third Feminist Book Fair in Montréal (1988), and on so many other occasions. Yes, the subject of this conference reminds me by contrast of women and words. lt echoes all that has been said and written by feminists over the last twenty-five years on women who have been silenced in life, history, art, politics, and science. It reminds me of all the work that has been done in order for women to speak loud and clear about their gender, their needs, their desires, their anger, their visions, in order to evade the cultural silence imposed on them. This conference on silent moments and ill-communication definitely reminds me of the moving and vibrant act of speech, cette prise de paroles des femmes nord-américaines et européennes at the end of this second millennium.

⁛

If you will allow me I would like to take a few moments to talk about silence, for this is the word that triggered my positive answer when I received your invitation.

Silence has always been an ally for me. In fact it is an ally for poetry. It provides moments of fullness and of plenitude when the pleasure of feeling alive is at its peak. If, for some people, silence is a synonym for fear and anxiety, for me it is essentially related to poetry and a spiritual quest. Silence has to do with a time-space dimension and gives me a good excuse to believe in eternity no matter what. Silence is about being able to listen to black holes and to do fine with the idea that bones and ashes travel through time, language, and perfect moments. Silence and poetry have a lot in common. In fact I believe that there can be no poetry without silence and the space it allows for concentration, focusing, meditation, for thoughts and emotion. Adrienne Rich, in her book *The Dream of a Common Language*, has an extraordinary poem titled 'Cartographies of Silence' in which she says (and I quote): 'Silence can be a plan/rigorously executed /the blueprint to a life/It is a presence/it has a history a form /Do not confuse it/with any kind of absence.'

In each culture, silence is meaningful. In each moment of silence, existence takes precedence over culture, for silence projects us in space, pushes us gently in the vast movement of time and its fluidity. In fact, silence reminds us how small we are and nevertheless how good it feels to be reminded because it comes with an incredible sense of openness. Everything that we achieve, even breathing, has silence for background. Life teaches us to focus our attention only on what human beings have achieved and so for one reason or another it is only when we are suddenly immersed in silence that we realize how many of the things we do are futile and vain.

It is amusing to think that I am being asked to lecture on silence at a moment in my creative life when the word *silence* has become, if not a key word, at least a very significant one in my most recent hook: *Musée de l'os et de l'eau*.[1] Today if one asks me from where do I speak, I answer: from where a strong desire for silence comes to me. Not that I want to be done with writing. To the contrary, I speak from a place, difficult to designate, but from which the words would organize themselves in such a way that their staging on the page would leave an impression of silence, a lowering of the volume of the ambient noises. As others satisfy their desires with daring gestures, so do I want to satisfy my penchant for silence with words that have a strong sensual resonance, literary connotations, and philosophical depth.

I am probably attracted to silence exactly the way I am actually looking for words able to convey reality and concrete references. Because it is so noisy outside, I need silence. Because everything will soon be virtual, I long for words that are concrete like olives, roses, shoes, dog sort of words that I would have never thought to use in my poetry.

No doubt silence stimulates a positive state of consciousness which can be related to harmony, calm, and peaceful emotions like those we find in nature but also in ourselves. Of course, and I will come back to this subject; I am not without the knowledge that silence can also be associated with anguish, fear, panic, or censorship. Indeed, silence can be scary.

> There is my fear
> of no words   of
> falling without words
> over and over   of
> mouthing the silence
>   – Michael Ondaatje[2]

---

1. Translated as *Museum of Bone and Water.*
2. 'White Dwarves' (70).

As I said earlier, silence is a precious ally of creativity. On this matter, David Le Breton, author of an essay titled 'Du silence,' writes: 'Le silence relâche l'emprise du sens, il désoriente les repères et restitue l'initiative à l'individu. Il exige de posséder les ressources symbolique pour en jouir sans céder à la peur sinon, à l'inverse, il ouvre les vanne du fantasme' ('Le Silence').[3]

In fact there are two kinds of silence: silence that comes from within and silence that is produced outside us. One we like to avoid, and one we seek. But one could also interestingly oppose silence to the noise produced by non-humans (machines, robots, electricity, wind, falls, thunder, and animals), as well as to the sounds produced by human beings with their breath and mouth, namely words, cries, laughs, murmurs, shouts, or scats like in jazz. In our society, we are used to noise, not to silence. In an urban environment, silent places are rarer and rarer: parks, churches, cemeteries. In hotels, silence is a luxury and a quiet room is often more expensive than other rooms. In a way we could say that silence is always there waiting for us to pay attention; in another way we could also say that silence is an invention because once the familiar noises are gone, others take over that we were not noticing before.

No wonder that in a recent article in which I was asked to write about the room where I write, I used the expression the 'exhilaration of silence.' I say there that I take pleasure in writing in a room of my own because I respond well to what I call the silence of the city. A shrouding silence which advantages those little sonorous compositions created by the sound of a car afar, the humming of a plane, a brief dialogue between passing-by neighbours. When the computer is on, the silence varies in intensity and in quality. Sometimes, I have to choose between the electric sound of my computer and the imperfect silence of the city.

When I choose silence, it gently fills the room, reducing all sources of stress for the benefit of a perfect listening, a slow descent at the heart of a perfect void which gives me a real appetite for language, the soft craziness of seeing myself bumping into another silence, that one interior. Nothing

---

3. 'Silence releases the sense's stronghold, it disupts the landmarks and restores initiative to the individual. It demands possession of the symbolic resources to enoy them without yielding to fear, conversely, opening the floodgates of fantasy,' 20.

then seems easy when I am faced with that silence, a curt scary silence watching my own silence. Yes, at that moment, one can talk of the white page as being a white space. But what astonishes me the most is that I have never encountered this silence in nature, not even in the most remote places. This disturbing silence, I sometimes imagine it like a warrant of a writing space which, although based on a work of precision, is nonetheless sheltering the most fabulous drifts that make literature a marvel of invention sculpted within the friable matter of silence.

THE BLANK AND THE WHITE: VIBRANT SILENCE

Somehow I have come to believe that when writers talk about the white of the page and the anxiety that comes along with it, they know that this is not about literature but about existence, their own existence, the idea of a void that can suddenly jump on you as raw questions about the meaning of life and a few unavoidable words, like death, for example. I also believe that silence can activate the white of the page, the light that makes it tremble around intimacy. In 1970 in a book of poems titled *Le Centre blanc* I wrote:

> tout se neutralise et s'éclaire se vide de
> tout sens tout la mort soufflé blanc silence
> de mémoire silence silence silence la mé-
> moire tout dans un seul souffle le dernier
> centre où tout se peut enfin concentrer
> centre blanc sans surface le temps le temps
> ne transforme rien désormais le temps
> durcit blanc[4]

---

4.   'all things neutralize illuminate and empty themselves of
all meaning all death breath(ed) blank silence
of memory silence silence silence me-
mory all in one breath(e) the last
centre where all things can at last concentrate
blank centre without surface time time
transforms nothing henceforth time
hardens blank.'

Almost fifteen years later, in *Journal intime* (1984), the notion of white comes back and I write this:

> from one moment to another, I am in the process of inventing myself like this morning, sunny, glacial, white before noon. Blinding. White. Terribly white. […] The light fills the entire space, infiltrates the morning, silently seeping, soaking in, and it is as though I suddenly saw everything in detail. The whole room I'm in is invaded by a thousand structures that fill up the space, that empty the space, leaving the familiar objects without any shadow. In this room, moreover, there is only the indispensable: paper, pen, table, and me. Not even a dictionary, not a single ruler. And the frost blinds me, it's the frost; don't ask me what my life will be, don't ask me what it has been. I won't tell anything. The journal is blinding me. What a strange morning for someone who loves to write. […] What can one say in a journal that one couldn't say elsewhere? What memory do we address when we claim to bring the past to life again, however near the past might be? What is so intimate about a journal that it could not be shared, opened by someone else's reading? Intimate. The Japanese have an expression, *Mono no aware*, that signifies the 'moving intimacy of things.'[5]

Understanding the intimacy of things has cost me enormous energy and despair. But I had one advantage: I was able, by writing, to slow down the act of writing. I've always done this. It is by slowing down between each word that I learned how to identify, to compare. To laugh. I also learned to see the whites coming, to hear them without ever being completely able to sound their echo. The whites that one calls white spaces are in fact so filled with thought, with words, with sensations, with hesitation, and with chances to be taken that it is only possible to translate that by a tautology, that is by another white, this one visual. It is in the white that whoever writes, trembles, dies, and is reborn. Before and after the white everything's fine because there's the text. And that fills up a life

---

5. Trans. Barbara Godard

so well, a text! Each text is a sample, that is a little bit that one shows to give an idea of the whole.

Before and after: this is exactly when they say silence occurs. Most of all it is said to appear before and after important events, beautiful, moving, tragic moments, before and after love, before and after a storm. Before and after a concerto, before and after a firework.

Silence is an invisible fluid moving slowly but surely always in the direction of the soul. It's everywhere, bit by bit, it hides in cloisters, it roams in gardens, it lodges itself in people's hearts and souls as a child throws herself in her mother's arms. Even though it seems paradoxical, silence is often accompanied: a few drops of rain on the ceiling, a fountain and its murmur, the whistling of a locomotive, the beat of a heart, a dog barking in the night. In fact, we say that music is a choreography of sounds on silence as a screen, we could easily say that reality, the sense of existing, is shaped out of the silence. Silence as a background will always be there, making us look good or foolish depending on how we project meaning on it. But I guess we can say that in the future it will be more and more difficult to obtain the effect of depth because the layers of noise are getting thicker and thicker, in fact so thick that we simply have learned to surf on a surface of parasitical noise.

BETWEEN SILENCE AND ILL-COMMUNICATION: VOICES

In her suicide note, Virginia Woolf complains about voices that give her the impression that she is going crazy. She says that she hears voices and cannot concentrate on her work. She probably is not the first writer nor the last to be troubled by voices. Writers have often complained or simply acknowledged the fact that they were sometimes under the spell of voices. If the voice is not too loud they call it inspiration; if the voice amplifies, multiplies, and becomes a continuous burden they call it hell, where of course there is no place for silence. But the voice is not always in opposition to silence. Sometimes it simply exists outside the control of the writer. The Quebec poet Denise Desautels writes in *Cimetières: La Rage muette*:

De plus en plus souvent, la nuit, ma voix parle toute seule, sans moi et danse à côte de moi, et virevolte, et s'emballe, et monte. Parfois très haut. [...] Comme, si montant très haut, trop haut, atteignant des sommets quasi impossibles à atteindre pour une voix, elle parlait en mon nom et m'excluait tout à la fois.[6]

It is interesting to note that, in the seventeenth century, it was common for writers to bear a voice sometimes accompanied by a vision that would speak so clearly about what they should do. Pascal, Descartes, Marie de l'Incarnation, all of them have been able to name the precise date and the time of that voice inspiring them, a turning point in their lives. Of course, when one hears the voice of God I suppose it's difficult to forget when it was.

But what voices did indeed speak to Virginia Woolf? Was it the noise of the voices which was annoying or the fact that meaning was covered by sounds? Was it about meaning or about the chaos of voices? Hearing voices is a documented fact in schizophrenics. But definitely we can say that many creative persons have felt that they were commanded by a little voice to say such and such a thing. Where shall we situate the voice of remorse, voice of desire, voice of another in oneself? The ghost in *Hamlet* is a voice and Hamlet's first reaction is to resist it because the voice is always demanding. Therefore, as soon as the ghost appears, Hamlet questions: 'Whither wilt thou lead me? Speak, I'll go no further.'

Victor Hugo wrote a whole book of poems titled *Les voix intérieures* (1837).

Strange voices inhabit a space normally occupied and shared by silence and by our own interior voice. Together they constitute a fertile discursive terrain for consciousness and powerful emotions. But when strange voices expulse silence and invade the inner space of our soul, they also appropriate and alter the interior voice that we hold as a symbol of our own validity

---

6. 'More and more often, at night, my voice talks all on its own without me and dances next to me, spins around, winds itself up, and rises. Sometimes very high [...] As though, by climbing very high, too high, reaching summits virtually impossible for a voice to reach, it speaks in my name while excluding me at the same time.'

in this world. The Quebec poet Line McMurry writes: 'In silence you suffer from loud speech.'

FROM SILENT EMOTION TO TALKING VOICES

In the history of cinema, it is interesting to notice that what have been called silent films have not been silent films at all, for most of the time they were filled with a piano music used to punctuate and influence the audience's moods and emotions. When silent films became talking films there were comments to the effect that speech has no more to do with film than literature or that speaking films could be of no concern to cinema. Even the famous writer and art critic Andre Malraux said, strangely, talking films would not improve cinema any more than elevators would improve the skyscraper. Obviously the human voice covering silence and music or taking the forefront of the soundtrack first seemed to irritate critics, especially in Europe. Or was it simply a habit that they felt was difficult to change? Nevertheless, as soon as characters would be able to engage in loud and clear dialogues and communicate feelings pertinent to the understanding of sophisticated narratives, silence would be relegated to the background. Decades after, silence would reappear, especially in European films, as a dramatic tool. Silence would then monopolize the screen and would only be interrupted once in a while by dialogues and realist sounds. Here, I especially think of lngmar Bergman's 1963 film titled *The Silence*. But in most of his films, Bergman uses silence and the powerful tension it creates to dramatize the relation between the characters. And so, his characters are often immersed in silent moments that seem to slowly swallow men and women as moving sands would. Bergman's silences are almost unbearable, because they are thick with ill-communication. On the other hand, I could as well say that silence in Bergman's work requires a lot from the viewer because it is deep as sorrow, intense as inspiration, vital as music. Silence then offers us a space in which the tension is renewed and that tension functions as a learning device for us to understand and observe ill-communication.

Silence can also be visual. For example, I think that stone, whether in sculpture or in architecture, is a material full of silence as if it were in the nature of stone to absorb silence, the silence of night, of dawn, the silence of grass and of the blue sky. I believe that stone can even absorb the silence in us when we walk by it and more if we touch it or caress its porous hard grey surface.

When I use the expression 'visual silence' I spontaneously think of Mark Rothko, Balthus, Edward Hopper, and of a postcard by Duane Michals. Rothko has always been my favourite painter. I guess it is because he was able to transform intensity (a vibrant luminous intensity) in his work. An intensity in which darkness would be part, more or less in all his painting, most of them being titled *Untitled*, which for me is in his case a synonym for Silence. I have never been in the Rothko Chapel in Houston, Texas, but I am haunted by the fact that more than anywhere else this is where we can contemplate his silence, because only there is it exposed with no mercy.

At the opposite end is the painter Balthus, whose work installs silent moments and leaves a disturbing impression of ambiguity and of ill-communication. You might have seen some of his work where children or young adolescents are represented. Most of the time by themselves, some-times with an adult, a music teacher. The characters read, play a musical instrument, or play cards. In most of the paintings one of the characters, usually the young boy, is hiding something, telling us, we who are looking at the scene, that he is cheating, has been or will be masturbating, or that he has unfriendly thoughts toward the little girl sitting on the sofa. Because we suspect his intentions and those of the girl as well, we enter the silence of the room, we enter the silent fantasy hidden in the head of both the girl and the boy. We cannot even escape the silence and the sexual wandering that the painting itself has introduced in our gaze.

While Balthus exploits silent moments of ill-communication, Edward Hopper translates visually still moments where time seems to have stopped around faces and gestures.

I also think of a photo by Duane Michals. The photo shows two women close to an open window. A breeze is blowing the curtain. The women look in two different directions. Until I went back to look at the picture for the purposes of talking about it in this speech, I thought the title of it was *Silence*. In fact, the title is *Certain Words Must Be Said*.

I remember buying the postcard because it featured two women, proba-bly lesbians I thought. But I felt uncomfortable with the women in the picture as if they were mannequins. Nevertheless I had the postcard reproduced in a book that collected writing on women and culture from *Tessera*. Edited by Barbara Godard, it was called *Collaboration in the Feminine* (1994).

CULTURAL AND SOCIALIZED SILENCE

The use of silence and cultural places where silence is required varies in each culture. I am not an anthropologist but I know that silence can serve many cultural purposes, be it to facilitate studies, law and order, or to initiate prayer, pleasure, and violence, or to anchor solitude and discipline of the self. In our culture, we know that silence is usually expected in libraries, churches, hospitals, cloisters, and monasteries, for better concentration, meditation, or rest.

As an example of a social use of silence, I would think of the minute of silence required from an audience to honour the memory of someone who has just died. Or I can think of the minimal amount of silence required from everyone for the audience to enjoy a film, a concert, a show, a play. That silence and the quality of it will vary depending on whether you're attending the projection of a cult film like *The Night of the Living Dead* or a Tomson Highway or Ann-Marie MacDonald play. I also see, as a cultural silence, the silence expected within official hierarchical relations (for example whose role is it to initiate the conversation in an embassy, in the army, in the parliament, at the Vatican, etc.). Culturally, silence is a sign of respect, of reverence. Not remaining silent when expected to can be seen as a sign of disobedience and of disapprobation.

Among the cultural types of silence, there is of course the one imposed by patriarchy. Depending on how patriarchal the culture is (whether it is a hard patriarchy or a soft patriarchy), silence will be imposed on women on different occasions, during certain activities, in certain places, and in the presence of males. We all know the famous: '*Sois belle et tais-toi.*'[7] It is unbelievable how much men have mocked women's speeches. The jokes seem endless. Women's verbal exchanges among themselves have been called

---

7. 'Shut up and be pretty.' Like the English expression 'Women should be seen and not heard.'

gossip and it is strange to think that probably most 'gossip' was about silent moments or ill-communication between husbands and wives. But we can also think that gossip was also full of precious information on all sorts of subjects concerning surviving.

ILL-COMMUNICATION

'Le silence favorise un retour du refoulé quand le rempart du sens que fournit le bruit se dérobe en partie.'[8]

– David Le Brun

Because it is different to be silenced by cultural tradition than by another individual, I have chosen to distinguish between socio-cultural silence and ill-communication, no matter how much it can sometimes resemble the sexist socio-cultural relation. I believe that there is a difference between cultural socialized silence and ill-communication. I will reserve the expression ill-communication for dual relation, which is to say relation between two persons who for some reason have to talk to each other or are said to cultivate a relation, whether deep or superficial. And it is certainly not because a relation is superficial that it cannot go wrong or be contaminated by ill-communication.

To tell you the truth, ill-communication as a topic does not really inspire me. Why? Because it is so obvious that it exists and that it will go on existing widely. It makes people unhappy and frustrated. It can put an end to long-term relationships; it can also create disasters (pressing the wrong button, insulting someone against one's will). Life is full of ill-communication situations because most people are forced to communicate with people they don't necessary want to communicate with: parents, professors, bosses, colleagues, neighbours, etc. I suppose that politeness has been invented to attenuate the frictions or indifference that would naturally occur between citizens had they not been taught that living in society requires a minimum of effort. Of course, good communication has nothing to do with telling all

8. 'Silence favours a return of the repressed when the defence of the sense that noise provides partially strips away.'

about yourself, believing that the other will understand more about you. I can hardly stand the idea that new lovers, new friends, will tell each other their life story in the first hours of their encounter. It's an insult to imagination, to a creative relationship.

Life is full of ill-communication because we use words to conmunicate and meaning is alive like fishes that keep slipping from our hands when we believe we hold them for good. Meaning changes constantly depending on the context. Affective meaning is always on the move, has to be staged and re-evaluated all the time like a theatre production.

No doubt in my mind that ill-communication is nourished by hierarchy, roles, unequal affective needs, ambition and its strategy, shameful pasts, social class, unmentionable desire, envy, pride. In one word, ill-communication is nourished by guilt, by strategies of manipulation and by fear of losing something (a tooth, a job, or love), the three reasons working their way in language through omission, lies, and fictitious inventions. In each scenario of ill communication a narrative is kept secret and activates words in a sublimininal way. Either you control the story or you don't. But it is possible that for both parties, fictive passages (not lies) will be used as a strategy allowing for positive justification in response to complaints, accusations, or reproaches. And so, when fictional passages are integrated in ill-communication as positively real, they somehow contribute to reactivate communication.

But what is the role of silence in ill-communication? Well, for example, it certainly affects communication by interrupting it. Silence can be used as a punishment, an objection, a blunt refusal, or it can leave space for a renewal of communication and invigoration of it. But very often in ill-communication silence should not any more be called silence, but should be called muteness.

There is a distinction to be made between silence and muteness. Silence envelops important events while muteness veils them. Silence gives things grandeur and majesty, muteness depreciates and degrades them. Silence is a fabric of emotions, muteness is refusal of emotions. In all cases, muteness as opposed to telling while silence can be an instrument to enrich a dialogue. For we all know that silence can be full of love, tenderness, seduction, admiration, especially when accompanied by a very special look.

Silent moments can play different roles in communication but they could certainly be listed under the name of the unsaid, shame, omission, interruption, or as a tool for censorship and humiliation. But its most interesting role to me is silence as punctuation in a dialogue. Because of that, punctuation creates emotion, expectation, and sometimes reflects our own dubious silence. Silence is also a place where tears assemble and mysteriously fade away after a moment or two.

DIALOGUES IN REAL LIFE/DIALOGUES ON STAGE

There are not many places where you can hear dialogues and at the same time look at the people engaging in them. Of course those places are in real life and in theatre. In real life, dialogues can be observed in public spaces like in cafés and in restaurants but as well at the beach and in parks where they seem a little different because in open air voices and silence move differently than indoors. But no matter the subject, the communication, or the lack of communication, silence and dialogue cannot do without one another.

In his book *The Dialogic Imagination*, Bakhtin discusses the fact that '[w]hen we attempt to understand and make assessments in everyday life, we do not separate discourse from the personality speaking it (as we can in the ideological realm), because the personality is so materially present to us. And the entire speaking situation is very important: who is present during it, with what expression or mimicry is it uttered, with what shades of intonation?' (340-41)

In real life, we care about real people but also about characters of fiction. Even though it seems paradoxical, we might not pay attention to dialogues among real people; but at the same time we feel responsible to intervene if the dialogue turns dangerously sour. At the theatre, we pay careful attention to the dialogues among the characters, but no matter what happens between them we remain comfortably sitting on our chairs, knowing that we do not have to worry about anything else than our emotion.

Of course, in real life, most of the dialogues surrounding us are boring or of no importance to us. They are made of silly details, of nasty comments, of 'she said, I said, he said.' They are made of what others do and say. While in the theatre dialogues are made of what causes other people to resemble us which is emotion: love, pain, joy, despair, anger. Dialogues in the theatre initiate a dialogue with ourselves.

For me, there are two writers whose dialogues are about silence or incommunicability. Samuel Beckett is one of them, and I particularly think of *Waiting for Godot*. In a different way, I would also think of Marguerite Duras. Whether in her novels or in her films, silence seems to build up in her sentences and the characters give the impression of emitting silence as a code for surviving. *Il y a une telle lenteur dans ses phrases. On dirait que le silence s'installe partout et fabrique sournoisement un destin à chacun.* Perhaps it's all about an irrepressible melancholia. *C'est la lentuer qui nous séduit.*[9]

Time goes by and every time a sentence says so, it allows silence to close on it. By depriving her characters of a name, by them she, the woman, he, the man, Marguerite Duras imprisons them, their emotions, and their bodies in time and in silence. *Elle les isole dans un autre monde.* She isolates them in a world which seems unreal, diaphanous, which forces us to keep our distance yet to feel strongly moved.

In that sense I believe that the silence 'we hear' in a novel can never be faked because that silence can only exist if it is already in the writer's blood and breath. Then the sentences take over and the writer's silence becomes ours, for a short time or forever.

REAL LIFE AS IN DIALOGUE

– I love theatre and I am fascinated by dialogues, be it among strangers, family members, lovers, or friends. I like to observe how silence progresses, how it can stumble or drift on a word, I wait to catch the moment when it becomes false, artificial, symbolic, or readable at a second level. I like to vatch silence sculpting non-said, uneasiness, shyness, how it puts holes in violent thoughts and changes the muscles of the face. How it builds walls round characters, how it chokes them.

---

9. 'There is such a slowness in their phrases. It is as though silence settles in everywhere and slyly crafts a destiny for each one [...] It's slowness that seduces us.'

– But why do you like to watch, don't you practise dialogue yourself in real life? (Silent moment on my part.) Are you afraid of dialogue? Real dialogues with real people. (Silent moment.) Are you writing to avoid real dialogues?

– Maybe writing is all that matters to me?

– I think this is the kind of sentence one must regret saying in front of her child or her lover. (Silence.)

– To tell you the truth, I think you have been avoiding the real question of this conference, which is how silent moments are symptoms of ill-communication?

– I don't believe that silent moments are only symptoms of ill-communication. In any case I don't like to concentrate my thoughts and my time on people who cannot communicate properly. I am not a doctor or a psychologist.

– It is not a reason to close your eyes on the poison called ill-communication.

– I know, I know what you want. You want me to explain things about women and silence. How we have been silenced because of the patriarchal system. But haven't you read 'Constructing Women's Silence' in Dale Spender's book *Man Made Language*? Haven't you read *On Lies, Secrets and Silence* by Adrienne Rich? You want me to find solutions to ill-communication. Are you kidding? Most of the people, healthy ones like you and me, are suffering from the simple fact that they once were children, from the fact that people don't pay enough attention to them. Why is everyone so desperately seeking love and affection? And I am not even mentioning those who have been really, badly hurt, who have reason to be suspicious when required to communicate with others. Why is it that most people would like to rewrite their lives? Why is it that people beg for love like dogs and bark for food?

– What is it that rebuffs you in the idea of writing about ill-communication?

– I simply feel impatient about it.

– But don't you think that it is a writer's responsibility to take into account such a reality?

– You mean the darkness, the trouble zones of human relationship? The drama. Yes, in art I don't mind. But in real life I find it unbearable. I would rather break up with someone than keep the relationship by sinking into the stupid silence of ill-communication.

- You have changed. Nicole, I think you have changed. I can remember a time when you would do anything to find a solution to ill-communication because you used to say: the sparkle of life in someone's eye is what makes it worthwhile to find solutions for life to be better.

– OK I've changed. I don't want to have anything to do with 'la misère de vivre des autres.'[10] (Silence.) Life is too short. Let people find their solution in language. Or in silence. (Silence.) Or in solitude. (Silence.) Or in work. Or in pleasure. By the way, did you make a reservation for tonight at that little restaurant we went to last summer? It was such a wonderful evening, the food, the conversation. You had just bought Daphne Marlatt's most recent book, *Readings from the Labyrinth*. And I remembered talking a lot about *My Paris* by Gail Scott.

– Of course, I remember. It was a very special moment. Now I can tell you, I was so sad at that time because Mother had just died a few weeks before. I was devastated.

(Silent moment.)

– Do you still remember the taste of that *Suprême de brochet à la dijonnaise?*

– '*Pour notre souper, nous avons simplement commandé un poisson poché au beurre noir, une salade de légumes et des frambroises. Le repas était satisfaisant. Nous nous sommes promenées aux limites de la ville et avons été echantées. [...] Un soir, une femme très belle s'est assise à la petite table à côté de la notre, son livre tourné vers nous.'* [11]

– You won't fool me. I know this is a quote. Yes, that's a quote from the French translation of *Alice B. Toklas's Cookbook*. (Silence.)

– Why didn't you say anything then about your mother.

– I couldn't. People get nervous, uncomfortable when you talk about intimate matters. It would not have been about my mother. It

---

10. 'I do not want to be company to other people's misery.'

11. 'For supper, we simply ordered a fish poached "au beurre noir," a vegetable and raspberry salad. The meal was satisfying. We wandered around the outskirts of town and were enchanted. [...] One night, a very beautiful woman sat down at the table next ours, her book turned our way.'

would have been about images of agony and death. Anyway, I did not want to upset you.

– But I am your friend. Am I not? (Silence.)

– I am still uneasy with the subject. (Silence.)

– Earlier you said that you felt uncomfortable, with the photo that Duane Michals had made of two women. Do you know why?

– The women in the photo don't look natural.

– Art is certainly not about objects or people looking natural.

– Silence between woman is often a space of desire that only women can imagine. Imagining silence among women is as difficult as imagining lesbian desire. Silence between mother and daughter seems to be more familiar because the relation is unavoidable. Sooner or later, it falls on each woman. (Silence.) Do you know that last year at the same time, I was beginning a novel by saying: 'It is through the space opened by my mother' silence that I look at the world, that I've learned that another world exists into which I could plunge, laugh at will, and survive all ordeals.

– Sharing silence with someone creates a powerful bond because somehow it is like sharing the intimacy of a person. More it is like recognizing in her the aptitude to understand the beauty and the necessity of silence. It's hard for me to understand people who use silence as a threat to the other.

– Unpleasant things have to be said and are never easy to communicate.

– I don't think that ill-communication comes from the fear of saying unpleasant things. Ill-communication is rooted in existence itself. It's in our pride, in our fears, and mostly it takes root in our ability to imagine and to make up stories about reality.

– I'd rather think ill-communication is basically a matter of bad translation.

– You know something! I wish we could spend more time together.

– In silence?

– In silence.

2002

THE FRAME WORK OF DESIRE

from *Theory, A Sunday*

tr. Erica Weitzman

in every word, rests only the meaning we make for it

However one defines the word feminism, it's impossible to ignore the motivating factors behind it, those motivations that make every woman apt to become a feminist. Whether taught about feminism or not, it's easy to suppose that every woman has been brought up receiving, in her flesh and her subjectivity, in the form of many disdainful words and humiliating gestures, all the information she needs to initiate her revolt. On the other hand, it should be kept in mind that every woman simultaneously receives all the information necessary to maintaining her inferiorization and all the misinformation required for her subordination. No woman really gets used to violence; few women accustom themselves to contempt and insult; most women accustom themselves to dependence, and thereby validate the patriarchal tradition. Still, one can still say that throughout the course of history, and despite all of the economic, legal, moral, and religious constraints that consigned women to a 'secondary role' and to their own effacement, women have managed to speak out and take action. Whenever women have done this, it has been for the sake of life, sometimes in their own name, demanding rights for their own gender, rights that would be not exclusive to them but equal for all.

The feminism that we have been experiencing in the West for more than twenty years now presents us with a wholly new historical phenomenon, because it questions the imaginary, symbolic, and psychological construct of everything through which the inferiorization of women has been programmed. What is more, in its validation of the individual as well as the collective subjectivity of women, this feminism has allowed for the blossoming of women's creativity and the affirmation of their identity, and has created a basis for the formation of solidarity. In other words, we can say that contemporary feminism, even as it undertakes the task of the advancement of women and the extension of their rights, has also and above all become an idea, a moral system, an ethics. By a curious coincidence, this happened at the very same time as male philosophers and thinkers came to grace their books with titles like *The Defeat of the Mind*, *The Age of Emptiness*, *The Future of a Negation*, *The Empire of Fashion*, *The Death of Genre*, as if, having made the grand tour of the garden they once mapped out and cultivated, now they insist upon its barrenness and desolation.

That said, my intention here is not so much to talk about feminism as to try to understand how feminist consciousness functions, so as to identify the various difficulties that it encounters as it claims, affirms, or proposes. How can a feminist consciousness *deal with* reality in such a way that we can inscribe our convictions and perspectives within it, convictions and perceptions that comprise the cumbersome and creative subjectivity of a totally new world?

In order to answer these questions, I feel that it is necessary to single out three elements on which the coherence of the work of feminist consciousness depends: motivation, decision, and concentration.

MOTIVATION

Motivation is defined as 'the action of (conscious and unconscious) forces that determine behaviour.' We ought therefore to ask ourselves what is the source of our motivation, so as to identify the *reasons* and *motives* [les *motifs* et les *mobiles*] that generate and nourish feminist consciousness, and at the same time to understand how these two factors affect and control the evolution and the relevance of our thoughts.

REASONS

Philosophy teaches us that, as opposed to motives, reasons are easy to objectivize and thus identify. To comprehend them, one only has to look around and gather information. If one grants that motivation increases in proportion to the number of reasons for acting, one would also have to agree that a feminist must constantly keep her eyes open and update her knowledge. The past and the present basically provide us with a certain quantity of *raw* data about what the condition of women is and was. Statistics, legal texts, television news programs, advertising, various facts, pornography constitute reasons for intensifying our anger and our revolt on a daily basis, thus reaffirming both our will to act and the urgency of the need to take action. Other reasons for acting can be found buried in history and literature: it is the task of feminist consciousness to identify and analyze them. These reasons add up to an immense iceberg of injustice and violence: most women are only able to see the tip; feminists have the ability to take its whole measure.

There is also another source for reasons, one which has the power to orient our desire and inspire us. These are the words, writings, actions, and gestures of liberation produced by women throughout history. And closer to our own time, one can say that every book written by a radical feminist, a lesbian feminist, or a radical lesbian is motivating material, blowing fresh wind into our sails.

MOTIVES

Motives differ from reasons in that they are unrecognized or unconscious, and deeply private. As the name indicates, motives are constantly in motion and travel through us like something undetectable. Correspondingly, it is more difficult for us to isolate them from among the mass of emotions and sensations which we experience and which have the power to strengthen but also to diminish our motivation. Thus motives can influence our energy levels, our feelings, and our subjectivity all at once without our even being conscious of it: a fact that is obviously not without consequence for how we invest and/or disinvest in feminism. To the extent that they are unconscious, however, it seems easy to define motives (the emotive) as personal factors and thus give up on evaluating the real impact they have on our collective motivation.

However, one can also consider the fact that the solidarity of women, the pleasure we experience in being together, our identification with other women, the state of mind in which lesbian love can immerse us all equally constitute substantial motives for acting. In another sense, we can also say that the sorrow, suffering, and anger that come to us out of the accumulated violence and contempt against the female sex and thus against that which we are, also evoke in us the energy that arises from the 'sense of honour.'

While reasons have to do with facts and circumstances, motives are inextricably linked to faces[1] and to forms[2] whose relative emotional proximity has the power to multiply attraction or threat, well-being and discomfort – private expressions and figureheads are never neutral; their nearness has the effect of eliciting complicity or rejection, drawing us closer or pushing us away. In this way, reasons (in the public sphere) and motives (in the private one) organize, so to speak, our caution and our daring, our self-censure and our taking liberties, our reserve and our exaltation.[3]

DECISION

Concentration is that which bring together under one meaning, that which is called the convergence of things. It could also be defined as the 'total application of intellectual effort to a single object.' Even though one can make a case for the possibility of being conscious of two things at the same time (comprehension), one can't maintain the possibility of concentrating on two realities at the same time (judgment). Yet this is exactly what determines the radical *ambivalence* and the *inadmissible certitude* of feminist consciousness as soon as it tries to articulate itself as an idea. Thus, it is worthwhile to think about what can impede or encourage the decision-making process.

A feminist diagnosis, which concludes that women have been and are still dominated by men, correspondingly necessitates the valorization of women and the devaluation of men and their institutions. Such a diagnosis also has the effect of making the *duality* of men and of women into something *real* and *active*, and of making present the atavistic *antagonism* that the idea of complementarity could never hide: a complementarity that amounts, in the patriarchal system, to saying that woman (as supplement) completes man (as subject).

---

1. Mother, father, brother, sister, lover, friend, enemy.

2. Heroine, hero.

3. One can observe a woman's motivation grow or diminish respective to the arc of events in her life (childhood, romantic relationships, life as a couple, motherhood, friendship, work). Among other things, this explains the moments of withdrawal or recommitment that are part of the fluctuations of the feminist movement. This also explains the diversity of approaches and definitions feminism has been given.

DUALITY

Duality is the coexistence of two units of differing natures. The human race constitutes two groups, men and women. But whereas male thought was able to discount the idea of sexual duality by simply making the female gender inferior,[4] feminist consciousness can't simply endorse a similar obfuscation in return. Moreover, even while validating the existence of women and discrediting the logic of the male imaginary, feminist consciousness is still obliged to pose the question of difference as a series of careful statements that, on the one hand, takes care not to deny men their humanity, and on the other, tries not to hold women in an exaggerated esteem. In short, by virtue of the very nature of its humanist aspirations, feminist thought finds itself forced to a certain degree to grant men that which is not just a kind of ontological immunity, but also the consideration to which every human being has a right. This is not without consequence for the consistency of our argument, for even as we are *morally* obligated to include and respect men, we also have to vehemently reject and despise the arrogance, the baseness, and the hypocrisy that they have shown us. Also, our thinking gets lost in what to include and what to exclude; it is as reluctant to make generalizations as it is to particularize. In return, by refusing to *overestimate* women, feminist thought deprives itself of a form of representation that is essential to every mythology, to every imaginary, and as a consequence renders itself incapable of propagating itself. In this way, feminist thought holds itself hostage. Without cultural and institutional supports, without a mythic space or an anchor in the imaginary, feminism can only remain something limited and occasional: in other words, subjected to the fluctuation of reasons and motives. Hence the feeling that feminism is incapable of achieving the goal of creating a second generation of women as radical as the first.

What is more, if one accepts the fact that our knowledge and language spring from a common masculine subjectivity, we have to recognize that whenever we make use of these things, we are using instruments whose

---

4. In refusing to acknowledge the duality of the sexes, i.e, by making women their inferior, men have been forced to take recourse in the antagonistic binaries body/mind, nature/culture, and intuition/reason, always giving the inferior of the two positions to the dimension of phenomena they designate as feminine.

trustworthiness is highly questionable and which risk – at every moment, in every statement – turning against us. I refer for example to the definition of the word 'feminist' given by the Petit Robert.[5] 'That which relates to feminism. E.g.: feminist propaganda. Noun: Partisan of feminism.' What is the word *propaganda* doing here, considering that the word has a pejorative connotation, and that its use generally serves to designate the distribution of *false* information for the purpose of influencing opinion? Why the use of the word *partisan* in the masculine form, even though it's perfectly obvious that feminists are mainly women – if not exclusively, then at least in the vast majority of cases? Of course, one could argue that if feminism is a 'humanism,' it should be possible to mobilize just as many men as women and thus the use of the word *partisan* in the masculine is justified. But here is an example that nicely illustrates at once male antagonism (propaganda), comprehensive duality (feminism is valid for all), and the *general rule* that privileges the masculine over the feminine. A semantic victory has been won that can only be undone through our resolve.

My conclusion is that if it wasn't for our *motivation* (anger against men, identification with women, love and sexual attraction for women), our feminist consciousness alone could never have dared to articulate the affirmations and propositions that have been our prerogative for the past twenty years. This means that even if we are conscious of two things at the same time, the duality, we still can't do without antagonism; the latter allows us to discover our versatility and to declare our difference on our own terms.

ANTAGONISM

If every antagonism carries within itself the terms of its own contradiction, what do we feminists stand to gain by adopting a binary style of thinking that blindly discredits and generalizes? How could we possibly think that, where a misogynist antagonism has succeeded in keeping women apart from their own identity and integrity, a feminist antagonism would be able to bring us any nearer? My own answer to this question is that, insofar as

---

5. The standard dictionary of the French language, roughly equivalent to Webster's.

every oppositional process generates a justifying and/or accusing equivalent, such a process also creates a *narrative*.

'The form of narrative,' writes Roland Barthes, 'is essentially marked by two powers: that of extending its signs through the whole of the story, and that of inserting unforeseeable developements within these distortions.'[6]

Thus relations of opposition, by intensifying through mutual tension the dimensions of 'women's folly' and 'men's reasons,' for example, or, conversely, men's violence versus women's tenderness, open up the space of a semantic virtuality in the narrative we are creating that provides an opportunity for a referential anchor other than the one that until now has diverted our attention and thereby suspended our power of *judgment*. In fact, if it weren't for what this subjective (diaries, biographies, letters) and novelistic narration of our lives exposes to our consciousness, we would have no other alternative, for lack of any other perspective, than to debate amongst ourselves using the contradictory and hierarchical binaries that the male imaginary constructs.

In short, we can say that by finding its resolution in narrative, antagonistic tension enables us to glimpse the polysemic images from which the breadth of our options and our presence of mind in the body of language can arise.

CONCENTRATION

For our thought to be able to attentively listen to the narrative we carry within us, and for us to understand all the existential ramifications and ontological import of such a narrative, we have to focus our subject of interest and identification in such a way that we create an image that makes ONE [UNE] of us. We have to bring into focus the double image of the woman and the feminist, the blurry form, at once near and faraway, that speaks its presence within us; to bring into focus: to make our pathos/logical presence something real, i.e., to make visible the logic of our passion and accept our deviation from the patriarchal norm until it is nothing more than a tiny insignificant point, a tiny scar on the species' back.

---

6. Barthes, Roland. *Poétique du récit*. Paris: Seuil, Collection Points, 1977. 46.

Concentration allows us to bring together our mental and our affective faculties. It is the synchrony of energy and desire. It is a privileged moment in which knowledge, intentionality, and inner conviction meet.

The Latin word *focus* is the root of three different words in French: foyer, fire, and focal. The first has to do with a place, the second with a form of energy, the third with optics. So one could say that the place from which one looks out (distance), the intensity with which one apprehends the object (speed), and the perspective from which one goes toward the object (goal) all influence the act of focusing itself.

Yet, separated from ourselves, from other women, from our own history by men and their institutions, at the same time joined to men by heterosexuality and its institutions, from what position, what base, can feminist consciousness situate its gaze? What sort of distance does feminist consciousness have to overcome in order to draw close to women, what sort of energy does it have at its disposal, and what kinds of interference does it run up against?

It is obvious, for example, that lesbian desire syncs distance, energy, and motivation into a single reality that literally brings image and presence into immediate focus. One can't overestimate the extent to which sexual desire intensifies energy, attraction, and motivation. But since among lesbians it is the principle of pleasure *itself* that allows them to focus and to fix their attention on women, must one then conclude that in female heterosexuality the same principle leads to the splitting apart of image and presence, rendering distant the subject of interest, identification, and desire? Must one call this a context of distractibility that blurs the gaze, suspends thinking, and elicits melancholia?

But what is actually at stake here is not so much what one has to reflect on but what one has to be in order to reflect upon oneself. For since it's a question of being, all women have to be able to set aside the male gaze, whether this appears in an approving or a disapproving form. Without this ability to set it aside, there is only distraction, that is, the semantic event that either painfully divides or (g)ratifies (being) 'right.' In both of these cases, concentration has been lost or a semantic spark has been extinguished that could have kept our attention focused on the immanent and virtual feminine, that is, on the spiral curves of the heavy and aerial bodies which are ours the moment we commit ourselves to the imagistic space of the self and its propositions.

This effort of concentration is particularly required of us because every setting is a patriarchal one: institutions, language, customs, and traditions. Everything that creates meaning around us either effaces our presence or subordinates it to a primary identity, cause, entity: be it the heterosexual couple, the family, the nation, one's race, one's social class, even one's professional position. The phallocentric crime of minoritizing and marginalizing women from reality or of enclosing them within a masculinized humanity results in the fact that in 'that situation' our thoughts are constantly displaced and dubbed over.[7] And even if we do manage to find the right tone when speaking about the locus of feminist consciousness, our voice is still vulnerable to being doubled by an effeminate voice that alters its rhythm and its relevance.

Concentration is essential to the emergence of our plural singularity, and to the way in which we will be able to give shape (thought) and manner (ethics) to our convictions and thus far unspeakable intuitions. Concentration is initiation into a mode of thinking that would take us away from the binary and linear modes of masculine logic. Concentration is a challenge calling us to the creation of entirely new metaphors.

Overall, while reasons and motives are what organize our motivation (movement), and duality and antagonism are what generate our rich

---

7. One would think that our gestures of resistance and liberation would be able to garner the same sympathy that any other group working toward its emancipation and dignity receives. However, this is not the case because from the perspective of patriarchal society, women do not constitute a *minority* whose sufferings one could circumscribe within a political-historical chronology; they do not make up a *nation* in danger of disappearance or extermination on whose behalf one could be outraged and whose eventual loss one could lament; they do not constitute a homogeneous economic class that could go after specific political and economic aspirations; nor do they form a *race*, for the uterus is not a distinctive racial characteristic. Even though such analogies might seem valid on the surface, none of them really apply. Indeed, what our own struggle produces is essentially *movement*, in other words, 'a change of position in space through time, in terms of a system of reference.' But since this system of reference is based on the power/domination value, we are constantly forced to work in a state of emergency: to save democracy, to fight racism, to defend the rights of minorities, etc. In this way it becomes extremely difficult for us to focus our attention, since our own subject of interest is subordinated to emergencies.

narrative (our history, analysis, and telling of events), concentration is what produces the presence, meaning, and image of ontological and poetic emergence.

By way of a conclusion, I will say that if the feminist struggle forces us to think up strategies and to confront the weight of the real (organization, action, negotiation), feminist consciousness, for its part, requires a continual movement toward the unknown [vers de l'inconnue]. It binds us creatively to the *essential* [*L'essentielle* and, like writing, demands that we relentlessly face the inner necessity that compels us to exorcise our nightmares, sketch out dreams and utopias, add colour and meaning to the craziest angles of desire, weave bonds out of language so strong and durable that sometimes we don't dare to move for fear and for joy.

It is through feminist consciousness that a *moral* suffering enters our lives like a painful rite of passage. It is frightening and exhausting. Yet it is also through feminist consciousness that the creative dimension of our lives, their meaning and dignity, can begin: for as soon as it breaks the sound barrier of patriarchy, feminist consciousness finds itself relentlessly on the side of creation.

La Théorie, un dimanche
1988, tr. 2013

SALON:
CATHERINE MAVRIKAKIS TALKS WITH
NICOLE BROSSARD AND NATHANAËL

tr. Katia Grubisic

NATHANAËL: Listen, for me, the question of community, the very word *community* ... I'm a bit reluctant about it, even though I threw myself into things in the nineties. But for me it's really something I'm more wary of than I try to approach. I really like Derrida's idea of *esseulement* – that is, there are encounters, and friendship, yet the idea of being part of a group is often defined in homogeneous terms, which makes me uncomfortable. It's clear that the choices I have made have often been choices of departure. There have been many traversals, I've left many places, and it wasn't to go looking for something necessarily outside of writing, but it's not ...

CATHERINE MAVRIKAKIS: Yes, I agree, but you also have a lot of friends who are writers.

N: Yes, yes.

CM: But those are just friendships?

N: More so, yes. As far as I'm concerned, the idea of community can be defined in different ways, I know, but for me it's a rather homogeneous thing, and it can be defined otherwise, but it's really in relation – it's in the encounters, exchanges – but for me it takes place one on one. That's why I like the word *esseulement*, aloneness. I like it because it acknowledges a state of solitude, which, for me at least, must be borne in order for me to be able to do my work. I find it creates a terrible sense of dislocation to find oneself ... First to go from a text to speaking, and in addition to solitude, to a verbalized relationship with the world. I find it very trying, very demanding. So encounters like this require a lot of me, even if I find it important, I do agree with Nicole ...

CM: You find it draining, that's what you're saying?

N: It's very demanding, yes, but I also do it far less often.

NICOLE BROSSARD: As for me, I've played basketball and tennis, happily, and handball too …

[*Laughter.*]

NB: But what I wanted to say, too, is that there are also historical moments that depend not only on our relationship to writing. In any case, you're always alone in the writing. When I was twenty years old and I started publishing, there was an absolutely boundless enthusiasm, and a great deal of turbulence in Québec society. It was so rich and so full of promise – the meetings we had, whether at *La Barre du jour* or with other groups, which were more about politics than literature. It was always important. As for working with other women, there too … It's about sharing, but there is also the project. I've always had projects. Whether it was the *Anthologie de la poésie des femmes* with Lisette Girouard, or with others, authors and actresses in *Le Nef des sorcières*, or with Luce Guilbeault in the film *Some American Feminists*. It was intense, and I felt good in those kinds of exchanges. Of course, when you write, you're alone, no one can do it for you. Friendships can be stimulating, as you said earlier. But today things have changed. We're much more individualistic. I would even say that there's a different atmosphere between encounters among poets (poetry festivals, readings) and the literary festivals attended mostly by novelists. Basically, they sell books, while poets sell very few. [*Laughter.*] One thing that has always fascinated me is that between poets, while some differences remain, aspects of age and social class disappear in light of what is essential – of being, of each singularity. Which is incredibly beautiful, and I believe it happens more easily among poets.

CM: Following up on what Nicole just said, I want to throw out a question that's a little tongue-in-cheek: why is poetry the superior form of literature?

I don't entirely disagree, but I want to ask you why. What is it to be a poet? What is it you have that I don't?

[*Laughter.*]

NB: The French poet René Daumal said, a novel says something while poetry does something. The whole posture is different, certainly in terms of language, and of the tension in language. Because a writer can shift from one genre to another, we can also ask the question of prose poems, for instance. Why not write a poem, why write a prose poem? It's because prose balances the peaks of tension, whereas the poem always exists because of the tension in meaning, and therefore in grammar, syntax, and rhetoric. It's always in the present when you're reading it, and when you write it. Even if it takes six months to work on a poem, you're always in the present, you are always in the moment. When you read it, too. And you can't negotiate with a poem, you can't say, *I love this part of the poem*. You love it, or you don't. A novel – you can like parts of a novel, while other parts you don't like so much, but it's negotiable. And it has to do with the span of the text, obviously, its length. It really is a different way to relate to the world, to look at the world, and of course another way to live in the present, to experience one's own present moment in the language, I think.

CM: [*to Nathanaël*] Would you like to speak to that?

N: Yes, well, I think I conceive of it a little differently, and I don't agree with what I myself might believe, which is to say I wouldn't put poetry at the top necessarily, and before even addressing that question I'd ask myself what poetry even is. Already, with poetry – if that's the term that must be retained, and I'm not … Personally, I've been distancing myself from it for several years now. I wouldn't limit it to a particular genre. The poetic, if perhaps that term could be employed, crosses multiple genres.

CM: One might ask, Nicole, whether you've actually written novels at all, whether you haven't just written poetry.

N: But it could also be said that there's a lot of writing that claims to be poetry but is not at all. In fact, you don't have to look very far. Whether in Canada, Québec, or the United States, there's a whole machine that produces poetry that has nothing to do with poetry. We could talk about that for hours. And so what interests me much more personally in my writing and in my reading ... I read more philosophy than – and here again, it's 'philosophy' – than I do poetry. I don't distinguish between genres, and yet what interests me are the slippages, where genres become dislocated and don't resemble themselves. Because as soon as a text compels me, it's because it's already exceeded the limits of its genre. From that moment on, the generic distinctions, for me, are no longer really of much interest, especially since they increasingly serve the corporate university machine, of creative-writing MFAS and the like, which for me have nothing to do with literature. They have nothing to do with thought, and everything to do with questions of commerce – marketing this or that, capitalizing on books, which is of no interest to me, and is completely beyond me.

NB: If I can be even more outdated ... Large multinationals are using what is called storytelling. It's a mechanism. Corporations used to have a logo, but now they have to have a story, so they need a narrator for their story to be able to sell their products. We're talking about people, but we're also talking about creativity. Technology has made it a commercial activity, a commercial must. I don't know if you've noticed, but for some time now, everyone has to be very creative, and so people are creative. Creativity has become another consumer product. This goes even further, but it's the world we live in. There's been a shift. An activity that is extremely rich in spirit, thought, and emotion has shifted and is now increasingly placed in the service of big multinationals, or of mercantile excess, of an ever-increasing commercial meanness. It's hard to accept, or believe, but that's how it is. To come back to poetry, I've always said that what makes a novel lift us up and carry us away is its poetic dimension. Sometimes it can be excessive. But if you think for instance of Pascal Quignard, his work is at once narrative, philosophical, and has a great poetic charge, because he operates with symbolically charged words and knows how to move them about, either in the narrative or in philosophical reflection. So, sure, a bad collection of poems is quickly spotted. But the fact remains that these are postures. They are postures, and sometimes our postures are also in flux, because we need both the storyteller – For example, if we look at women's writing, the narrative aspect was so important. They had to be fearless, and to have gone through a poetic turn, but they also needed to tell, to speak. There is a practice of prose poetry among women. I'm thinking in particular of France Théoret, who came of age around 1975 to 1980, and developed that feminist consciousness, which maybe required being in both postures, in fact, at that time. Because the world had to be remade.

CM: So it's not only about poetry versus narrative.

NB: You write poetry because it's your way of being in the world in language. Poetry isn't written against narrative. I may have had a few moments here and there when I said horrible things about the novel, but it was surely very unfair.

CM: I think that poetry – I'm not going to defend the novel, because I don't really care. [*Laughter.*] The novel doesn't need to be defended right now; the novel is doing very well on its own. Even if it's struggling, I mean, it doesn't need to be defended. Forgive me, as an outsider, but what always makes me smile a little is the relationship to poetry. I'm teasing again, but it can be a bit sectarian, no? It is because poets have a very sectarian relationship with literature? And among them there are those who write poetry, those who don't. You said earlier that there are bad poets, or poets who are not poets. I'm teasing, but from the outside, anthropologically, there's something about that. Yet at the same time, as someone who loves literature, it's true that there's a kind of high admiration for poetry. I think poetry somehow compels a kind of worship.

[...]

N: The identity politics of the 1990s as I experienced them were very fragmentary. And that's precisely where my mistrust of this idea of community comes from. I may well have participated in the demonstrations, et cetera, but I found it to be very divisive. Nor am I convinced that where we are now in the discourse, which is heavily influenced by post-structuralism, is necessarily – It's a topic that's always hard to situate. I don't know if that's the answer either.

NB: It's very interesting because I'm trying to understand where you're coming from, if you're speaking as a writer, if you're speaking as someone who presents as a woman, even if you identify as androgynous or whatever. But it's about where we're speaking from. I've always said that, when the feminist or the lesbian lacked for words, often it was the poet who could find them. That is certain. But it's an enigma, a problematic question. In *La Lettre aérienne* [*The Aerial Letter*], I was trying to understand why women always move away from other women. One says, a woman is a woman – a tautology, meaningless. Another says, a woman is a man – which of course is a nonsense or a contradiction pointing in the direction of a double bind. Another one says, it's simple, I am woman, and so we fall back onto individualism, and once again we're separating women from each other, which means that solidarity is difficult to achieve.

CM: Or like saying a lesbian isn't a woman: it separates straight women from lesbians.

NB: There's been that, too, yes. I've always said that I work in the *polis*, the city of men where laws are made, indeed the city where the laws that control us are written. I want to remain in the city to erase, change, or renew the law. Symbolically, that's what I've always said. I couldn't just withdraw to the island.

CM: So we have the poet, who may be able to speak otherwise. But there's an aspect of citizenry with you, of civic engagement.

NB: Of a poet who is very engaged publicly. I've always said that I write on two pages: one page is the page of desire and utopia, and another page, which describes what's happening in the status of women, among women. Everything that has been stolen from women since the beginning of history. For me these two pages operate at the same time. That is where the expression 'the thought of emotion and the emotion of thought' comes from – that is, I can't think without emotion and I can't have only emotions. I wouldn't be comfortable. This whole question of the feminine is very complex, but one thing is certain: the feminine is debased and it is marginalized. In all the changes we've seen regarding women and violence against women, society seems to need to neutralize or masculinize (that is, humanize) the victim in order to to make a change. For example, say that women are victims of rape. Oh yes, but there are men too, there are children who are victims of sexual assault. And once you can neutralize or masculinize the victim, then society says, ah, I understand. So in a way feminism is still condemned to being marginalized rather than universalized. When it comes to something that applies only to women, society pretends it's harder or impossible to understand it, or that it's a false problem. Therefore it either dismisses or marginalizes it.

[...]

NB: I recently met a young, thirty-five-year-old actress. Her anger was immense. We were saying the same thing thirty years ago, but her anger was immense.

N: I wanted to say something maybe a little bit provocative or not very interesting, but I think it's possible to be disgusted with both regimes – the masculine regime ... – or else recognize how entangled the two are, because –

NB: Excuse me ... Regime?

N: The regimes, yes.

NB: Two regimes?

N: It could be up for debate. You could say there's only one, or you could say there are several. I think. I'm not going to dispute the fact that society is structured as a patriarchy. But I believe that in spite of all efforts, in spite of the efforts that have been made, I believe that as soon as an ideology … That's what scares me, ideology. And in fact, for me, the city [*cité*] refers to the public square, and the public square is foremost – even if it wants to be the locus of democracy – it is also the space of the gallows. That, too, has to be taken into account. And whoever holds the power – As soon as feminism became institutionalized, as soon as queer studies became institutionalized, as soon as postcolonial studies became institutionalized, that is, found a legitimate place within universities, all of them only propagated the same power structures of oppression, suppression, et cetera. I think there is … Well, it's the human, whatever it is, that is meant to be addressed. And I'm never going to question what you're saying in regard to politics, about the city, about the public square and so on, but I think it's a problem of – Honestly, for me, it's a problem of consensus. And I fear consensus. Because in that moment somehow there is always a suppression [*extinction*] of voices.

NB: Obviously. Now you're talking like a writer. I think that's what makes us speak in an individual, singular way. It's absolutely normal. I'm not a writer so that I can accept the voice of the majority. There is still a marginality that I cultivate. Because you can be marginalized, but you can cultivate your marginality and learn a lot from that marginality. There have been three elements in feminism. There was the gathering together of women and of their personal, individual experiences, which made it possible, on the basis of these experiences, to understand a system, a part of the system. There were political positions, because once we understood a phenomenon, we wanted to take action. And of course there are words, there are statements that are not at all pretty but that were politically effective. There is also philosophical thought, reflection, by women, with a feminist awareness, on the imaginary, on the symbolic, on language, and so on, and that's another thing. I understand very well what you mean: yes, but that is the human condition, which through daily simplification of thought reduces complexity to mediocrity.

CM: It comes down to the question of whether poetry and politics – or rather, poetry and the political – can align.

N: They have to, necessarily, since the poets have been expelled from the city.

NB: Well, the *I* and the *we* sometimes meet. In Quebec it was through the question of nationalism: Gaston Miron, Jacques Brault, Michèle Lalonde, Paul Chamberland. The *I* and the *we* crossed paths again through the question of feminism. When a woman said *I* everyone heard *we*, and when a woman said *we* everyone heard *I*. And the same thing was happening with 'colonized' Quebecers. It happened with Senghor, it happened with Depestres. It happened with Miron, of course. It seldom happens in history in general, this encounter of the *I* and the *we*, but it's always implicit, in some way, because when we write poetry, a part of the *I* is at work, it weeps, but there's a part of us as humans that is weeping or that is luminous. So there is always in our writing a part that belongs only to us. It's not the most interesting, it's how the sharing takes place, reaching to the core of each being. That's where it's shared, where it can be shared. And the language is made to learn to share as well. Or, how can I say, we write in order to be able to share. I was going to say to convey experience, but that's not it at all, it's sharing, because even we don't understand it. The sharing happens because of the ambiguity of language. And maybe that's the beauty of language, that it always leaves a space for translation, for interpretation. It's never closed. No word is closed. All words have at least two, three meanings, and often five or six; they have a root, etymology, so there's always a possible opening with every word, every sentence.

CM: [*to Nathanaël*] For you, in regard to aloneness [*esseulement*], is there something political, in your work? How do you understand your – I don't want to say your public participation, because that's not at all what you're trying to do, but how do you, do you ... Maybe I've misunderstood, but you don't see what you do as withdrawing completely from the world, do you, even if the work of actually withdrawing is warranted. Do you still see the effect of what you do? Does some part of you hope that it's also a political stance? Or maybe the better term for you would be 'ethical'?

N: Well, there's an accountability in regard to something I despise, actually, in fact that's a major contradiction, I won't hide it. I don't think … There is simultaneously a reach [*élan*] and a retreat. It's not easy. But I feel summoned – there, it's a word – I mean … It's very banal, it's not especially elevated, but it's possible in fact that I may be in a period of exaggerated reticence, it's possible.

NB: We might ask you the question too, Catherine. That sense of accountability in writing. You've written about people who are sentenced to death, you've gotten involved on several levels. May we ask you the question?

CM: I have a very romantic vision of writing, I think. Writing for me must have some sovereignty. It is possible for me to write – it's very different, but it would be possible to write a totally violent, politically disgusting text that would be literally interesting for me. I believe in that, I really believe in the sovereignty of literature. I don't think ideology should come first, not that that's what you're doing at all, that's not what I'm saying, but for me the aesthetic is more important than the political. Which isn't to say that an aesthetic project is not a political project. I was thinking of a surprising book – a lot of people didn't like it – I was thinking about Yves Gosselin's *Discours de réception*. Maybe you read it: Germany has won the war and it's Céline's speech to the academy. I had a colleague who wrote extremely critically about this man, while I wanted to defend him, on behalf of – Because his text isn't bad, first of all, and because it's an interesting text. Here's someone who is well placed, but who is utterly unknown in Quebec, even if he's from Quebec. I don't know why his voice has been stifled, but, I mean, literature has the right to do that. Céline remains a great writer for me, I can't think otherwise. But literature can do that. So there's an ethical aspect I don't like about Céline, but maybe what I like about my favourite writers is when the aesthetic allows me, albeit perhaps indirectly, to think about the political. But of a political aspect that isn't merely … The effects of literature on me aren't always immediate. It's not always in line with the times. I think literature is always anachronistic, despite everything, even during an era when we were the most closely aligned with time. I think it is always anachronistic because otherwise it's always ahead or behind; it can't be just in time – because that is discourse without literature. That's why I see literature as being able to navigate the political without presenting the political, creating gaps.

NB: Able to navigate meaning, to make it tremble ...

CM: Exactly. So if I'm doing something interesting when I talk about death row inmates, it's not by talking about death row inmates, it's by making God talk. Trying to find a voice for God, because I'm ridiculing God. It wasn't so much that the theme is interesting, but the work I was able to do around how to present God's narrative voice. That was it. And in poetry I think it's the same, because poetry isn't necessarily political right away. It is above all an aesthetic, it's an art. It's a practice too. That's why I was saying that I have a rather romantic vision of art.

NB: It can't do any harm!

[*Laughter.*]

CM: I see art as being capable of great things. Whereas the world is not capable – I don't believe that the rest of the world is capable of great things. And I've come from teaching. In teaching, I think it's the books that count: there are only the books. People have to – We could just pass along the books, impart the books. I think that's it.

2014, tr. 2019

LOREM IPSUM

From *Luminous Ink: Writers on Writing in Canada*

tr. Susanne de Lotbinière-Harwood

Poetry is the formal and semantic intuition our desires put forward even though unaware of their own laws.

Poetry is the highest probability of desire and thought together in synchronized time.

'Political language is destined to make lies sound truthful and murder respectable, and to give an appearance of solidity to pure wind.' – George Orwell, *Politics and the English Language*, 1946

SOMETHINGHAPPENEDTHATTRANSFORMEDOURSAPI-
ENCEOURREVELRYOURDREAMSWEOFTENFINDOUR-
SELVESONTHEFOLLOWINGDAYSHAPEDBYTHEARTI-
CLESWEREADTHEPREVIOUSDAYWHICHCOMEBACKA-
TUSWITHTHESMELLOFCOFFEEANDFRESHNEWSPAPERS-
THESENTENCESWEREMOREANDMORESIMPLEASSIM-
PLEASEACHONEOFTHECAMERASSPYINGONOURLIVESIN-
PUBLICPLACESANDSOMETIMESININTIMATEONESTHE-
SENTENCESBECAMEMOREANDMORESIMPLEWITHACORE-
CALLEDSAPIENCESAPIENCE

Whether we like it or not, the writer is a symbol of humanism regardless if he or she is rebellious, transgressive, or immoral. Eventually, because of the freedom available in democracy, the writer is expected to fulfill her/his obligation to remember (*devoir de mémoire*), and ethical and linguistic obligations as well as the dual solidarities, identity-based and universal. Theoretically, the writer is a symbol of humanity because, from the inside and from the remotest locus of the species, he/she seeks the laws that govern emotion, beauty, evil – meaning to everything exploding before our eyes, inside our chests. To seek from the inside, to listen to the resonant flow of conscience. To introduce into language leaps and bounds and somersaults of joy and astonishment, an abyss of fear and dread, to translate the infinitesimal slowness of the desire scrutinizing the enigma at the very core of this desire.

A writer is always of his [sic] time, wrote Gertrude Stein. How could it be otherwise? As for me, I have always wanted to be of my time, meaning that very early on I assigned myself the task of understanding the world I live in. What are the values, the standards, the social and literary currents that have transited through me? How have they contributed to my existential stance, the one hiding within the body and its many folds of meaning, in the gestures, sentences, and thought processes that make one gloomy or happy? And how did this stance generate my behaviour, attitude, and narrative logic regarding writing, language, and literature?

Only over time does it become possible to grasp the facts and recurring evidence of our existential postures and attitudes, of our formal behaviour in language, and of the aesthetic and ethical consequences rendered toward writing itself as well as toward language and others.

Some writers write with the raw material of their childhood, of their singularity, others with their thoughts and questions. Others accuse or marvel, while others write their inner life; that is to say, with a narrative and emotion that keeps them circulating from inside to outside and vice versa, so their thinking becomes perpetual movement, a vertiginous vividness immersed in the subterraneanvastness of language. This being said, one must not confuse a private life with an inner life.

The present, I must discuss the present. I have long said: I am a woman of the present, meaning by this that the present makes me happy and/or stimulates my clarity of vision. The present as a source of well-being that brings the joy of extreme presence. And now, so very suddenly, after just a few decades into digital civilization, the present is deleting all prior eras to become, all on its own, a bottomless pit of the ephemeral, of consumerism, an invasive means of distraction. And yet the present is not ephemeral once it vibrates in language.

Now that the idea of present has set in. I can no longer dislodge it. I am the ambience of the text and of my own existence. Impossible to separate them. This atmosphere serves a single purpose: the vibrant spirited well-being of the present. Some welcome it without words, others require words that raise body temperature.

Yes, one must, beyond reality, risk one's own insertion into the vastness. You say it, you do it.

So, then, does consciousness really need our bodies? It no doubt circulates the same way as do cosmic waves, which now are easily captured. Therefore, how is it that the so highly knowledgeable consciousness of Europe has transformed into the chaos of war, of dull noises, and the ceaseless stridency of violence. In the night.

Can knowledge temporarily delay the repeated evacuation of our singularities by the ephemeral and thus save us from total amnesia, from that state of ethical and philosophical weightlessness that seems to be looming over us? Knowledge as an infinite resource, bruising and renewing the imaginary landscape and our abiding melancholy.

Yesterday, amid the cypress trees, beside a joyful little turquoise fountain, in the tranquility of the terrace at Casa de Velázquez in Madrid, I wrote. Writing fills me with a well-being I had almost forgotten. Or does living in the freedom of floating, astonishing, ingenious, and sensory thoughts also give life meaning? Between yesterday's writing of desire and today's controlled writing (whose processes of performance and consequently of marketing[1] are well known) lies a semantic and time-space zone that effectively throws me into a paradoxical criss-cross of ambivalent logics, ethical certainties, and fierceness which, although real, sensual, rebellious, and innovative, seem less and less viable semantically, whereas in times past, the heart and emotions, Eros and Thanatos, origins and memory, displayed our vulnerability as a species.

In the hallways of Casa de Velázquez that week there was an exhibition titled *Las maletas de Walter Benjamin.* The suitcase is us, inside-outside,

---

1. The vocabulary and referents concerning literary writing have been incorporated into neoliberalism: storytelling, fiction, morphing of the self, emotion, shifting of meaning for specific political or commercial goals.

content which is fragile or not, a heavy weight to carry; manuscripts, a survival instinct, or an urge to be elsewhere or for travel with dawns fragrant of lilies and lilac. Since the twentieth century, the sound of trains has resonated through our conscious minds, the noise of convoys in the suitcase, but also a surrender of the self, reaching the world's ends, a figure of speech that intersects with matter, metaphor, and virtuality, as if we were no longer going to die from having done it so often before. The suitcases made me think that women often must choose between the suitcase and the child.

Beginning in 2000, I often said that the world had changed. The leitmotif was still mysterious; it elicited questions, a veritable jolt of concern and of an excitement bearing lyricism. Then the world kept on changing, but with the difference that it started to seep into me, to fragment my use of time, to disjoint and unravel my gestures, my projects, to change me into a drone soaring above knowledge, history, my feelings and emotions. Little by little the relationship to time, to space, but also to others, to the idea of humanity, was transforming as if we were soon going to have to choose between our old humanism (grow its secret gardens of emotions, beliefs, compassion, solidarities with the species) and the concept of post-humanity (grow its algorithms without shifting moods, intelligence nonetheless remaining attentive to the *last call* for freedom, justice, and democracy); intelligence casually recycling fire bombs of lies and *fake news*.

In every century, women, be they docile or not, have been massacred simply for being women. This was rarely mentioned in a twentieth century plugged into death, nihilism, and destruction. In any case, for men and women entering life in 1943 and who would begin to discover literature, the values of rebellion, transgression, and deconstruction prevailed, from Tristan Tzara to Alfred Jarry to Emil Cioran to Samuel Beckett to Jean-Paul Sartre, then differently with Gaston Miron, Léopold Sédar Senghor, James Baldwin, Aimé Césaire, then differently again with Virginia Woolf, Monique Wittig, Mary Daly, Adrienne Rich, and Louky Bersianik.

Two world wars and a holocaust, ongoing misogyny and sexism at the heart of Western civilization have made humanity repellent and humanism deceptive. Technology and the anthropological knowledge we have of our species have done the rest. From now on we can get an aerial view of our species in most of its behaviours. Just like a good designer transforms the 'table' principle, or the 'chair' principle, into an aesthetic object, we will soon be in a position to design the basic materials of our inner self far beyond the idea of fiction. What I mean is that, conceptually speaking, we will be able to, and desire to, not so much express ourselves in order to discover our self, but more so that our self will be sufficiently aroused by the idea of an 'I' that it will create itself as a work of art.

In the second half of the twentieth century, many of us in Quebec culti-vated and retained a form of hopefulness linked to a search for identity, renewal, and an ownership of speech, thus giving the impression that we took root at the same time as tenderness at the heart of the North American landscape, of the French language and of modernity. But just as suddenly came the disenchantment of the Western world absorbing memory's slow-moving time at a speed never before known. Today quan-tic, biogenetic, and cybernetic mysteries juggle with the shadows and smiles of our species which, nonetheless, continues to love salt, apples, turmeric, the sea, caresses. A species which, in any language capable of philosophy and theology, crosses out, deletes, still does not love women. And yet I am a woman.

I am constantly redesigning my life, I mean the life of others, giving me the impression of inventing mine. A non-invented life does not exist, cannot belong to our species. Our happiness comes from knowing how to invent, to move here and there or someplace else where freedom flows into the pleasure of solving enigmas. Each one of us is free to pretend we live in the space reserved for us without complaining or in a different manner. The idea is to maintain our status as a free person for as long as possible.

Every writer inserts their presence, an imprint, on the world. Be it insignifi-cant or significant. How do we insert our significant presence in the world now; how do we allow our gaze to convey the excitement of extinction that dwells in our eyes?

Desiring, imagining for some time to create sentences, narratives, enthusiasms that temporarily unburden the human condition. How, with our angel wings, do we thread our way through the wounds, circulate between the stories, the deaths, and our skilful sentences? How to express that we are breathing and that this is something simple?

How to hide pain behind a story, how to use it to imagine, to walk around, in a living body, in smart cities, to play at 'sowing a vital spark' some small seed of happiness throughout the existential labyrinth. Must we hide pain to avoid thinking about it? Certainly we can conceal it in a tree trunk, in the sand, under a pebble, at the edge of a cliff, under our tongue, or inside our chest. This is more complicated in literature, where it must be downplayed in order to retain only the viable part, for our humanity will agree to rejoice only once a certain pain threshold is reached. Below that point, it will just ruminate.

The viable part of our humanity hides somewhere in the cosmos and in our genes, in some village along the St. Lawrence River, in a tiny microphone pinned to the wool sweater of a woman who is recording a poem in front of the little Koksoak River. In the brief description of an artificial palm tree behind a hotel on Okanagan Lake, on the dark, vibrant surface of the fourteen paintings in the Rothko Chapel, in the drawer of a bedside table in a Tadoussac hospital, in a reply from a Chekhov play, in the belly of a woman, in the grand staircase of the Palazzo Grassi, in the abusive use of the word *absolute*, between my lips about to kiss you, in the ongoing poem.

Will there come a day when algorithms are able to act as meaning and emotion, to design sentences so perfect that all of art will simultaneously take the shape of desire and enchantment? Maybe, but then why all these serene scars in our thoughts: *dawn's rosy fingers, the rapture of deep middays, the cinco de la tarde, night and its glimmerings of syntax.*[2]

Oriane Ossilk tends to worry about her lack of sensitivity. She envies Hilda Sogol's ability to live with disturbing images which she seems to naturally cultivate like the one of her son laid out, chest offered up on an operation table, awaiting the scalpel and the oblivion that will shift

---

2 . Homer, Anna de Noailles, Federico Garcia Lorca. Translations by SLH.

him to an elsewhere with a thousand names, surfaces and myriad planets. **For Hilda, death is at work everywhere, she sees it or she doesn't, but forever seeks to understand how the darkness, how it inserts itself into light so far as to aspirate its every manifestation, infinite comings, infinite goings, which the invisible and the visible map inside her without her awareness.**

Therefore writing, therefore I should say 'Why' and 'How I do it.' I have done it, I can do it again, I can even summarize: extreme present, pleasure of language, and progressive immersion into complexity, the enigma of presence. That pleasure will admit certain constraints but will not tolerate any coercion. It is because we go to the far reaches of ourselves that we are able to throw ourselves into the void.

My notes, your thoughts: LIPSING.

Basically I know nothing about my ties to others. I have never investigated their solidity or their fragility. I know or don't. One thing is certain, I confuse my relationship to others with prose and narrative. I never really talk about other people, only about what can arise from the simple fact of being together. I do not seek out encounters with others, and so there is little left for me to describe, understand, interpret, regarding their presence. Nonetheless, I know that every gesture, word, or silence counts as do the landscapes where we come together, the time of day, the light, the noise, have meaning and occasionally this gratifies me. Wounds, pain, misfortunes, and little joys make sense only once organized in language, otherwise I die.

I don't want to be me in a text. I want only the essential of what can make me say 'I'; and to live from this by combining grammar, punctuation, breathing words, and a point of view on the world. Dust, resplendence, etymology, verb. Then redesign the sentences with the emphasis that writing is the most refined of the technologies that concern our species, a form of *jouissance*, body and soul. Grant me one more minute in the body's logic. Grant me one more moment in the logic of happiness.[3]

---

3. Thinking of this quote from Albert Camus: 'Happiness is generous. It does not feed on destruction.' Caligula. Translation by SLH.

Something happened that transformed our sapience, our revelry, our dreams. We often find ourselves on the following day shaped by the articles we read the previous day, which come back at us with the smell of coffee and fresh newspapers. The sentences became more and more simple, *so sorry I forgot to talk about my self,* as simple as each one of the cameras spying on our lives in public places and at times in intimate ones. The sentences became more and more simple, with a core called sapiencesapience.

2018, tr. 2018

AND SUDDENLY I FIND MYSELF REMAKING THE WORLD

tr. Oana Avasilichioaei and Rhonda Mullins

(tr. Oana Avasilichioaei)

Why is translation a subject unlike any other? Why is it so conducive to a genuine fervour of meaning that can sometimes turn argumentative, as though every word contained a life challenge, a miniature vision of the world within it?

I am not a translator. True, I have occasionally translated a few Irish, American, and Canadian poems for special issues of literary magazines. Until very recently, I didn't understand why I was asked whether I translated my own poems, as though this implied an insult: are there no translators interested in your writing? Or even: a good, humble poet does not translate their own work. In fact, my relationship to translation has developed to a large extent through fiction and through my fascination with this activity, which, in my opinion, entails the same emotional and associative circuits as writing. The considerations I project onto translation stem from thinking about literary creation.

There are certainly many ways of approaching translation: for me, it involves examining the gears of words, thoughts, images, and meanings and immersing myself in the dreamy meanderings generated by any literary reading. It also involves tackling the cultural contours of language, identity, and a certain kind of thinking practice. Simply put, it involves valorizing the constant virtual state in which we live, a state that increases the possibilities of approaching life with intelligence and wonder. Wonder not because life is necessarily wonderful, but because life is complex, diverse, and mysterious enough for us to develop an attraction for it that is something other than instinctual.

Every translation of a literary work is a bulwark against ethnocentrism. Like writing, translation protects humanity from its own erosion since it guarantees circulation, dialogue, and regeneration across space and time.

Every translation is also a potential tease, arousing desire, memory, comparison, and imagination.

Translating is a privileged means of entering the universe of one's own language and being able to explore in all directions by traversing the varied terrain of its origins and major historical narratives: its regionalisms, modernity, timidity, arrogance, rage, and always, always the gleam of a thousand small inventions that, whether they are joyful or cynical, give one pleasure.

Translation is a reading practice taken to the extreme, a practice that, let's be frank, has real power to stimulate and revitalize our inner life. Every translator is a reader first and foremost – that is, someone who takes into their inner world another world along with its mysteries, ambiguities, dazzlement, and danger zones.

RESPONSIBILITY

'Difficile, en effet, la traduction. On ne sait pas si on a le droit d'imaginer.'   – Yves Bonnefoy

Responsibility is paramount in any field when it comes to producing, constructing, and transmitting meaning. Meaning is by definition ambiguous. It is often the outcome of some misunderstanding, an accident along the way, ignorance. Meaning is also the living core of desire. Desire revitalizes it, betrays it, clarifies it. Life naturally flows in all directions, and it is only by exercising willpower and making crucial decisions that we can channel our understanding of the complexity and virtual energy charge that meaning contains.

The meaning of responsibility varies according to the time period, function, ethics, and cultural environment that put things in a specific light – let us say the light of the era. Is responsibility in translation elastic? Is translation free of censorship? Is it likely to uphold ethical standards at the expense of the text? Can a conventional translator raise the level of an ordinary text? How original can one get before translation becomes transcreation? At what level of conformity does translation lose its vivacity, its energy?

> 'Je conçois les textes traduits en langue française comme faisant partie de la matière intrinsèque de la création en langue française parce que le savoir-être de l'autre, dans son paysage linguistique, ses mises en scène existentielles et cognitives, excite mon propre savoir-être lorsqu'il s'immisce dans le centre blanc de ma langue. De cela je ne peux me passer.'
>
> in *Poésies de langue française, 144 poètes d'aujourd'hui* (Paris: Seghers, 2008)

How can one know where innovation begins, where error slips in, where semantic banality infiltrates under the cover of otherwise perfectly adequate vocabulary?

A double personality of sorts: I read you in a foreign language; I will take you with me into my mother tongue. I is always an other in the act of becoming. What will I do with you once you have entered my universe? Will we go some of the way together? How far?

This leads me to say a few words about what I call the circles of intimacy present when working on a translation, before I delve into the question of translating poetry. An intimacy relative to our knowledge of the work, the author, their biography and idiosyncratic references. Also an intimacy relative to the aesthetic, identity, ideological, sexual, ethnic affinities. Of course, these affiliations don't have to be made explicit. Let us simply say that they often motivate the attraction to certain texts and the desire to translate them.

CIRCLES OF INTIMACY, AFFINITIES, AND COMFORT

Translation belongs not only to a linguistic space but also to an emotional one. Whoever translates stays very close or at moderate distance to or very far from the author and their universe. There are circles of proximity, let us say of affinity and comfort with the writing. Is a good translator one who can come close to the intimate ground zero? Does maximum proximity guarantee a successful translation? As we know, there are no rules. Does knowledge of the language, intuition, experience, a brief or long acquaintance with the work ensure a successful translation?

In speaking about these circles of intimacy, I am thinking of conversations I've had with a translator who, whenever she needed to find a

ML: Je peux vous reprocher ce qui existe dans votre livre.

LA: De quel droit?

ML: De vous lire me donne tous les droits.

LA: Mais, traductrice, vous n'en avez aucun. Vous avez choisi la tâche difficile de lire à rebours dans votre langue ce qui dans la mienne coule de source.

ML: Mais lorsque je vous lis, je vous lis dans votre langue.

LA: Comment pouvez-vous me comprendre si vous me lisez dans une langue et transposez simultanément dans une autre ce qui ne peut adéquatement trouver place en elle? Comment croire un instant que les paysages qui sont en vous n'effaceront pas les miens?

ML: Parce que les paysages vrais assouplissent en nous la langue, débordent le cadre de nos pensées. Se déposent en nous.

Dialogue entre la traductrice Maude Laures et l'auteure Laura Angstelle (fictives) dans *Le Désert mauve*, Montréal, Éditions de l'Hexagone, 1987; Montréal, Typo, 2010.

solution, knew where to look in my poetic universe and had in mind an idiosyncratic lexicon of the recurring themes in my writing. As she had thorough knowledge of my feminist trajectory and lesbian texts, she did not hesitate to use words that shifted the text into the realm of female love and solidarity as well as anything that could suggest a life force. Therefore, it was possible for her to delve more deeply into the circle of intimacy, in part due to her knowledge of my work, but also due to the personal commitment she had made to this work. Everyone knows what it means to commit to a text, a work, namely to dive into it as though it were a matter of life or death, a space so unsettling we can't tear ourselves away from it since it merges so intensely with our sense of reality and regenerates our intimate perception of it, our intuitive sense of true or false, and our intoxication with words. There is undoubtedly an entire world between reading the writer's thoughts and projecting oneself into them.

The encounter produced by an intense reading alters, confirms, regenerates how we see and feel reality. Certain attitudes and behaviours toward a text and its meaning reveal an attraction and intention, and sometimes an ethical stance. I have tried to identify a few:

- The non-approach: meaning as is
- The identity approach: desired meaning
- The permissive playful approach: ubique meaning
- The responsible interactive approach: reinvented meaning
- The free interactive approach: writing of rewriting

THE NON-APPROACH: MEANING AS IS

'La prose dit quelque chose, le poème nous fait quelque chose.'

– René Daumal

In an excellent essay by Maria Sierra Córdoba Serrano[1] on the Spanish translation of my novel *Baroque d'aube* (1995),[2] the author wonders why the book has not reached its natural feminist/ lesbian/avant-gardist audience, taking into account the Spanish reality of feminism. All she knows is that the book has been published by a major publishing house. She then examines the circumstances that led to the selection of the Spanish translator and discovers that the translator, as often happens, simply received a contract to translate a book whose author she didn't know, nor did she know her previous work or the context for the many questions and intentions that had fed the novel. Serrano comes to the conclusion that *Baroque d'aube* is adequately translated into Spanish, but that its energy and rebelliousness is in a way neutralized in the translation. The translator has conveyed meaning without holding the reader in a state of tension and alertness: the translation is impeccable but 'soulless,' devoid of knowing allusions or inventions. In short, a Teflon translation, in the sense that 'it doesn't stick.' Sometimes I think that the non-approach is the one most commonly taken in our social relationships, everyone keeping the essential to themselves or transforming the other's varied identity terrain into

---

1. Maria Sierra Córdoba Serrano, '*Baroque d'aube* traduit en Espagne: une "re-belle et infidèle"' ['*Baroque at Dawn* Translated in Spain: An Unfaithful Rebella'], *Le Québec traduit en Espagne: Analyse sociologique de l'exportation d'une culture périphérique* [*Quebec Translated in Spain: A Sociological Analysis of Exporting a Peripheral Culture*] (Ottawa: University of Ottawa Press, 2013).

2. Trans. by Patricia Claxton as *Baroque at Dawn* (Toronto: McClelland & Stewart, 1997).

cliché or prejudice and thus neutralizing the vibrant or beautiful fervour that can arise even in our briefest interactions.

THE IDENTITY APPROACH: DESIRED MEANING

Several times, women who are not professional translators have told me: 'Your book should circulate. It should be read by women in other languages.' This occurred with my first collection of feminist essays, *La Lettre aérienne*[3] (for the English translation), as well as with *Amantes*,[4] a collection of lesbian love poems that gave rise to an unauthorized translation in Italian. In both cases, the desire to disseminate specific content was the driving force behind the translation.

That said, I think that the same phenomenon of identifying with a work also affects criticism and publishers' manuscript choices. It comes down to the pleasure and emotion of recognizing the essential in itself, living with it, and then reintegrating this essence into a circuit of exchange and validation. True, the identity approach is more subtle and complex than the mere desire to disseminate a message. This approach consciously or unconsciously activates connections between the book and the reader, a reader interested in immersing themselves in a text, in a world word by word, knowing that something in this universe belongs to them, resembles them. It can be a country, a city, a key theme (grief, motherhood, melancholy); it can be a way of being, a certain perspective on the world. In these translations, there is a powerful encounter between the unspoken of the author and the unspoken of the translator, which are then clarified and revealed through the translation. There is also the idea of the palimpsest in the sense of the Greek word *palimpsestos*, which means 'scraped and cleared for new writing.' Who becomes whom by translating, by being translated? What might it mean to say becoming another through writing, through translating?

We are now getting to the heart of a fascination I've had since the 1980s and whose traces can be found in *Journal intime* (1984), *L'Aviva* (1985),

---

3. Translated by Marlene Wildeman as *The Aerial Letter* (Toronto: Women's Press, 1987).
4. Translated by Barbara Godard as *Lovhers* (Toronto: Guernica Editions, 1986).

fait de langue tourmente
rattrape-moi dans ma tradition
dans la durée de la phrase
le plaisir en douceur espacé
rattrape-moi dans ma différence

Vertige de l'avant-scène, Trois Rivières/Paris, Écrits des Forges/L'orange bleue, 1997.

Baroque d'aube (1995), and of course *Le Désert mauve* (1987),[5] a fascination that is definitely tied to the question of identity, which is very complex and, like the aurora borealis, is in constant motion. It is this movement, this dynamic of secret development, like a mysterious device lodged in every being, every language, that has always stirred me and that stimulated the challenge I took on of translating myself from French into French, a challenge which was at first playful in *L'Aviva*, a work of ten pages, and which then transformed into the raison d'être for writing the novel *Le Désert mauve*. I like the idea that language can make us say what we don't believe to have thought and that, in turn, we can make it shed its habitual nature and fly off the handle.

(tr. Rhonda Mullins)

THE TO AND FRO OF LANGUAGE

Every day we go out with two dimensions to our being: our body and our language, whether mother tongue or second language. Everyone lives intimately in their minds in their own language, a bit like everyone does what pleases them in their bedroom: sleeping, crying, caressing themselves, reading, drawing, putting on perfume, gazing in the mirror. Everyone lives in society at an intersection of languages. Everyone translates the best they know how.

Languages seep into us through smells, silences, sounds, and faces. They are faces and landscapes. Beauty, agony, like the language of insanarchy of Antonin Artaud or explorian like that of Claude Gauvreau. Yes, I read a lot

---

5. Published in English as *Intimate Journal*, trans. Barbara Godard (Toronto: The Mercury Press, 2004); *Aviva*, trans. Anne-Marie Wheeler (Vancouver: Nomados, 2008); *Mauve Desert*, trans. Susanne de Lotbinière-Harwood (Toronto: Coach House, 1990, 2006, 2015).

in translation. First and last names: Fyodor Dostoevsky, Emily Dickinson, Ovid, Jorge Luis Borges, Sappho, Sándor Márai, Dante Alighieri, Ivo Andric, Djuna Barnes, Rainer Maria Rilke, Antonio Tabucchi. The languages detach from expanses of imagination and civilization so we can soak up their flavour and marvel at their endless chasms and contours. Yes, I also know that the contour of languages depends on whether they are spoken from the margins, the periphery, or the centre. They age and rejuvenate with technologies that transform our relationship with time and space, the body and death; they nestle in our old humanist cells, fragrant with melancholy and hope. Yes, I know that we will speak of it again, ear pressed up against the idea that meaning keeps changing, because we conflate it with our dreams and our fascinating capacity for sharing and meeting.

We say French language, we say francophonie, we say mother tongue, we say that's not my language, we say I remember: *je me souviens*; we say I love you: *je t'aime*; we say it again, anything can happen in language: the present, the future, war, friendship, even a child who will make their way between the words of a language called mother tongue. Why am I so moved by language, like the day someone showed me the DVD of the French theatre company Le Poème Harmonique? This troupe dedicates itself to reproducing as accurately as possible the plays of Molière as they must have been staged (lighting, music, staging, and, above all, the language of the seventeenth century, when every syllable was pronounced, every *s*, every *r* rolled as long as possible). Within seconds, ancestors appeared. Intense emotion crept in between what I know about the history of Quebec and what I know about France and its literature.

Emotions, yes, questions, of course. What is it you are trying to keep me from by making that *e* – a clue to the feminine – silent, concealing millions of women behind the masculine and therefore also obscuring a part of reality? Why do you want me to believe that a *cuisinière* is 'a kitchen appliance used to heat and cook food' and a *traductrice* is a 'translation machine, also, pocket translator'? What do the core and contours of my language look like? What role does its history play in the fears and joys that prowl in my thoughts?

Occasionally one facet of us speaks louder, knows – out of urgency or need – how to better unfold in awareness. 'Affective resonance' is also a way of understanding the metaphor that allows us to see and imagine ourselves from different angles.

It is the nature of all writers – particularly novelists – to enjoy becoming other, sometimes under the pretext of discovering/ rediscovering themselves. In the verb *écrire, to write*, there is the idea of becoming other by taking risks with meaning, language, and oneself. Some will say: I want to be myself. I choose to translate you because your words create the right landscape around me, or simply because I see in your words a kinship that takes me near and far.

Rimbaud's 'je est un autre' resonates because it sums up a natural possibility that points to the invisible part of us, a secret lab where our most intimate and brave thoughts come to life. Literature is indeed one of the ultimate sites where invisible life can reveal itself and let the writer pretend to be another, a strange doppelgänger, monster or angel, as they exercise their freedom of movement and speech in the illusion of a new body, borrowing someone else's words. Only in literature and theatre can we plausibly don a new identity. Only in language can we become the spy, the double, the alter ego of the me who inspires or stifles, who inhales or asphyxiates.

Likewise, the subject of the other in itself is studied mainly within the framework of language, because it is its theatre, its stage. In 1983 I wrote in *Journal intime*: 'To be translated … means I have to question myself about the other I might be if I thought in English, Italian, or another language. What law, what ethics, what landscape, what picture would then come to mind? And who would I be in each of these languages?' Twenty-five years later, I would say in *Fences in Breathing*: 'I have put some distance between my mother tongue and reality. I am valiantly trying to imagine how pleasures and joys, fears and frights, can be built in a language not at all familiar. [...] Who am I becoming in another language? Who translates what in the alternating pattern of words' shadow and desire's infinite renewal?'

How does this to and fro of the self involve what I call the invisible part, the submerged narration and the connections that need to be made between the invisible, the inexpressible, and our relationship with language? The invisible part may be what is most alive within us. We

Toute langue quand nous la respirons est brève comme on dit sa mère jusqu-au fond du retour.

should not mistake it for the unconscious, because it is a narrating voice that takes part in our decisions and constantly organizes our actions. Our intelligence of the world hides in the invisible part of our thoughts; our identity is nestled within it.

(tr. Oana Avasilichioaei)

THE PERMISSIVE PLAYFUL APPROACH: UBIQUE MEANING

Every text subliminally tells us how it wants to be read as it produces certain effects that we cannot rationally identify but whose impact is very real. A text tells us if it wants to be used for pleasure, for thoughtful reflection, for emotional effect. It says *I am gentle, I am violent, learn how you can know me. Feel free to transform me, to be virtuosic yourself.* A text that generally triggers a permissive playful approach often presents itself as ripe terrain for wordplay, a sort of Rubik's Cube. It says *I exist to be assembled, dismantled, rebuilt.* It offers itself as a unique jigsaw puzzle open to any reader who wants to joyously interfere in its structure. It invites players in. Take, for example, poet Caroline Bergvall with her translation of *Typhon Dru* (U.K.: Reality Street Editions, 1997). Or Fred Wah with a 'transcreation' of my poem 'Si Sismal.' Or Daphne Marlatt with the translation of *Mauve* (1985) and Anne-Marie Wheeler with the translation of *Aviva* (2008). Or more recently, Jennifer Moxley and her translations in *Nicole Brossard: Selections* (University of California Press, 2010). In the case of Wah and Marlatt, we are dealing with two modern Canadian poets who know very little French and are therefore in literary cahoots, where everything is permissible, anything is possible. In the case of the other three translations, two of them are poets and one is a translation professor and scholar; they all know French very well, which allows them to stay within the scope of translation while also titillating the words and subtext. For example, in her translations of poems from *La partie pour le tout* (1975), Moxley emphasizes the erotic dimension of these texts. One could even say that in all these translations, the translators are playing with fire because they know that the author, who has often been playful in her own writing, will probably be game. I should also mention that in two cases, the publications are chapbooks and a third adds up to a few pages published in an anthology. None of these three instances relate to a full book in the usual sense. Might this imply that such risky translation has value only as long as the game is circumscribed, somewhat the way misbehaviour is accepted during the major celebrations that every society gives itself to mark some mythical or temporal passage?

THE RESPONSIBLE INTERACTIVE APPROACH: REINVENTED MEANING

Some will say, but isn't all translation interactive, particularly when one has access to the author or when, in reading a second or third translation of a classical text, one can nevertheless converse with the first translation despite its distance in time? Every translation is dialogical. Yet through the expression *interactive translation*, I want to indicate the constant back and forth flow between the source language and the target language, a movement between the lexicons, references, and particularities of each language. I'm thinking of poems translated by Robert Majzels and Erín Moure, in which the references also pass through other languages, other flavours besides those of English and French. I would use the expression *responsible interactive translation* when the translation is done by a translator and the expression *free interactive translation* when the translation is done by the author. In both cases, however, I would say that dialogue is the processing mode that allows one to 'translate the writing' and not just the text. The eighteenth-century German philosopher-translator Friedrich Schleiermacher identified three elements in translation – hermeneutics, dialectics, and ethics – and I particularly like these dimensions, especially if we translate them as reading, comprehending (grasping together), and entering into dialogue to examine the value and meaning of words.

Also, in speaking about a dialogue and a responsible interactive approach, I want to highlight the confluence of trajectories: that of the author who has led the text to its final version and that of the translator who intends to find its route, whatever semantic, grammatical, or syntactic labyrinths may be encountered along the way. Essentially, whatever escape attempts, infatuation, bursts of enthusi-asm may first arise, whoever translates will have to enter into dialogue, negotiate, and define the scope of their field of action within the field offered by the virtual machine, which is itself infinite. The route of many versions starts here.

Just as a creative manuscript has several versions, so does translation, I assume. In fact, we are increasingly study-ing not only the genetics of translated texts, but also of the translation itself. What is a version? Does it entail beginning from a more refined place every time or

A Tilt in the Wondering. Montréal, Vallum Chapbook Series, no 15, 2013.

at this point again it's time for notes & translation
close reading had been an idea
heart started searching
beyond gravity spelling too fast
the use of oneself strongly related to
la tite langue chaude du désir

being forced to begin from a misstep, a false start, a false octave? I am constantly fascinated by the variety of ways we can read a text, particularly poetry. By how we accept or reject something depending on the mind's level of fatigue, resistance, availability, and openness at the time. For even if the text tells us how it wants to be read, the fact remains that the attention we bring to it is what creates tension and in part gives it its volume and varied terrain.

THE FREE INTERACTIVE APPROACH: WRITING OF REWRITING

English literary journals often ask me for poems. Two possibilities present themselves: either I write in French and then have it translated into English, or I write directly in English. I recently found myself having to make this choice. But instead of writing a new poem, I reworked some poems that were lying fallow in my manuscripts. Then I decided to trans-late them. How can I describe what an immeasurable pleasure it was to rewrite and translate these texts! Why did this pleasure seem greater than the normal sense of satisfaction one feels after a successful translation?

Perhaps the unfinished aspect of the initial poems and a premature launch into their translation triggered a new writing process, since a

L'aviva

l'aviva son visage et les relais
de connivence l'ampleur des images
toute penchée sur l'attrait, sa bouche
or les lèvres il y a normalement mots
au bord de l'émoi une phrase reliée
tapie et à l'insu caressée
tout en longeant les bras d'excitation
s'appliquer, l'idée tenait tenace
car lier

l'en suite traduite

l'anima l'image et les effets
d'alliance teneur du visage
toute pensée sur les traits se couche
or les livres singulièrement toi d'aloi
au loin l'émoi qui s'écrie
a l'infinie d'utopie l'ainsi caresse
d'excitation longe le geste au comble
langue sujet vorace s'appliquer ignée,
ç'allier

L'Aviva, Montréal, Éditions NBJ, 1985; reprinted in *À tout regard*, Montréal, Bibliothèque québécoise, 1989.

dialogue began as of that moment between English and French and suddenly, I found myself redrafting the French text so that it could adapt to the translation. Or deciding not to change the fine French rhythm even if that meant sacrificing certain resonances in order to obtain a better semantic balance between French and English. I believe that was the moment when the two texts became living organisms, sometimes existing in perfect agreement, sometimes evolving at their own rhythms. A kind of improvisation of writing and translation. A subtle, very subtle dialogue: I change, I alter when it suits me, in the places I want. The translation becomes a real creation, a game of interactive languages.

Clearly here, I am re/writing through the translation, which in turn demands reformulations of the original language because they improve the text or are formally more appropriate. In this case, re/writing is a sign of freedom, transforming the tone and spontaneously allowing itself to make minor or daring transgressions. This explains why the free interactive approach is the one that most resembles the dynamics at work in translating poetry.

'Translation, unlike art, cannot claim permanence for its products.'
– Walter Benjamin

THE VIBRATING THRESHOLD OF THE POEM

Inquiring into the specificity of poetry translation means scrutinizing both poetry itself and the reasons why a line, image, or clause is poetic or not. In other words, it means trying to understand why and when in the text a grammatical and semantic shift takes place that endangers meaning by making it ambiguous, drifting, uncertain, and polysemic, and yet the effect of which is the certainty that something, right there, is true and inexplicable for the simple fact that it has unsettled us. This 'obvious inexplicable truth' can be detected only through the effect of reading produced in the form of emotion, a sensation, intuition, a flash of meaning, a clear or chaotic echo. A text can be called a poem when in a few words it produces a *vibrating semantic zone*, a blurred area that may or may not be amplified depending on the sensitivity of whoever reads or translates it. This is the zone in which one has to work in a state of alertness questioning the poem and the *poem's mystery*.

Now we are turning to reading and its impact on translation. Of course, there is knowing how to read, but there is also sharing at least some sensibility that can not only take in the poem but also ensure its artificial reproduction, whether imaginary, utopian, mental, or plausible, in another language. That is undoubtedly what is meant by *translating the untranslatable*, the untranslatable being that vibrating, energetic resonance *that changes everything*. I have often said that what we read in a poem is its energy, and that is what is most difficult to translate, because energy is what radiates from calibration, the expenditure or restraint in a text; it is this incandescence, the fine silk of living, that must be translated. Energy is the form of the living poem, meaning constantly shifting, which one has to pin down without seeming to. I assume this is also what makes the difference between a reading of Bach by Glenn Gould and by someone else. What happens to the performer in reading, during the hours of rehearsal, during the performance itself? Should I refer to the meaning that appears, ephemeral and yet rooted, born of the alternation between outburst and silence that lends any emotion its truth and, paradoxically, its enigmatic

J'avais aussi remarqué que, bien qu'ayant le même nombre de syllabes, une des deux phrases était plus longue à prononcer. Trois syllabes n'égalaient pas toujours trois syllabes. Il y avait là un indice que dans chaque langue, le temps pouvait tout à la fois être étiré ou se contracter de manière à faciliter le déchiffrement de l'encombrante monotonie du quotidien et l'énigme tenace des passions.

La capture du sombre, Montréal, Leméac, 2007.

flavour? Between falling and flying, the performer creates her own choreography, and that changes everything in the thinking body of the other who reads, watches, or listens. I like to use the work *interprète* for performer – interpreter – 'someone who clarifies meaning, who orally provides the equivalent in another language of what is said; someone who makes known the feelings, desires of another.'

This changes everything depends on the person translating, but also on the historical time elapsed between the text to translate and today's translation.

For example, it changes everything whether Paul Celan is translated by André du Bouchet or Martine Broda. It changes everything whether Shakespeare is translated by Pierre Letourneur between 1776 and 1782, or by François-Victor Hugo between 1859 and 1866, or by Yves Bonnefoy between 1951 and 1998. It changes everything: our language changes, because we breathe the *air du temps* differently, all the feelings and emotions, acts limited in time and by fashion that have a contemporary moral, ethical, or ideological quality. Peace time, war time: we vibrate differently, like when we learn to use new technologies that transform our actions and desires. And this applies even more now that we have stopped measuring time the way we used to – that is, beyond the binary and desire in three tenses (before, during, and after). Translating poetry is being and *not* being in the history of *being there* in the language. Translating poetry is 'immediately the sensation of a wound,' like a painting by Lucio Fontana, or 'immediately it disappears again,' like a video by Michael Snow. It changes everything because life changes: the life of the pliant and the rebellious, the life of the buoyant and the bored, the life of the oldest and the most recent words, not to mention the ones that disappear from real life to go live in the dictionary, the way that stamps, mail carriers, phone booths, inkwells, pens soon will.

More than any other genre, poetry promotes risk taking, escalates the tension of choice, and whets the appetite for freedom. We are familiar, of course, with translations by poets who, unfamiliar with the poem's language of origin, develop their translation from a first, minimalist version: Guillevic translating Attila József, Gilles Cyr translating Korean poets, French poets translating a wonderful anthology of Armenian poetry. Does this mean that poets translate in the *approximate* and that in poetry this notion is valid? Yes, if we think of the vibrating zone, yes again if we think that the poet who translates another gets at the essence, and this approximation is in fact rooted in a zone of sharing where two formal and existential postures meet. I can see that imperceptibly, quite naturally, I have moved from the word *translator* to the word *poet*, as if both were always working at the essence of the word and its music, trying to absorb into their own language the poetic words of their brethren. Poets have always needed to translate other poets, because they are eternally fresh readers, by which I mean that for them the foreign language they translate is always new, a source of wonder, play, surprise, potential mistakes, and false friends. This fresh language is what they will try to bring alive in the hollows, creases, rhythm, mysteries, hurdles, and hazards of their old language. Challenge, sharing, friendship, empathy, and aesthetic solidarity are the life of translation, and of literature, too. The curiosity that prompts one to want to translate the other poet is a curiosity that feeds what we call national literatures.

So why do poets initiate poetry in translation? What fascinates so many poets that this happens? Does *the other language* represent riddles to solve, sounds to transpose, to make appear and to hear in one's own language? Does it generate enjoyment that can make the fragments of story and landscapes emerge, even long narratives around a single word

La tentation est permanente de m'adonner à ce déguisement linguistique que George Steiner voit dans le mouvement moderniste comme « une stratégie d'exil permanent ». Quoi qu'il en soit, j'aime voir des mots étrangers surgir inopinément dans mes textes comme une intrigue en condensé dont le ton étonne, relance la difficile promesse d'exister en parlant de vivre au-delà de sa propre existence.

L'horizon du fragment, Trois-Pistoles, Éditions Trois-Pistoles, 2004.

and its etymology, as well as ethical questions about its rules of grammar? Could comparing two languages become a form of play and a philosophical inquiry into usage, the possible and the exceptional? *You don't say that in French.* Okay! *You don't think that in French.* Really? In French the masculine dominates the feminine, which can create problems even for someone who writes in French. In English, you always need to specify whose hand, whose eye; you cannot necessarily remain conceptual. In Spanish and Slovenian, you need to know whether the hand is feminine or masculine. And suddenly I am remaking the world, full of questions, happy to move around in the complex beauty that connects with, collides with, and is reborn on the side of the living.

OTHERNESS: EVEN MY LANGUAGE IS ANOTHER LANGUAGE

'What is this gap that slides between me and me?'
— Fernando Pessoa

Otherness is a word that offers space that is at times intimate, at times expansive, attractive, and that constantly reconfigures our potential. In principle, the word does not contain *resemblance*, and yet, if otherness has a meaning like existential space, it contains a centre, a kernel likely to resemble us, which is why it is fascinating. I use the word *fascinate* here because it conveys the mystery that persists despite our understanding of the other poet or the other text. In other words, this fascination may not be far from beauty, in the sense that the artist Rothko meant in his thinking about beauty and his mysterious *apperception*, because he said it required adjusting the tension between pleasure and pain to experience it. But chances are what I call fascination with a poem, with the otherness of the other poet in their language, relates to beauty. A bit like when I said the poem produces something in us that is unreadable and yet shakes and destabilizes us. And make no mistake, in poetry, otherness is woven from resemblance and resonance, which, paradoxically, operate in the form of a riddle.

Of course, there is also that other phenomenon of otherness that says 'je est un autre,' but I am not thinking in particular of Rimbaud. No, I am thinking of Fernando Pessoa and his heteronyms (Alberto Caeiro, Álvaro de Campos, Ricardo Reis), and of Erín Moure (Elisa Sampedrin), for whom the source of 'je est un autre' is not psychology but the practice of poetic language in the variety of linguistic intersections she engages in for pleasure, intersections at times of translation, at times of creation. This occurs in a number of texts, including *Secession/Insecession*, which is in fact a translation of the Galician poet Chus Pato. A translation of Chus Pato's text appears on the right page, and '*echolation-homage and a biopoetics*' by Erín Moure appears on the left. The entire book is in English, but we know that part of it was written in Galician. In fact, Erín Moure lays bare what until now has remained in the subtext: me, translator, poet, I live, I hear, and I respond at many levels to what I translate; in short, in every translation, I respond to my own life of reality and thought. There is also the phenomenon I call *language is even another language.* I am thinking here of *Or Carbon Slides: Anagrammatic Translations of Work by Nicole Brossard*, a sixteen-page book by Bronwyn Haslam that offers anagrammatic translations in which each poem translated to English uses the same letters and the same number of letters as was used in the French.

I personally experienced this attraction to a fictional other, of self or language itself, with *Mauve Desert* and *Fences in Breathing*, the former demonstrating my desire to translate myself in my own language, and the latter associated with the idea of writing in a language other than my own. In both instances, it was a case of 'depicting a fictional self' against a backdrop of absence of me. More recently, writing a short book of poetry in English, *A Tilt in the Wondering* (2013), again showed my fascination with this posture of hesitation with *identity* that secretes its own restlessness.

Perhaps I should also discuss language migrants, those who have chosen to write in a language other than their mother tongue, not as a game but as a new life, a complex translation of creation itself. There are many

Dans la langue étrangère, je continue de creuser des trous et à tisser de courts récits dans lesquels je suis heureuse, multiple et inquiète, parfaitement libre. Il y a des sensations qui disparaissent en laissant des cernes autour des mots. D'autres naissent aux mêmes endroits. Dans l'autre langue, je multiplie inutilement les pronoms, étreins l'obscurité comme une chose précieuse, une petite ombre de la grande peur.

La capture du sombre. Montréal, Leméac, 2007.

Le désert est indescriptible. La réalité s'y engouffre, lumière rapide. Le regard fond. Pourtant ce matin. Très jeune, je pleurais déjà sur l'humanité. A chaque nouvel an, je la voyais se dissoudre dans l'espoir et la violence. Très jeune, je prenais la Meteor de ma mère et j'allais vers le désert. J'y passais des journées entières, des nuits, des aubes. Je roulais vite et puis au ralenti, je filais la lumière dans ses mauves et petites lignes qui comme des veines dessinaient un grand arbre de vie dans mon regard. (*Le Désert mauve*, récit du personnage de Laura Angstelle, dite l'auteure.)

Le Désert mauve, Montréal. Éditions de l'Hexagone, 1987; Montréal, Typo, 2010.

such migrants, so I will name just a few: Paul Celan, Vladimir Nabokov, Benjamin Fondane, Samuel Beckett, Nancy Huston, Yann Martel, Ying Chen, and countless others from what we call post-colonial literature.

In literature, there is therefore a dream of moving toward another self, another language, another identity, essentially to be transported somewhere else, to be carried away, by and in the language itself. Having said that, let's look at what happens today in poetry translation by other poets, most of whom are anglophone and part of a moment of writing as translation that generations before them may have dreamed of (I am thinking of Barbara Godard, Fred Wah, Daphne Marlatt, Anne Carson, and the Luxemburgish-American Pierre Joris).

Historically we have observed a closeness, an attraction, and a tacit agreement between poets who stimulate the desire to know the other in their literary intimacy, magic, barricades, dignity, universe, way of holding a cigarette or glass of wine, of holding one's child in one's arms, of walking and smiling, not exploding into a thousand shards of sobs.

But is it possible that the other to translate spares us the agony of the blank page and provides material for transgression? Increasingly we engage literarily and culturally in translation, as if it were a new space for fantasy conducive to creation and transgression. Once the hierarchy has 'fallen' between the author and the translator, the space that is gained, the emancipation from the desire to respect the text and be faithful to meaning, can be reinvested. For example, a quote from Antena (a collective made up of Jen Hofer and John Pluecker created in 2010) that opens the excellent issue 3.23 of the *Capilano Review* reads: 'We translate into our language to rewrite our language.'

Similarly, Antena's *Manifesto for Ultratranslation*, which appeared in the same issue, also conveys this reinvestment: 'Ultratranslation is messy. Ultratranslation is excessive. Ultratranslation is unruly. [...] Ultratranslation labours to translate the untranslatable, and also to preserve it: not to reduce the irreducible. Not to know but to acknowledge. The untranslatable as starting point, not ending point. Ultratranslation does not replace translation ... '

The use of the word *manifesto* in this context says a great deal about the unruly, transgressive, ironic posture, as well as about the scope of projects to invent and the possibility of saying the opposite of what we say, because we want to encompass everything: what is beautiful, exciting, and inspiring.

So this is another writing space, created from translation as a practice that mentors writing and an attitude toward the world. This new space was created by poets translating poets. It is the result of poetic language enhanced by the understanding of its own trajectory and unfolding in the cycle of language and the psyche that keeps us there on constant alert. Being able to say the opposite of what we are saying acknowledges the effect of the global vision produced by our use of new technologies and by the quantum space (as opposed to the dualistic space) in which we circulate, some days knowing it, other days completely unaware. Yes, I believe we have entered the era of *quantum translation* (intervention on meaning and reappropriation of meaning through small doses of discontinuous

> Le désert est indescriptible. La lumière avale tout, gouffre cru. Le regard fond. Aujourd'hui, pourtant. Très jeune, je désespérais déjà de l'humanité. À chaque jour de l'an, je la voyais se disperser dans l'espoir et la démesure. Très jeune, je filais dans l'auto de ma mère et j'allais vers le désert ou je m'obstinais devant le jour, la nuit et à l'aube, a vouloir tout. Je tissais la lumière. Je roulais vite et aussi lentement; je suivais les petits fragments de vie qui s'alignaient dans mon regard, horizon mauve. (*Mauve, l'horizon*, traduction de ce même récit par Maude Laures, dite la traductrice.)
>
> *Le Désert mauve*, Montréal. Éditions de l'Hexagone, 1987; Montréal, Typo, 2010.

meaning). Which would be the suspense of meaning advancing and engaging from one language to another in intimacy, etymology, and tradition, creating a coming together, a potential for sharing where previously the impossible translation (unfaithfulness) inhibited it. Translation is therefore a new sort of impossible, as were and are our return trips between the world of the imagination and fiction and that of reality.

Our power to move between the words of the dead and the living, between centuries, cultures, works, and their authors, is enormous and terrifying, because it enhances our capacity for horizontal presence and is accompanied by an increasingly global vision that is an invitation to plunge, an absolute mise en abyme where we can glide, fall, brush against, collide with, or, simply move around.

Et me voici soudain en train de refaire le monde
2015, tr. 2019–2020

PERMISSIONS

Logical Suite (pp. 30–35): From *Suite logique,* published in French by Les Éditions de l'Hexagone (1970). English translation by Pierre Joris, as published in *Nicole Brossard: Selections* by University of California Press (2010). Courtesy of University of California Press, and Pierre Joris.

The Part for the Whole (pp. 36–38): from *La Partie pour le tout,* published in French by Les Herbes rouges (1975). Translation by Jennifer Moxley, as published in *Nicole Brossard: Selections* by University of California Press (2010). Courtesy of Les Herbes rouges, University of California Press, and Jennifer Moxley.

Calligrapher in Drag (pp. 39–40): From *Mécanique jongleuse,* published in French by Les Éditions de l'Hexagone (1974). Translation by Larry Shouldice, published as *Daydream Mechanics* by Coach House Press (1980). Courtesy of Nicole Brossard.

June the Fever (pp. 41–44): From *Amantes,* published in French by Éditions Quinze (1980). Translation by Barbara Godard, published as *Lovhers* by Guernica Editions (1986). Courtesy of Groupe Librex/VLB, Guernica Editions, and the Estate of Barbara Godard.

Sous la Langue/Under tongue (pp. 45–49): Published in French and English as *Sous la Langue/Under tongue* by L'Essentielle/Gynergy, English translation by Susanne de Lotbinère-Harwood (1987). Courtesy of Susanne de Lotbinère-Harwood.

Ultrasound (pp. 50–53): From *Piano blanc,* published in French by Les Éditions de l'Hexagone (2011). Translation by Robert Majzels and Erín Moure, published as *White Piano* by Coach House Books (2013). Courtesy of Coach House Books, Robert Majzels, and Erín Moure.

Scenes (pp. 54–65): From *Le Désert mauve,* published in French by Les Éditions de l'Hexagone (1987). Translation by Susanne de Lotbinère-Harwood, published as *Mauve Desert* by Coach House Press (1990), reissued by McClelland and Stewart (1998) and Coach House Books (2006, 2015). Courtesy of Coach House Books and Susanne de Lotbinère-Harwood.

Hotel Rafale (pp. 66–74): From *Baroque d'aube,* published in French by Les Éditions de l'Hexagone (1995). Translated by Patricia Claxton and published as *Baroque at Dawn* by McClelland and Stewart (1997). Courtesy of Nicole Brossard and Patricia Claxton.

Sixth Bend; Ninth Bend (pp. 75–76): From *La Nuit du Parc Labyrinthe,* published in French, English, and Spanish by Les Éditions Trois, 1992. English translation by Lou Nelson. Courtesy of Nicole Brossard.

The Aerial Letter (pp. 78 -94): From *La Lettre aérienne,* published in French by Les Éditions du Remue-ménage (1985). English translation by Marlene Wildeman, published in *The Aerial Letter* by Women's Press (1988). Courtesy of Les Éditions du remue-ménage, Nicole Brossard, and Marlene Wildeman.
  'La Lettre aérienne' was a text written for presentation at Cerisy-la-Salle in August 1980. Passages of the texts within are to be found in: 'The identity as science fiction of self,' *Identités collectives et changements sociaux* (Privat, 1980); 'L'épreuve de la modernité,' *La Nouvelle Barre du Jour,* no. 90–91 (May 1980); 'Un corps pour écrire,' *Le Devoir,* 24 November 1979.

6 December Among the Centuries (pp. 95–101): First published in *La Presse,* 21 December 1989 under the title '[La fusillade de Polytechnique]: le tueur n'était pas un jeune homme,' then collected by Louise Malette and Marie Chalouh in the book *Polytechnique, 6 décembre* (1990), then translated by Marlene Wildeman for *The Montréal Massacre* (1991) and reprinted in *Fluid Arguments* by the Mercury Press (2005). Courtesy of the Mercury Press and Marlene Wildeman.

From Shadow: Soft and Soif (pp. 102–106): From *Ardeur*, published in French by Écrits de Forges/ Éditions Phi (2008). Translated by Angela Carr as *Ardour*, published by Coach House Books (2015). Courtesy of Nicole Brossard and Angela Carr.

Femme d'aujourd'hui (pp. 107–108): Transcription of a Radio-Canada interview, 16 mai 1975. English translation by Genviève Robichaud. Courtesy of Archives Radio-Canada.

Paris, 27 November 1975; 19 March 1983; 20 March 1983 (pp. 110–112): From *Journal intime, ou, Voilà donc un manuscrit*, published in French by Éditions les Herbes rouges (1994, 1998). Translation by Barbara Godard, published as *Intimate Journal, or Here's a Manuscript* by the Mercury Press (2004). Courtesy of Éditions les Herbes rouges, the Mercury Press, and the Estate of Barbara Godard.

Worn Along the Fold (pp. 113–118): From *Le Sens apparent*, published in French by Flammarion (1980). Translation by Fiona Strachan, published as *Surfaces of Sense* by Coach House Press (1989). Courtesy of Fiona Strachan.

Screen Skin Utopia (pp. 119–122): From *Picture Theory*, published in French by Éditions Nouvelle Optique (1982) and Les Éditions de l'Hexagone (1989). Translation by Barbara Godard, published as *Picture Theory* by Guernica Editions (1991). Courtesy of Nicole Brossard, Guernica Editions, and the Estate of Barbara Godard.

Just Once (pp. 123–141): From *French Kiss*, published in French by Éditions du Jour (1974) and Éditions Quinze (1980). Translation by Patricia Claxton, published as *French Kiss, or, A Pang's Progress* by Coach House Press (1986) and reissued by Coach House Books in *The Blue Books* (2003). Courtesy of Groupe Librex/VLB, Coach House Books, and Patricia Claxton.

Chapter Two (pp. 142–147): From *Sold-out*, published in French by Éditions du Jour (1974) and Éditions Quinze (1980). Translation by Patricia Claxton, originally published as *Turn of a Pang* by Coach House Press (1976), reprinted in *The Blue Books* (2003) by Coach House Books. Courtesy of Coach House Books and Patricia Claxton.

Harmonious Matter Still Manoeuvres (pp. 148–150): From *Typhon dru*, published in French by Collectif Génération (1989, 1990). English translation by Caroline Bergvall, published in *Typhon Dru* by Reality Street Editions (1997). Courtesy of Éditions du Noroît, Reality Street Editions, and Caroline Bergvall.

Soft Link 1, Smooth Horizon of the Verb Love, Every Ardour (pp. 151–153): From *Cahier de roses et de civilisation*, published in French by Les Éditions du Sabord (2003). Translation by Robert Majzels and Erín Moure, published as *Notebook of Roses and Civilization* by Coach House Books (2007). Courtesy of Nicole Brossard, Coach House Books, Robert Majzels, and Erín Moure.

Theory, A City (pp. 154–159): Written by Lisa Robertson as an introduction to *Theory, A Sunday* (2013), a translation of *La Théorie, un dimanche*. Courtesy of Lisa Robertson and Belladonna*.

Yesterday (pp. 160–166): From *Hier*, published in French by Éditions Québec Amérique Inc. (2001). English translation by Susanne de Lotbinère-Harwood, published as *Yesterday, at the Hotel Clarendon* by Coach House Books (2005). Courtesy of Coach House Books and Susanne de Lotbinère-Harwood.

Mauve (pp. 168–172): Originally published as a chapbook in a bilingual edition by Éditions NBJ/Writing (1987), republished in *À tout regard* by Bibliothèque Québecoise (1989). English by Daphne Marlatt. Courtesy of Nicole Brossard and Daphne Marlatt.

Polynésie des yeux/Polynesya of the Eyes (pp. 173–182): Originally published in both languages, translated by Nicole Brossard, in *Notus*, vol. 2 no. 2, 1987, and reprinted in *À tout regard*, published by Bibliothèque Québecoise (1989). Courtesy of Nicole Brossard.

Polynesian Days (pp. 183–185): A 'translation' of 'Polynésie des yeux' by Charles Bernstein. Published in his collection, *With Strings*, by University of Chicago Press (2001). Courtesy of Charles Bernstein and the University of Chicago Press.

If Yes Seismal/Si Sismal (pp. 186–187): 'Si Sismal' was published in French in *À tout regard* by Bibliothèque Québecoise (1989). Transcreation by English by Fred Wah published in *Absinthe*, Summer 1992, Vol. 5. Courtesy of Nicole Brossard and Fred Wah.

L'Aviva/Aviva (pp. 188–193): Originally published in French in *La Nouvelle barre du jour* and reprinted in *À tout regard* by Bibliothèque Québecoise (1989). English translation by Anne-Marie Wheeler published as a chapbook by Nomados Literary Publishers (2009). Courtesy of Nicole Brossard, Anne-Marie Wheeler, and Nomados.

Silk Font 1 (pp. 194–195): An anagrammatic translation by Bronwyn Haslam of 'Soft Link 1' from *Cahier des roses et de civilisation*, published in a chapbook, *Or Carbon Slides: Anagrammatic Translations of Works by Nicole Brossard* by no press in 2007 and then in the January 2016 issue of *Asymptote* for their Experimental Translation Feature. Courtesy of Bronwyn Haslam.

A Book (pp. 196–206): From *Un Livre*, published in French by Éditions du jour (1970) and reissued by Les Éditions Quinze (1980). Originally translated by Larry Shouldice as *A Book*, published by Coach House Press in 1976 and reissued in *The Blue Books* by Coach House Books in 2003. This is a retranslation by Katia Grubisic, unpublished in book form. Courtesy of Nicole Brossard, Groupe Librex/VLB, and Katia Grubisic.

Figure (pp. 207–210): From *L'Amèr, ou Le chapitre effrité*, published in French by Les Éditions Quinze (1977). English translation by Barbara Godard, published as *These Our Mothers: or, The Disintegrating Chapter* by Coach House Press (1983). Courtesy of Groupe Librex/VLB and the Estate of Barbara Godard.

Reconfiguration (pp. 211–215): From *L'Amèr, ou Le chapitre effrité*, published in French by Les Éditions Quinze (1977). Retranslation by Robert Majzels and Erín Moure as *SeaMother: or The Bitteroded Chapter*, published in *Asymptote*, as yet unpublished in book form. Courtesy of Groupe Librex/VLB, Robert Majzels, and Erín Moure.

Typhon Dru (pp. 216–19): From *Typhon dru*, published in French in a limited run by Collectif Génération (1989, 1990). English translation by Caroline Bergvall, published in *Typhon Dru* by Reality Street Editions UK (1997). Courtesy of Nicole Brossard, Reality Street Editions, and Caroline Bergvall.

Typhoon Thrum (pp. 220–222): From *Typhon dru*, published in French in a limited run by Collectif Génération (1989, 1990) and reprinted in *Musée de l'os et de l'eau* by Éditions du Noroît/Cadex Editions. Retranslation by Robert Majzels and Erín Moure, published in *Museum of Bone and Water* by House of Anansi (2003, 2020). Courtesy of Éditions du Noroît, House of Anansi (www.house-ofanansi.com), Robert Majzels, and Erín Moure.

Site, Knowledge, Encore, Redundancy, Repetition, Tomorrow (pp. 223–225): From *Installations (avec ou sans pronoms)*, published in French by Écrits des Forges–Le Castor Astral. English translation by Robert Majzels and Erín Moure, published by The Muses' Company (2000). Courtesy of Écrits des Forges, Robert Majzels, and Erín Moure.

The Marginal Way (pp. 228–231): From *La partie pour le tout*, published in French by Éditions de L'Aurore/Les Herbes rouges (1975). Translation by Jennifer Moxley, as published in *Nicole Brossard: Selections* by University of California Press (2010). Courtesy of Les Herbes rouges, University of California Press, and Jennifer Moxley.

Field of Action for New Forms (pp. 232–236): From *Mécanique jongleuse,* published in French by Les Éditions de l'Hexagone (1974). Translation by Larry Shouldice, published as *Daydream Mechanics* by Coach House Press (1980). Courtesy of Nicole Brossard.

The Most Precious Things in the Future Will Be Water, Silence, and a Human Voice (pp. 237–254): This text was written in English by Brossard and first presented at a graduate student conference entitled 'Silent Spaces and Ill-Communication,' which took place at the University of Western Ontario on February 10–12, 2000. This text was also presented under the title 'Around Silence and Precious Words' at the Department of English at the University of Alberta on October 5, 2001. In 2002, another version appeared in 'The Nicole Brossard Issue' of *Verdure* devoted to Brossard's work, and a shorter version appeared under the title 'Silence,' in the Montréal newspaper *Le Devoir* on July 29 as part of a summer series, *Le Mot de L'Académie.* It appeared in *Fluid Arguments,* published by The Mercury Press. Courtesy of Nicole Brossard and The Mercury Press.

The Frame Work of Desire (pp. 255–264): Brossard's contribution to *La Théorie, un dimanche,* published in French by Les Éditions de remue-ménage (1988). Translation by Erica Weitzman, published in *Theory, A Sunday* by Belladonna* (2013). Courtesy of Nicole Brossard, Belladonna*, and Erica Weitzman.

Salon: Catherine Mavrikakis talks with Nicole Brossard and Nathanaël (pp. 265–275): A translation by Katia Grubisic of the transcription of 'Catherine Mavrikakis tient salon au cercle avec Nicole Brossard et Nathanaël.'

Lorem Ipsum (pp. 276–283): An essay written by Nicole Brossard, 2018. First published in *Luminous Ink,* edited by Tessa McWatt, Rabindranath Maharaj, and Dionne Brand, published by Cormorant Books (2018). Translated by Susanne de Lotbinière-Harwood. Courtesy of Cormorant Books and Susanne de Lotbinière-Harwood.

And Suddenly I Find Myself Remaking the World (pp. 284–304): Published in French as *Et me voici soudain en train de refaire le monde* by Mémoire d'encrier (2015). English translation by Oana Avasilichioaei and Rhonda Mullins (2019–20). Courtesy of Mémoire d'encrier, Oana Avasilichioaei, and Rhonda Mullins.

WORKS BY NICOLE BROSSARD

POETRY

'Aube à la saison.' Trois. Montreal: Presses de l'AGEUM, 1965.

Mordre en sa chair. Montreal: Éditions Estérel, 1966.

L'Écho bouge beau. Montreal: Éditions Estérel, 1968.

Le Centre blanc. Montreal: Éditions d'Orphée, 1970.

Suite logique. Montreal: Les Éditions de l'Hexagone, 1970.

Mécanique jongleuse. Paris: Génération, 1973; *Mécanique jongleuse: Suivi de masculin grammaticale.* Montreal: Les Éditions de l'Hexagone, 1974. // *Daydream Mechanics.* Translated by Larry Shouldice. Toronto: Coach House Press, 1980.

La Partie pour le tout. Montreal: Éditions de L' Aurore/Les Herbes rouges, 1975.

L'Amèr, ou Le chapitre effrité. Montreal: Les Éditions Quinze, 1977. (Reissued as *L'Amèr, ou Le chapitre effrité. Théorie/fiction.* Montreal: Les Éditions de l'Hexagone, 1988.) // *These Our Mothers: or, The Disintegrating Chapter.* Translated by Barbara Godard. Toronto: Coach House Press, 1983.

Le Centre blanc. Poèmes 1965–1975. Montreal: Les Éditions de l'Hexagone,1978.

D'Arcs de cycle à la dérive, poèmes. Gravure de Francine Simonin, Saint-Jacques-le-Mineur; Éditions de la Maison, 1979.

Le Sens apparent. Paris: Éditions Flammarion, 1980. // *Surfaces of Sense.* Translated by Fiona Strachan. Toronto: Coach House Press, 1989.

Amantes. Montreal: Les Éditions Quinze, 1980, 1998. // *Lovhers.* Translated by Barbara Godard. Montreal: Guernica Editions, 1986.

Double impression: Poèmes et textes 1967–1984. Montreal: Les Éditions de l'Hexagone, 1984.

Domaine d'Écriture. Outremont, Quebec: La Nouvelle Barre du Jour, 1985.

L'Aviva. Montreal: La Nouvelle Barre du Jour, 1985. // *L'Aviva / Aviva* (bilingual edition), translated by Anne-Marie Wheeler. Vancouver: Nomados Literary Publishers, 2008.

Mauve, with Daphne Marlatt. Montreal: *La Nouvelle Barre du jour/Writing,* 1985. Collected in *À tout regard,* Bibliothèque Québécoise, 1989.

Character/Jeu de lettres, with Daphne Marlatt. Montreal: *La Nouvelle Barre du jour/* Writing, 1986.

Sous la langue/Under Tongue (bilingual edition), translated by Susanne de Lotbinière-Harwood. Montreal/Charlottetown: L'Essentielle/Gynergy Books, 1987.

À tout regard. Montreal: Bibliothèque Québécoise, 1989.

Installations (avec et sans pronoms). Trois-Rivières/Pantin: Écrits des Forges/ Castor astral, 1989. *// Installations (with and without pronouns).* Translated by Erín Moure and Robert Majzels. Winnipeg: Muses' Company, 2000.

La Subjectivité des Lionnes. Brussels: L'arbre à paroles, asbl identités, 1990.

Typhon dru, with illustrations by Noël Dolla. Paris: Collectif Génération, 1989. Republished, with photographs and collages by Christine Davies, 1990. *Typhon dru* (bilingual edition), translated by Caroline Bergvall. London: Reality Street Editions, 1997.

La Nuit verte du parc labyrinthe/Green Night of Labyrinth Park/La Noche Verde Del Parque Laberinto (trilingual edition). Laval: Les Éditions Trois, 1992.

Langues obscures. Montreal: Les Éditions de l'Hexagone, 1992.

'Flesh, song(e) et promenades,' *Lèvres urbaines*, Vol. 23, 1993.

Vertige de l'avant-scène. Trois-Rivières/Paris: Écrits des Forges/L'Orange bleue, 1997.

Au présent des veines. Trois-Rivières/Herborn/La Réunion: Écrits des Forges/ Éditions Phi/Grand océan, 1999.

Musée de l'os et de l'eau. Saint-Hippolyte/Saussines: Les Éditions du Noroît/ Cadex Éditions, 1999; 2008. *// Museum of Bone and Water*, translated by Erín Moure and Robert Majzels. Toronto: House of Anansi Press, 2003; 2020.

Cahier de roses et de civilisation. Trois-Rivières: Éditions d'art Le Sabord, 2003. *// Notebook of Roses and Civilization*, translated by Erín Moure and Robert Majzels. Toronto: Coach House Books, 2007.

Je m'en vais à Trieste. Trois-Rivières/Echternach/Limoges: Écrits des Forges/ Éditions Phi/Le bruit des autres, 2003. (Republished: Trois-Rivières: Écrits des Forges, 2005.)

Après les mots. Trois-Rivières/Esch-sur-Alzette: Écrits des Forges/Éditions Phi, 2007.

Ardeur. Trois-Rivières/Differdange: Écrits des Forges/Éditions Phi, 2008. *// Ardour*, translated by Angela Carr. Toronto: Coach House Books, 2015.

Lointaines. Paris: Éditions Caractères, 2010.

Piano blanc. Montreal: Les Éditions de l'Hexagone, 2011. *// White Piano*, translated by Erín Moure and Robert Majzels. Toronto: Coach House Books, 2013.

A Tilt in the Wondering (chapbook). Montreal: Vallum, 2013.

Lumière, fragment d'envers. Montreal: Éditions de la Grenouillère, 2015.

Temps qui installe les miroirs. Montreal: Éditions du Noroît, 2015.

A cappella (chapbook), translated by Erín Moure and Robert Majzels, Toronto: Someone Editions, 2018.

NOVELS AND NOVELLAS

Un livre. Montreal: Éditions du jour, 1970. (Republished: Montreal: Les Éditions Quinze, 1980.) // *A Book*, translated by Larry Shouldice. Toronto: Coach House Press, 1976. (Reissued in *The Blue Books*, Toronto: Coach House Books, 2003.)

Sold-out. Étreinte-Illustration. Montreal: Éditions du Jour, 1973. (Re-edited: Montreal: Les Éditions Quinze, 1980.) // *Turn of a Pang*, translated by Patricia Claxton. Toronto: Coach House Press, 1976. (Reissued in *The Blue Books*, Toronto: Coach House Books, 2003.)

French kiss. Étreinte-Exploration. Montreal: Éditions du Jour, 1974. (Republished: Montreal, Les Éditions Quinze, 1980.) // *French Kiss, or, A Pang's Progress*, translated by Patricia Claxton. Toronto: Coach House Press, 1986. (Reissued in *The Blue Books*, Toronto: Coach House Books, 2003.)

Picture Theory. Théorie-fiction. Montreal: Éditions Nouvelle Optique, 1982. (Republished: Montreal: Les Éditions de l'Hexagone, 1989.) // *Picture Theory*, translated by Barbara Godard. Montrral: Guernica, 1991.

Le Désert mauve, Montreal: Les Éditions de l'Hexagone, 1987. // *Mauve Desert*, translated by Susanne de Lotbinière-Harwood. Toronto: Coach House Press, 1990; McClelland and Stewart, 1998; Coach House Books, 2006, 2015.

Baroque d'aube. Montreal: Les Éditions de l'Hexagone, 1995. // *Baroque At Dawn*. Translated by Patricia Claxton, Toronto: McClelland and Stewart, 1997.

Hier. Montreal: Québec Amérique, 2001. //*Yesterday, at the Hotel Clarendon*, translated by Susanne de Lotbinière-Harwood, Toronto: Coach House Books, 2005.

La Capture du Sombre. Montreal: Leméac, 2007. // *Fences in Breathing*, translated by Susanne de Lotbinière-Harwood, Toronto: Coach House Books, 2009.

ESSAYS

Double impression. Poèmes et textes 1967–1984. Montreal: Les Éditions de l'Hexagone, 1984.

Journal intime, ou, Voilà donc un manuscrit. Montreal: Les Herbes rouges, 1984. (Republished: suivi de *Œuvre de chair et métonymies*, Montreal: Les Herbes rouges, 1998; 2008.) // *Intimate Journal, or Here's a Manuscript*, translated by Barbara Godard. Toronto: Mercury Press, 2004.

La Lettre aérienne. Montreal: Éditions du remue-ménage, 1985. // *The Aerial Letter*, translated by Marlene Wildeman. Toronto: Women's Press, 1988.

Elle serait la première phrase de mon prochain roman/She Would Be the First Sentence of My Next Novel (bilingual edition), translated by Susanne de Lotbinière-Harwood. Toronto: Mercury Press, 1998.

La Théorie, un dimanche, with Louky Bersianik, Louise Cotnoir, Louise Dupré, Gail Scott, and France Théoret. Montreal: Éditions du remue-ménage, 1988, 2018. // *Theory, A Sunday,* New York: Belladonna*, 2013.

L'Horizon du fragment. Trois-Pistoles: Éditions Trois-Pistoles, 2004.

Fluid Arguments, edited by Susan Rudy. Toronto: The Mercury Press, 2005.

Et me voici soudain en train de refaire le monde. Montreal: Mémoire d'Encrier, 2015.

THEATRE AND CINEMA

'L'Écrivain,' in *La Nef des sorcières* with Marthe Blackburn, Marie-Claire Blais, Odette Gagnon, Luce Guilbeault, Pol Pelletier, and France Théoret. Montreal: Éditions Quinze, 1976. // *A Clash of Symbols,* translated by Linda Gaboriau. Toronto: Coach House Press, 1980.

Some American Feminists (documentary), with Luce Guilbeault and Margaret Wescott, 1977.

Célébrations, with Jovette Marchessault, presented at the Théâtre du Nouveau Monde (in Montreal). Montreal: Théâtre Expérimental des Femmes, 1979.

Je ne suis jamais en retard, with Lise Roy, Louise Bombardier, Marie-Eve Gagnon, Nicole Lacelle, Dominick Parenteau-Lebeuf, and Marilyn Perreault, Théâtre d'Aujourd'hui (in Montreal). Montreal: Groupe Ad Hoc/Lise Roy and Markita Boies, 2015.

Le Désert mauve, with Simon Dumas, premiered at L'Espace Go (in Montreal), Quebec: Production du Rhizome, 2018.

ANTHOLOGIES

D'Aube et de civilisation. Poèmes choisis, 1965–2007, edited by Louise Dupré. Montreal: TYPO, 2008.

Mobility of Light: The Poetry of Nicole Brossard, edited by Louise Forsyth. Waterloo: Wilfrid Laurier University Press, 2009.

Nicole Brossard: Selections, Oakland: University of California Press, 2010.

ANTHOLOGIES EDITED BY NICOLE BROSSARD

Les Stratégies du réel/The Story So Far 6. Montreal/Toronto: *La Nouvelle Barre du jour* / Coach House Press, 1978.

Anthologie de la Poésie des Femmes, with Lisette Girouard. Montreal: Éditions du remue-ménage, 1991, 2003.

Poèmes à dire la francophonie: 38 poètes contemporains, Bordeaux/Paris: Castor Astral/CNDP, 2002.

Baiser vertige: Prose et poésie gaies et lesbiennes au Québec, Montreal: TYPO, 2006.

Le Long poème, Quebec: Éditions Nota bene, 2011.

Sina Queyras is the author of *My Ariel, MxT, Expressway,* and *Lemon Hound*, all from Coach House Books. They were born on land belonging to the Nisichawayasihk Cree Nation and live and teach in Tiohtià:ke (Montréal).

Geneviève Robichaud is the author of *Exit Text* (Anstruther Press, 2016), a nano-essay on the errant and secret life of ideas. Her research focuses on twentieth- and twenty-first-century writings with an emphasis on translation as the poetry of thought still to come. She holds a PhD in English literature from the Université de Montréal.

Erin Wunker lives, works, and teaches in K'jipuktuk (Halifax, Nova Scotia). She is the author of *Notes from a Feminist Killjoy: Essays on Everyday Life.*

The editors would like to express their gratitude first and foremost to Nicole Brossard, who reminds us to stay on the crest of desire with our eyes on horizons and our hearts reaching toward one another. Thanks to each of the people who have edited, translated, and published Nicole Brossard's work. Thank you to Productions du rhizome for the Désert Mauve *spectacle photos. Enormous thanks to Alana Wilcox and the Coach House humans. Finally, we would like to thank all the readers of Brossard's work across generations and generations to come: the future can be swayed.*

Nicole Brossard (b. Montréal, 1943) began publishing in 1965. She has published more than forty books since and twice won the Governor General's Literary Award. A consummate advocate for literature and feminist discourse, she cofounded and co-directed the avant-garde literary magazine *La Barre du jour* (1965–1975), co-directed the film *Some American Feminists* (1976) and co-edited the acclaimed *Anthologie de la poésie des femmes au Québec* (1991, 2003).

Her work has influenced a whole generation poets and feminists and has been translated widely into English, including *Notebook of Roses and Civilization* (tr. Erín Moure and Robert Majzels), which was shortlisted for the 2008 Griffin International Poetry Prize. Her most recent books to be translated into English are *White Piano* (trans. Erín Moure and Robert Majzels, 2013) and *Ardour* (trans. Angela Carr, 2015). Her work has also been translated into other languages including Spanish, German, Italian, Japanese, Slovenian, Romanian, Catalan, Portuguese. 2020 should see translations in Catalan and Portuguese.

Brossard's work is not limited to the page; she is committed to interdisciplinary collaboration. In 2018 she performed with Simon Dumas in a multidisciplinary show based on *Mauve Desert* (produced by Rhizome and directed by Simon Dumas) at the Montréal theatre l'Espace Go. She also published the art chapbook *A cappella*, with illustrations by Mauricio Corteletti (Someone Editions, tr. Erín Moure and Robert Majzels). 2024 should see the production of an opera based on *Mauve Desert* composed by Symon Henry.

Brossard's work has been recognized and celebrated in Canada and internationally. In 1989 and again in 1999 she was awarded the Grand Prix de Poésie du Festival international de Trois-Rivières. In 1991, she won le Prix Athanase-David (the highest literary recognition in Québec). She is a member of l'Académie des lettres du Québec and won the 2003 W. O. Mitchell Prize and the Canada Council of Arts Molson Prize in 2006. The same year, she published *Baiser vertige*, the first Quebec anthology of gay and lesbian writers. In 2010, she was made an officer of the Order of Canada and in 2013 a chevalière de l'Ordre national du Québec. In 2013 she received le Prix international de literature francophone Benjamin Fondane. That same year, her name appeared in the dictionary *Le Petit Robert des noms propres*, and the Gallery of Arnaud Lefebvre in Paris had an exhibition on her work titled *Nicole Brossard: portrait ou l'horizon du fragment*. In 2018, she was made Compagne de l'Ordre des Arts et des lettres du Québec. She was attributed the first Violet (LGBTQ) Prize by the Blue Metropolis Festival in 2018.

Most recently, in 2019, she received the Griffin Trust for Excellence in Poetry's Lifetime Recognition Award.

Typeset in Arno and Lingerie.

Printed at the Coach House on bpNichol Lane in Toronto, Ontario, on Zephyr
Antique Laid paper, which was manufactured, acid-free, in Saint-Jérôme, Quebec,
from second-growth forests. This book was printed with vegetable-based ink on a
1973 Heidelberg KORD offset litho press. Its pages were folded on a Baumfolder,
gathered by hand, bound on a Sulby Auto-Minabinda and trimmed on a Polar
single-knife cutter.

Edited by Sina Queyras, Geneviève Robichaud, and Erin Wunker
Seen through the press and designed by Alana Wilcox
Cover design by Zab Design & Typography

Coach House Books
80 bpNichol Lane
Toronto ON M5S 3J4
Canada

416 979 2217
800 367 6360

mail@chbooks.com
www.chbooks.com

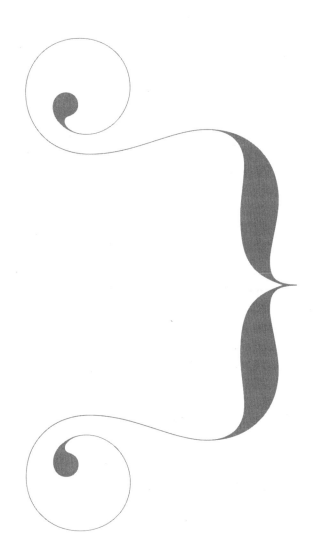